MY SIDE OF THE RIVER

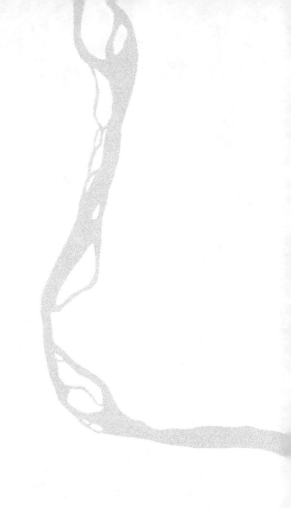

AMERICAN INDIAN LIVES

SERIES EDITORS

Kimberly Blaeser
*University of Wisconsin,
Milwaukee*

Brenda J. Child
University of Minnesota

R. David Edmunds
University of Texas at Dallas

K. Tsianina Lomawaima
Arizona State University

MY SIDE OF THE RIVER

An Alaska Native Story

ELIAS KELLY

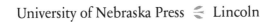

University of Nebraska Press ⋚ Lincoln

The University of Nebraska Press is part of a land-grant
institution with campuses and programs on the past, present,
and future homelands of the Pawnee, Ponca, Otoe-Missouria,
Omaha, Dakota, Lakota, Kaw, Cheyenne, and Arapaho Peoples,
as well as those of the relocated Ho-Chunk, Sac and Fox, and
Iowa Peoples.

Library of Congress Cataloging-in-Publication Data
Names: Kelly, Elias, author.
Title: My side of the river: an Alaska Native story / Elias Kelly.
Other titles: Alaska Native story | American Indian lives.
Description: Lincoln: University of Nebraska Press, [2023] |
Series: American Indian lives
Identifiers: LCCN 2022045150
ISBN 9781496235091 (paperback)
ISBN 9781496236340 (epub)
ISBN 9781496236357 (pdf)
Subjects: LCSH: Kelly, Elias. | Yupik Eskimos—Alaska—
Biography. | Subsistence economy—Alaska. | Conservation of
natural resources—Alaska. |
Traditional ecological knowledge—Alaska. | BISAC: HISTORY /
United States / State & Local / West (AK, CA, CO, HI, ID, MT, NV,
UT, WY) | LCGFT: Autobiographies.
Classification: LCC E99.E7 K415 2023 |
DDC 979.8004/9714092 [B]—dc23/eng/20221026
LC record available at https://lccn.loc.gov/2022045150

Set in Sabon Next LT by A. Shahan.

To my family . . .
and many elders who
guided me along the way

Contents

Abbreviations

Alaska fish and wildlife management is complex, influenced
by many organizations, and acronyms are unavoidable.
The tongue-twisters are easy to get garbled, so I include a
list for reference.

ADF&G Alaska Department of Fish and Game

AFN Alaska Federation of Natives

ANCSA Alaska Native Claims Settlement Act

ANILCA Alaska National Interest Land Claims Act

ASL age, sex, and length

AVCP Association of Village Council Presidents

AYK Alaska Yukon Kuskokwim

BEG biological escapement goal

BIA U.S. Bureau of Indian Affairs

BOF Alaska Board of Fish

BOG Alaska Board of Game

CDQ Magnuson-Stevens Act Community Development
Quota Program

CPUE catch per unit effort

FSB Federal Subsistence Board

FSL U.S. Forest Service Forest Science Lab

GMU game management unit

OSM U.S. Office of Subsistence Management

SEG sustainable escapement goal

UAF University of Alaska–Fairbanks

USFWS U.S. Fish and Wildlife Service

MY SIDE OF THE RIVER

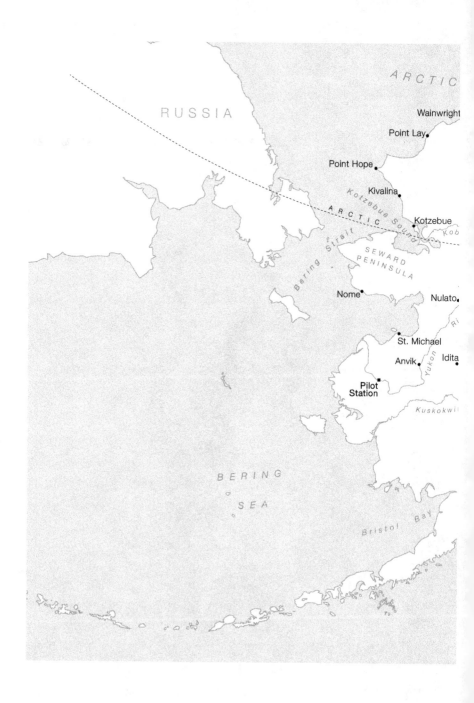

Alaska. Adapted from Mary F. Ehrlander, *Walter Harper, Alaska Native Son*

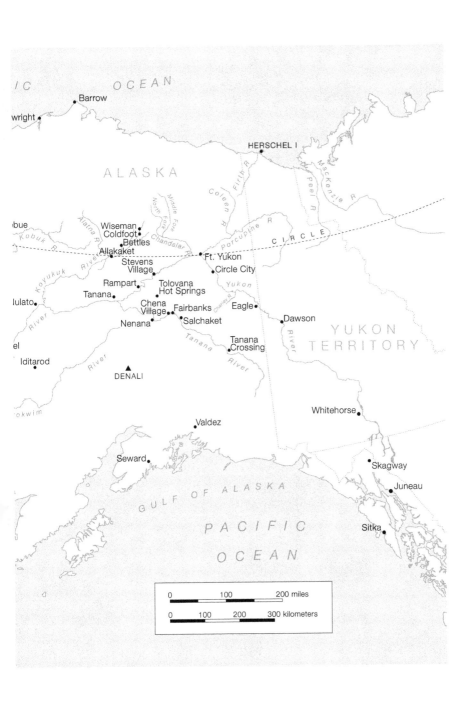

(Lincoln: University of Nebraska Press, 2017). Map by Dixon Jones.

Introduction

"We're going dip-netting for salmon; you should come with us," my sister Lucy said. I looked at the large dip net she was holding and wondered about this fishing method.

June 1980. I was visiting my sister Lucy and her family in Fairbanks. This was the first time I had heard of dip-net fishing for salmon. Driving the Richardson Highway to Chitina, I tried to imagine how this net could be used to catch fish. We pulled into Chitina Fish and Game to purchase State of Alaska fishing licenses and punch cards. The parking lot was busy with fishers, and I was comforted to know that we were not alone in this quest. Later, at O'Brian Creek, a happy fisherman walked to a grill holding a fresh-caught salmon and a dip net. I smiled at the urgency of his step.

As we carried our gear over the remnants of old railroad tracks to a more likely fishing spot, it was hard to imagine that train services used to exist between Cordova and this part of Alaska. I sat on the bolder rocks with a dip net resting in an eddy, and it was exhilarating when a fish thunked the net—I quickly twisted the net upright and pulled out a wiggling fish. When the fish are running, this was exciting. But when the fish are slow, it was easy for me to look across the river and remember what my in-law Jerry said when he slipped the dip net into the water.

"I know it looks foolish to see ourselves using this little stick on this river."

This river is over a half mile wide, with so much room for fish to swim. In hindsight, a traditional fishwheel, permitted for Alaska Natives, is not much bigger. This is the Copper River: the current is strong and swift, and the water is cold and glacial fed. The copper color glistened on the surface and the churning of the river was loud.

This is the river Katie John's story came from.

≋

In 1990 leaders in Alaska tried to address the needs of the state's rural Natives, arguing that the state constitution needed to be amended to recognize Native hunting and fishing. For the state government, the issue could not be ignored, and the language of the state constitution was at risk. This was when the misconception was created that Katie John was a criminal for fishing for Cooper River salmon to feed her family. Katie John had never violated any state or federal laws and was never issued a citation or pleaded "guilty" or "not guilty." At this time Katie John, an Athabaskan elder, filed a federal court case against the State of Alaska, claiming that for subsistence fishing, federal management responsibility applied on all of Alaska's navigable waters—not only on federal lands. The U.S. Supreme Court agreed with her. The name Katie John became synonymous with Alaska Native subsistence fishing rights on federal and state lands.

I am an Alaska resident and U.S. citizen. Many Alaska leaders agree that fish and wildlife management issues are complex and difficult. In the center of this complex identity is Native subsistence hunting and fishing. To the State of Alaska, "subsistence" has never been a kind word; when state leaders try to recognize Native subsistence users, they come up with unconstitutional legal issues. Although the Constitution claims "no person will be deprived of life, liberty, and property without due process of the law," this is misleading in the context of subsistence. When Alaskans stand together, we create a sense of solidarity, and the North Star on our state flag brightens our hope for the future. But when we sit and talk about hunting and fishing, there is too much legal jargon in the Constitution and lawyers only argue what the words mean or what they were intended to mean.

Since arrival of the first Russians, the natural resources of Alaska have shaped federal, state, and local governments. Alaska statehood in 1959 and the 1971 Alaska Native Claims Settlement Act (ANCSA) passed by the U.S. Congress recognized the major landowners and legalized federal and state management of all fish and wildlife. ANCSA extinguished aboriginal rights to hunting and fishing and created Native corporations to manage Native lands despite the concerns of Native elders. Many spoke and wrote about ANCSA and how Alaska Natives have no more hunting and fishing rights.

This is the reason Katie John shared her story in that court case. After the U.S. Fish and Wildlife Service and Alaska Department of Fish and Game claimed all wildlife management responsibility, many Natives have distanced themselves from management and use civil disobedience as a dare for subsistence harvests, whether or not the season is legally open or who has authority. Despite closures, Natives continue to fish for king salmon on the Kuskokwim and Yukon Rivers.

The use of any traditional ecological knowledge in current management schemes is trivial compared to the Western management doctrines that influence regulations. The challenge is how traditional information can be used compared to sound scientific information in federal and state management guidelines. Final management decisions are often influenced by non-Native hunters and fishers, whose like-minded perspectives support their convictions of how we all should live, forever changing the values and ethics of our ancestors with the way we now hunt and fish and the shared traditions of our harvest. After ANCSA, federally recognized tribes' claims of existence have created issues of hunting, fishing, and resource management responsibilities that are still questioned.

Although ANCSA extinguished traditional Native rights, it did not extinguish traditional stewardship obligations. This is the major misconception of ANCSA and the reason why many Alaska leaders agree that Alaska Natives have no management responsibilities. Indeed, traditional management doctrines are compelling, and it is time to compare these principles with current management applications for wild resources we all think are in jeopardy, such as wild Alaska salmon.

In 2014 the Kuskokwim River Inter-Tribal Fish Commission was created as a federal co-management agreement with Alaska Natives for *shared responsibility* of salmon. Then, in 2016, the Ahtna region also signed a federal agreement creating the Ahtna Intertribal Resource Commission. The Ahtna region is home to Katie John and her people. The agreement allows Ahtna Natives to help manage hunting and fishing activities on Native corporation and federal lands. The Richardson Highway, a major road system, connects the Ahtna region with the rest of Alaska, and the influence of non-Native hunting and fishing activities is unavoidable. This is the potential conflict the Ahtna Intertribal Resource Commission hopes to address.

The intertribal fish and resource commissions work with local tribes via co-management guidelines and pseudo-management responsibility. Although these agreements are only with the federal government, the State of Alaska is concerned for Alaska residents' interests. Provisions of these agreements apply on federal and corporation land and allow the intertribal commissions to circumvent corporation land as public lands subject to state regulations. The agreements do not involve the state, and the commission has no authority over state land or waters, so if any Native is caught hunting or fishing outside of this jurisdiction, the question of which regulations have precedents will need to be addressed. If these Natives use their state-issued identification cards where legal precedents have indeed extinguished aboriginal rights, their identity and the commissions' jurisdiction is at stake.

I am a tribal member of Pilot Station Traditional Village, from Pilot Station, a small Native village on the Yukon River. There are 229 tribes in Alaska, and every tribe is fragmented from every other tribe. Tribal identity is evolving and crucial to every Native issue, from child custody, education, social services, and economic development to food security. ANCSA created nonprofit regional corporations such as the Association of Village Council Presidents and Tanana Chiefs Conference to address and provide Native services and advocate for fish and wildlife concerns. These nonprofits offer their services only to tribal members.

Because ANCSA extinguished Alaska Native aboriginal rights, it is not unusual for Alaska Natives to talk of Native empowerment and the creation of a regional or statewide tribal government. During these events, federal and state agencies step back and wonder if Natives can use tribal sovereignty as a tool for unity.

I am also an Alaska Native Yup'ik Eskimo. Our Native elders are the center of every family, community, and cultural activity. Elders tell stories about hunting, fishing, and gathering resources with a message of being respected hunters, fishers, and gatherers: respected Natives.

Most Alaskans have heard about the many impacts of ANCSA. Despite the influence of Katie John's story, the intertribal fish and wildlife co-management agreements continue to use Western management doctrines of strict harvest regulations that are constantly changing and being refined. Unlike Western wildlife management doctrines, Alaska Native traditional wildlife management tools support community stability and enrich family values. I grew up learning to trust my culture. My family lives in Alaska, which I call home. The Yukon River is part of that home. Here is a story of my side of the river.

PART I

I am a subsistence hunter and fisher and also a
commercial fisherman on the Lower Yukon District
1 whenever the Department of Fish and Game
open our commercial fishing. When they don't,
then we just subsist. We try to mix our commercial
and subsistence because both of them are one. We
can't subsist if we don't earn a little money, then
we're stuck with what we're going to be doing.

A long time ago it wasn't like this. The subsistence
hunter or fisher a long time ago didn't have laws except
the Yup'ik laws, which we always had. The Yup'ik
laws are different from Department of Fish and Game
laws. They take care of the land, they take care of the
game, they take care of the fish and nobody overfishes.
That's how I was raised and I'm trying to do the same
thing for the Yup'ik people, but I get bumped into
Department of Fish and Game laws and then that's it.

— **JOHN HANSON**, Alakanuk elder, October 14,
2004, Region 5, AYK Regional Advisory Council–
Federal Subsistence Management Council

1 ⌇ Hunting, Fishing, and Resource Management in Native Alaska

"You cannot set net for fish today. Fishing is closed. You have to let the fish go."

My sister Agnes was trying to explain in Yup'ik to my *uppa* (grandfather) Walter Kelly what the white man was saying in English. The last spring ice had floated past Pilot Station, so families were busy getting fish camps ready, and many Yup'ik men had already set gillnets to catch a fresh taste of the first Yukon salmon. It had been a long winter; fresh salmon was a delicacy everyone looked forward to.

"My grandpa said there will be lots of salmon and the east wind and weather will be good for salmon."

Standing by the fish-drying rack, the wildlife trooper nodded his head and told Agnes to tell the old man that fishing was closed and that the sunny weather and wind had nothing to do with salmon.

He said, "Tell your grandpa to take his net out or we will take it away."

At the time Agnes was an eighth-grade teen who had learned to speak English at the U.S. Bureau of Indian Affairs (BIA) Elementary School in Pilot Station, and she happened to be with our grandfather to translate. Telling a respected elder that he could not harvest salmon because the non-Native said so would haunt her for the rest of her life. "My grandpa asks why you want to take away his net," Agnes said to the trooper as he walked away, asking a curious onlooker about the homes of Dan Greene and Noel Polty.

The Western assertion of power, order, and justice over all wild resources had arrived at our village. Like many villages Pilot Station is in the middle of nowhere: there are no roads to any other community, and airline transportation is limited.

Alaska became a state in 1959. In 1960 the state government claimed authority for all fish and wildlife management with enforcement help from U.S. Fish and Wildlife troopers. Uppa Kelly's date of birth was estimated to be around 1889. In his first encounter with the wildlife trooper, I can only imagine the devastation and confusion he must have felt when he was told he could not fish anytime. Before, fishing had been a practice centered to his way of life; when it was time to hunt, when it was time to fish was when we needed the food. Not tomorrow, next week, or next month. This is the same language Agnes used when she told her story, anguished that she was the one telling Uppa Kelly what to do. To Uppa Kelly, all fish and wildlife belong to Mother Nature. This is our traditional way.

≥

During Uppa Kelly's lifetime, dynamic changes to hunting and fishing practices came with the introduction of non-Native rules, enforcement, and punishment as a means of harvest regulation. These practices are central principles of colonial assimilation, and for Natives, the concept of all fish and wildlife belonging to someone was new and compelling—a colonial ownership based on powers of strength and claims of wealth in a divide-and-conquer nation. It was an alien concept.

To Uppa Kelly, the idea of his fishing gear being taken away as a lesson of obedience to the new law and order was arcane. If a trooper takes my net, I have no means to feed my family. Traditional Natives never took away valuable tools and means to harvest wild resources from others as a system of justice to Mother Nature or as punishment with the assumption that a Yup'ik tells Mother Nature what to do. Creating hardships for another family is not the Native way. Mother Nature has a way of taking care of herself. Elders know that fish and wildlife provide food, that we must respect and not waste the food or consequences will be dire. My parents would tell us not to waste food, or hardships will come and food will be scarce. The same lesson they learned from their parents.

One reliable tool of any resource management is to seek continuous feedback from involved participants to judge whether the management framework is successful—or not. In a manager's perfect world, feedback of information from users of the resource is considered useful to know if any regulation efforts are working. It is difficult to know if this management tool was usable before 1970 in Native Alaska for several reasons. The primary reason is the lack of a written record documenting Native tradition. Everything about my ancestors' way of life was passed with oral stories. Unfortunately, oral stories tend to change from generation to generation, like the whispering game, where one player listens and whispers into the ears of another, who then retells the story. Without conclusive evidence, many non-Natives accept the notion that it is difficult to support oral records and Native reasoning and dismiss them as nothing more than anecdotes of how things used to be.

Like the whispering game, these stories change due to a natural order of chaos theory where the least resistant path is one of disorder. Suppose you hear one storyteller with a conclusion that sounds acceptable. Later you hear the same story from someone else with a different conclusion but the message is similar. Like the fables of Aesop, the elders told stories with similar messages and Natives understood the meaning because they heard it before from someone else. This idea is intriguingly similar to the early stories of the Holy Bible. The challenge is interpreting the conclusion to those unfamiliar with Native customs.

Similarly, it is difficult to prove if there is a successful Native traditional management practice that has worked to sustain a particular species. A process with external application tasks helps manage the wild resource and assure replenishment to allow harvests the next season. Western academic fish and wildlife management principles call this practice "sustained yield," where enough of the renewable resources are allowed to be replenished every season as sustainable, and enough resources are harvested to allow some yield. In Western science, observations are written and documented, but Natives tell theirs as oral stories, making it difficult to prove management guidelines.

Early fish and wildlife managers in Alaska used the *Alaska Sportsman* magazine as the original scientific journal for fish and wildlife conditions and reports on rural areas—not all rural community, but those accessible to urban Alaskans on the road system or those used by Alaskans with their own air transportation to favorite areas for access to hunting and fishing. The *Alaska Sportsman* magazine taught Western doctrines of outdoor management principles and generalized all of Alaska as the same. The early managers assumed that management applications with positive results in one region would also work in other areas.

Eventually, managers recognized that biosystems along the road system had different hunting and fishing use and demand. With human population growth, as food security models and leisure activities developed in urban Alaska, different ideological management applications began to take precedent. As progressive human population growth became a concern with more hunting and fishing use and access, the economic idea of supply versus demand over all natural resources began to be addressed as part of the sustained yield principles of management. For rural Natives, fish and wildlife provide food, and all efforts for security focus on the next harvest. Urban development and a market economy food distribution system recognized hunting and fishing as leisure activities that produce wild supplements from domestic food sources.

A crowded society quickly becomes hungry for more, and only thinks about itself when talking about user access and how this privilege of riches and use should be divided. Overcrowding of hunters and fishers resulted in preferential access to wild fish and animals, nurturing the colonial concept of ownership responsibilities and need for conservation measures with a festering idea that resources are not finite. Overuse became a concern, and with any potential threat of overharvesting came a need for order and justice, accompanied by the idea that all wild resources belong to all Alaskans, that the privilege of access should be the same for everyone. As this developed, urban Alaskans recognized wild fish and animals no longer as primary food sources but as resources that could be managed to prosper the demands of population growth and access for leisure activities. With this trend, aesthetic appreciation and scenic attractions enticed visitors to travel to Alaska and see its beauty and plenty wild resources.

As the State of Alaska took wildlife management authority, preservation and conservation became principal management guidelines. The near decimation of wild buffalo in the Midwest provided reason for wildlife principles, and southeast Alaska's history of cannery fisheries and the impacts of a market economy on wild salmon provided reasons for fishery guidelines. We cannot make these same mistakes. The Alaska Statehood Act created management departments to regulate wild resources, powered by the concept of sustained yield. All Alaskans fell into one unit; all hunting and fishing regulations apply to everyone, regardless of affiliation with any group, ethnicity, place of living, and reason for use. Those who created these regulations did so under the assumption that no one would be discriminated, that no preference would be given, and that all this was done for the good of the resource. The wild resources of Alaska belong to everyone.

However, rural Alaska Natives were left to fend for themselves when management efforts ignored their concerns and their explanations of their existing hunting and fishing practices. The Natives' conventional thought processes may seem simple and illogical to the non-Natives who created all current regulations—and who accepted the mainstream concept that Natives have no management practices of their own. The Native way is seen as uncivilized, with none of the science and modern technology considered useful for Western management guidelines. Natives are seen to hunt and fish without law and order or stewardship responsibilities.

Conventional theory suggests that unregulated hunting and fishing is a constant threat to fish and animal populations, and that management is necessary to ensure that what Natives catch can be a sustainable resource for years to come. If Natives hunt and fish without management guidelines, the wild resources could become a conservation concern, and if there is a shortage, the burden of harvest restrictions will apply unfairly to non-Natives. Regardless of what Native ancestors practiced, management institutions continue to ignore Native concerns and recommendations.

Alaska leaders recognized the Native practice of respect to the natural world but continually misunderstand traditional management principles that have sustained harvest of wild fish and animal for generations. If these Natives have been harvesting wild resources for generations, what has kept them from overharvesting? The Native approach is influential, innovative, and unique: the idea is to harvest what is needed for sustenance and leave the rest of the resources for Mother Nature to manage so that the next season the resource will be replenished. Every season is a new cycle of life. State leaders recognized and incorporated this concept into the Alaska state constitution as sustained yield.

How can we prove what it is about Native ways that have allowed Natives to continue harvesting wildlife for generations? One management observation Natives talk about is respect for fish and animals. Respect for Mother Nature. Is respect a physical or spiritual task of Native management? Did Natives see Mother Nature as a deity, or do Natives see themselves as children of Mother Nature? Although non-Native leaders recognized the concept of sustained yield, they misunderstood and took for granted that Mother Nature needs to be managed to guarantee preservation of wild resources. When troopers take away any hunting or fishing gear, their ulterior motive is a lesson of obedience with the claim that to conserve the wild, we must take away the means of harvesting. To teach this lesson with more intimidation, non-Natives started to tell the Natives when, where, and how to fish and hunt. A practice of showing Mother Nature who is the real boss, who will protect her resources from these savages.

Creating hardships on others and asserting oneself as the boss of Mother Nature is not the Native way of showing respect. If intimidated, Mother Nature has a way of showing her fury, and there is nothing that humans can do to stop her.

The St. Mary's Mission was a Catholic boarding high school for Alaska Natives located in St. Mary's, Alaska. I graduated from the mission in 1982. Like many Natives, I grew up hunting and fishing and enjoying the outdoors. I participated with the University of Alaska–Fairbanks (UAF) Upward Bound, a summer program offered to Alaska Native high school students. After six weeks of intensive math, science, and English lessons, students could go on a road trip to visit the Alaska state capital of Juneau or hike the famous Chilkoot Trail, used by early gold rush pioneers at the turn of the century.

I've read some of Robert Service's bard tales of the gold rush, watched the black-and-white 8mm movie reels of Charlie Chaplin and the string of real pioneers climbing the Chilkoot pass. During the Upward Bound program, I chose to hike the Chilkoot Trail, and several of us convinced some students that we would find gold on the trail.

Waking up on the second day, some students complained about aching backs and sore feet. We had three more nights and had not started our climb up the steep and rocky pass. "Why did I pick this?" someone complained over breakfast. "I could have gone to Juneau with those others." Trying to be enthusiastic and encouraging, I asked if anyone had seen the fox skeleton hanging about a mile from the trailhead. It was ten feet up in a spruce tree, strung together like a taboo skeleton or a dreamcatcher in middle of nowhere. "You guys need to look around and pay attention," I told them. I was in my realm.

As we completed the Chilkoot Trail, the experience encouraged me to venture and leave home to see what life was like in many parts of Alaska.

"If ten years from now, you find no one speaking your language, don't come to me and ask me what happened. Ask yourself what happened."

This quote was posted on the classroom door of our high school Eskimo language teacher, Andy Paukan, our Yup'ik teacher and a respected Native from St. Mary's. Andy was a strong Yup'ik of tradition and culture. All the students at the school were Alaska Native. Andy's respect to elders, respect to others, and respect to his family taught many of us a strong will to honor our culture and tradition—to think Native.

After high school, I became a struggling young college student at UAF, where all my professors were non-Native and the challenge of trying to learn Western academia with my Native way of thinking was failing. As my major course of study, I enrolled in the natural resource management program. It is a broad subject, and I enjoyed the ambiguity of the classes I was required to take. As a young student, I was encouraged to study fish or wildlife, but I enjoy these activities too much to be bound working in them on a daily basis, and I reasoned to myself that I would have nothing enjoyable to do on my vacations from work.

Western education follows a set order of principles and doctrines. That this is the way it is and the only way it shall be acceptable was the motto of every college instructor. It was easy to feel rejected or self-piteous when my instructors told me I had a failing grade and needed to try harder. It sounded illogical as I thought about how to make my Native ways logical. I reminded myself that I speak and think in broken English and was still learning. Many elders had encouraged me to go to school, but it seemed like I had failed. When I was struggling and feeling rejected, I thought about quiet moments along the Chilkoot Trail.

My parents taught me to trust my traditions and my culture. In 1982 I was on the trail when Uppa Kelly passed, and I missed his funeral. The trail was a rite of passage for me from adolescence to young adulthood and helped nurture my way of thinking with Mother Nature. I learned to trust my instincts. There are no accidents; things happen for a reason. What compelled many non-Natives to hike over this Chilkoot Trail? I know many left families and homes behind. What were they seeking?

College is not the same as high school. My instructors gave me a failing grade. The university sent a letter expelling me, and this taught me a valuable lesson. I would have more challenges. I was already a Native and I knew my Native ways. If I was to succeed, I needed to learn to think like a *gussak* . . . to think like a white man.

2 Wildlife Management

"Man, you guys make moose hunting look easy." Ben Nukusuk was telling this to a group of Natives from Pilot Station.

There were several of us inside this little slough excursion. With my brothers James and Martin and cousin Ben Alick, we were a large group. Those of us from home had already caught our meat for the season, but this weather was too nice not to take a boat ride. Although each of us had gone our separate ways earlier that morning, we ended up together in this little dead-end slough, where moose and geese was always a reason to visit. Ben Alick and my brother James had grown up together, and this companionship made them excellent hunt partners. The beach in this slough was dry, and the beach grass and open setting made plenty of room to accommodate all of us. For some reason we enjoyed visiting this spot. Although there was no open meadow, the alder and willow were tall and thick and the moose were well fed and fat. There is one weakness about the moose: when we call them, they come out to see who we are.

There were enough of us that a long haul to carry out meat could be accomplished with one trip if a moose is caught far inland, by working together and everyone carrying a load. But we were not inclined to do so. From our elders we had learned a way to hunt that would make sport hunters skeptical and envy Native ways of helping each other. We used new tactics as a result of hunt regulations all Alaska residents must abide by. The first enforcement of these regulations was a dark period for traditional Native responsibility toward all wildlife. Elders felt resentment when Fish and Game came to Pilot Station and became boss of everything. With these regulations came a period of trial and error, and the skills learned were taught to young Native minds of our generation. As a result, we hunt as if the wild moose is tame. When we call it like domestic livestock, it comes willing, exposed, ready to be shot. Some may claim that the animals willingly give themselves to the hunter.

We were all in this small slough helping Ben Nukusuk and his hunting party from Hooper Bay.

Since 1999 the moose population numbers in this part of Alaska have been exceptionally abundant, and this did not happen by accident. The difficult stories happened before this abundant population growth. Some are not pleasant. Restrictive state hunting regulations imposed on the Natives shattered the trustworthiness of all federal and state wildlife management intents. According to the 1971 Alaska Native Claims Settlement Act, all Natives are to follow state regulations despite traditional Native harvest ethics and guidelines. For a period, Native hunting was done in secret. Legally this is called poaching. If we want to understand how we got to this current situation, we must learn where we came from and the hardships endured to learn these lessons. Through this difficult period Mother Nature was there guiding what the elders tried to explain to management and their regulatory methods.

My youngest son, Nicholas, was ten years old when he caught his first moose. With my wife, Janice, we were taking an evening boat ride. Hunting with small open skiffs is a way of life. We were cruising as we passed the entrance to this lake. The thick willow and alder allowed us to see so far into the brush. With time only for a brief glimpse, we saw a young bull moose with several female cows and calves as we passed the lake entrance. I slowed and allowed the boat waves to quiet and calm. We agreed that this was a good time for a first catch. Several times Nicholas had helped shoot at moose with a smaller rifle. This was not a large antlered bull, but it was adequate for a first kill. In Alaska Native cultures, first kills are a significant event. Janice was ready in case the animal was wounded, spooked, or made a run. I was there to teach a hunt with a guaranteed success.

I turned into the lake at idle speed. The moose came into view, eighty yards away. "Wait," I whispered. I watched the ears, as it was unsure of what we were. At idle speed the sound of the motor was quiet. At sixty yards the moose twitched its ears and was about to turn. I whispered again for Nicholas to wait and called to the moose. This was my first call. The moose turned and looked to my calling. In a calm voice I coaxed the animal and it stood willing. At forty yards Janice whispered to Nicholas to load his rifle and gave the okay to shoot. All our children learned to shoot with open sights; scoped rifles require extra care and maintenance. For Natives who travel and handle rifles every day, scopes will never guarantee any more accuracy than without. The first shot rang loud and hit the moose in a non-vital area. It turned to run into the brush with a limp. I told Nicholas to aim lower; all our rifles are sighted for accuracy at one hundred yards. I called louder, and the moose turned and stood broadside. At twenty yards Nicholas hit a vital spot and the moose fell, ten feet from the boat on dry beach grass.

With water from the lake, we gave the moose a taste of freshwater and praised its spirit for sharing Native traditions. All the meat was cut. Nicholas delivered meat to his namesake family, and elders shared choice parts such as the heart and liver. As this was a first kill, we kept none for ourselves but gave all meat away to teach our young hunters that in times of need, hunters will provide for elders and community. It is a lesson from Mother Nature that if the hunter respects the catch, Mother Nature has more lessons to teach and that being bossy, aggressive, and intimidating is not part of Native management. Sharing the success of our harvest teaches our young to be respected providers and respected Yupiit.

Early colonial America and Russian explorers' harvesting Native wildlife resources impacted coastal communities of Alaska. Dangers to wildlife numbers in Alaska is not unusual; animals have become extinct and reintroduced. Sea otters in the Aleutian Islands and muskoxen in western Alaska are examples. Although in the colonial period hunting focused on fur and large animals to help feed early whalers and fur trappers, the gold rush era brought a non-Native user with a different mentality: that Alaska offers instant riches, prestige, and wealth. Into the new century these new Alaskans developed the state, and the wild fish and animals provided food to them. The fur industry provided an economic stimulus for trapping, and wild salmon was developed into a market economy and exported. Salmon was packed, salted, shipped, and sold. Although non-Native Alaska played an influential role in management or lack of management in all wild resources, the post-ANCSA era has had the most impact to Native Alaska. If anything, this is a period of resentment that the 1971 ANCSA extinguished Native responsibility for wild resources and similar to the salmon experience with Uppa Kelly, it was non-Natives telling Natives what to do.

The Alaska Department of Fish and Game (ADF&G) Wildlife Division and the U.S. Fish and Wildlife Service (USFWS) hold all wildlife management responsibility. Wildlife management in Alaska is unique, especially true for Native Alaska. Post-ANCSA, these two agencies trying to help Natives often created confusion. For Native Alaska, there are two hunting and fishing regulation booklets, one from the state and one from the federal government. Each has different area coverage for management guidelines; ADF&G uses game management units (GMU), and USFWS use regions, giving broad areas where hunting regulations, seasons, and bag limits are set, depending on the condition of whatever wildlife is managed. Regions or units next to each other may have similar hunt guidelines and others may have completely different regulations or closures. Every hunter needs to be aware of these guidelines and whether a legal permit, license, or tag is required. Both agencies issue annual hunting regulation booklets with regional contact information for questions or concerns. It is the responsibility of every hunter to know the rules; otherwise, wildlife troopers may give hunters citations and fines for any number of reasons.

Ignorance is no excuse for an illegal harvest. Unconsciously this creates resentment for Natives that their every action is closely monitored as if the hunters are children. This is not a good analogy, but it is unfortunately the case. The phrase to describe this management tool is "wildlife micromanagement." What makes it complicated for Alaska Native hunters and fishers are the non-Native harvest ethics all regulations continue to represent.

Scrutinizing wildlife management efforts in other parts of the world is often necessary for recovery of numbers to acceptable levels after the wild critters have been overharvested. It is an issue between the hunters, users concerned about conservation, and managers responsible for the task. Efforts usually focus on large animals or their predators.

An example for my part of Alaska is moose management. Poaching of these animals was common before and more so after ANCSA, often because of Native resentment toward non-Native managers. Natives hunted out of season or shot the first moose readily available, including females and calves. The main excuse Natives claimed is that they need the food to feed their families. The 1960s to 1970s was not a good period for Native hunters; although the habitat for moose browse in the Yukon Kuskokwim region is considered excellent, the animal numbers were not as plentiful as this area could support. I remember stories of wildlife troopers peeking into the porches of suspected Native poachers. Stories like those, and of troopers' issuing citations and garnishment of equipment are difficult to listen to. Many elders know someone who went through this experience and it created resentment toward Fish and Game.

People who poach wildlife for any number of reasons are usually seen as disrespectful, and if they do it against current laws and regulations, they are often considered criminals as well. Although the poaching of small critters such as rabbits is not as noticeable as that of larger animals, anytime there is conservation or preservation concern, everyone who is involved with the resource in any way should have management responsibility.

Most elders familiar with Alaska wildlife issues have heard about the 1961 "duck-in" after a Native was cited for shooting a duck out of season and his shotgun and duck were taken away as lesson that this was now the law of the land. For USFWS, this story is a blemish to their respectable presence and responsibility over a public resource. As Natives heard about this citation, hunters turned themselves in with a duck and shotgun in hand and dared to be given a citation. Eventually, charges were dropped. Nonetheless, Natives continue to use this same footnote in history as a dare to current management. Hunting or fishing against regulations is civil disobedience.

In 2008 state wildlife troopers found caribou carcasses left to waste near the communities of Kotzebue and Point Hope. The troopers claimed the animals were killed by trigger-happy Natives and estimated one hundred animals were shot and the meat left to ruin. With crime scene investigation techniques, the troopers could only track the culprits to the community of Point Hope. Without the evidence to single out any primary suspect, the troopers tried to get community members to identify the culprit based on who was hunting in the area, but ultimately the troopers could not identify the culprits with only rumors. This is Alaska's current wildlife situation we must now live with.

≥

The regional nonprofit Association of Village Council Presidents (AVCP) is responsible for social service programs separate from the regional for-profit Calista Corporation. As Alaska Native corporations, both organizations were created as a result of ANCSA and encompass the Yukon-Kuskokwim coastal region. AVCP represent fifty-six villages and hosts an annual meeting to provide progress reports and programs for the region. AVCP also provides an award recognition event. In October 2016 my brother Abe was recognized with a hunter/fisher award. Although Abe is not a registered guide, he helps many Natives from other villages with successful catches and always makes sure that no one leaves this hunt area without meat. Native hunters from villages as far away as Newtok and Toksook Bay travel the Kashunuk River and camp for several days, and Abe and his family help as much as they can. Natives helping other Natives in this way is not unusual.

When Ben Nukusuk from Hooper Bay commented about how we Natives from Pilot Station had made moose hunting easy, we could only look at each other and smile. The slough excursion is a favorite because anytime we called moose, one would show. As I took out the prime stove and makings for a large pot of coffee, a good-size bull moose was spotted. My brother James and Ben Alick helped Ben from Hooper Bay using the same stealth technique and moose calling. They were close to the animal when Ben Nukusuk's uncle caught his first moose as a young elder. The success of this hunt struck him with awe and wonder about the skills developed over the years. The meat was cut and loaded into the boat as the coffee was ready.

In January 2017 the Board of Game addressed a proposal to open winter snow machine hunts for non-residents in my part of Alaska.

Given Native opposition, the board did not support this proposal. The seven-member BOG is the state governing body that creates all wildlife regulations. It is a major decision-maker for Native ways of life. When the board addresses regulation proposals, it is difficult to determine whether members intend to make it easy for hunters or to make it difficult, to make it a game.

The federal counterpart for the Alaska BOG is the Federal Subsistence Board. In 1980 the U.S. Congress created the Alaska National Interest Land Claims Act to regulate Native harvesters. Known as ANILCA, this created the second book of hunting laws and the Federal Subsistence Board (FSB). Although ANILCA instated Native management responsibility, the state continues to claim Natives as Alaska residents, meaning we must follow the same state regulations as non-Natives. To minimize disdain and conflicting laws, the dual management programs attempt to create mirror regulations to make it easier for Natives to understand the laws. Unfortunately, the majority making these regulations are non-Native and non-subsistence users. "Subsistence" is the key word that implies we are indeed supporting Alaska Native needs. Nonetheless, this dual management and special recognition create an identity crisis for Native hunters and fishers. Poaching remains common regardless of who is in charge.

As a result of poaching, moose numbers undergo a period of recession and take a long time to recover. After the passage of ANCSA, the presence of wildlife troopers became more visible in Pilot Station. ANCSA provided the legal arsenal to support all state hunting regulations, and many non-Natives would remind Natives that they had no more aboriginal rights to hunting and fishing. Natives have no more traditional stewardship responsibility.

The story about the moose in my part of Alaska is amazing. Scarcity created an economic recession for families. Costs for fuel, equipment, and supplies to harvest animals escalated, and meager incomes hampered hunters' success and thus decreased Native food security. Without options for recovery, in 1992 the Natives took action with guidance from the elders. No state or federal regulations existed for a group to self-impose a strict harvest closure, despite the presence and actions of BOG and FSB.

The managers looked to the regulations as guidelines and were at odds with the actions the Natives were taking. If any other group stood holding the state constitution before BOG, the action the Natives took would be more than sufficient evidence that the state cannot allow a complete restrictive closure. Lawyers would be ecstatic and legal courts would instantly agree that this restrictive closure was unconstitutional. There are no laws the Natives could use to help recover moose numbers. The recovery is no accident. Elders who provided leadership recognized the situation and implored a traditional management action based on principles of how Natives used to be responsible for our way of life. If we need to help our animals, we need to help ourselves.

Before recovery of these animals, the unpleasant stories about hunting in secret are difficult. But after the self-imposed action, we have learned much of our wildlife situations and what traditional stewardship meant to elders. In 2018 ADF&G and USFWS held a press conference apologizing to Alaska Natives about state and federal regulations that created hardships for Native food security.[1] Despite the claims of ANCSA, it is time for Natives to stand and take management responsibility of our subsistence resources.

NOTES

1. Alex DeMarban, "'We Got It Wrong': Governments Apologize to Alaska Natives for Banning Migratory Bird Harvests," *Anchorage Daily News*, September 13, 2018.

3 🦅 Yukon River Fisheries

"Hey, get up. It's foggy, they won't see us," Donald whispered, shaking me awake.

It was a calm, early Sunday morning in August 1970. The sun was just coming up and we knew Dad's boat was fueled with gas. We snuck away with Dad's eighteen-foot plywood skiff and his long salmon gill-net and went commercial fishing. We were kids then, at a time when seventy-two-hour commercial fishing was common. Neither of us had a commercial permit, but the five-dollar crewmember helper's licenses gave us a sense that we were young fishermen.

Although we had fished for more than ten hours the previous day, it still seemed like we were catching fish. But according to Dad, there was not much fish, and Dad wanted to quit and go home. Donald and I looked at each other. Tomorrow was Sunday, Dad didn't need to work at the U.S. Post Office, and commercial fishing would be open until noon. As young boys, we looked forward to fishing and especially staying up all night. We shrugged our shoulders and had no say in the matter. Dad sold our catch before midnight and we quit and went home.

A common weather phenomenon with calm early fall mornings is fog, and that day it was thick. Our fishing spot was upriver, seven miles from home. Cautiously, Donald started the forty-horse Yamaha outboard. We knew the sun was up—it was bright—but we couldn't see the other side of the bank. The river was calm and slow; the fog was eerie. Donald drove the boat slowly, and as we crossed the river, we could see the halo aura of the sun and dark silhouette of the tree line. Through the fog, I yelled something as Donald drove over a net. We laughed nervously and looked around to see if there was a boat. Someone had set their fishnet rather than drifting for salmon. At that time, setnets were allowed for commercial fishing. We were lucky our prop did not get caught or tangled in the net.

The fog cleared as we neared our fishing spot. There was one other fishing boat, and we recognize Uncle William, who we avoided to avoid answering questions about why we were fishing without Dad. We had made it this far and were reassured and confident. Donald drove in reverse toward the beach as I set out the 150-foot six-inch gillnet and watched for any tangles. After the net was set, I sat on the bow of the boat and enjoyed the calm views. The river current was slow and the warmth of the sun was nice. We smiled as bobbing buoys caught fish. Being younger than Donald, I was usually fortunate to get some catnaps and rest while Donald helped Dad do most of the fishing. Dad would let Donald drive to keep the net taught. With the soothing heat from the sun and constant hum of the outboard, Donald stated to doze and jerk awake as I smiled. He finally gave in and told me to drive, to watch the net and the beach, pointing this way and that to make sure I clearly understood. Like an idiot I smiled and nodded my head. This was my first time. I'd watched Dad and my brothers do this; I was excited.

As fortune would have it, nothing exciting happened. Our net was not caught in our motor prop and no underwater driftwood caught or tore our net. The river current did not pull us out to the middle deeper channel. The river was calm and smooth, not a ripple. No other boats came to check on us and no fish and wildlife trooper came by. We would have made Ron Somerville proud that day.[1] To keep awake, I started to whistle like Uncle William.

We drifted for two hours, which is not uncommon for that part of the river. Every bobbing buoy meant one more fish had been caught. As we neared the spot where we always pull in the net, I woke up Donald, who was dazed and confused. We pulled in the net and untangled our fish. It was 10 a.m., bright sunlight, and we could not hide the fact of what we had done. As we reached home, we saw a fish-buying boat tender at the lower end of town, but we needed a permit to sell the fish. We were scared as Donald woke Dad and told him of the catch and that we needed him to sell it before the boat tender left for the fish cannery in Mountain Village. Dad realized what we had done and was mad and reluctant. Fuming, Dad and Donald went to sell our fish tote of salmon. We made $150.00 for the salmon, at $0.10 per pound. After most commercial periods we got a little spending money, but our share helped pay for new winter school clothes and boots.

Although Donald and I did this on a whim, if we had been caught by the fish and wildlife troopers, the fish, boat motor, and gear would have been taken away. We would have become juvenile criminals, and Dad would have been fined and jailed. We saw this opportunity and took it. We never talked about it, so I can only imagine what it was like for Dad to sell the fish while he was still buzzed or drunk. Before rural Alaska communities legalized local options for alcohol importation, the U.S. post office delivered mail-order cases of green-bottled port wine and canned beer. Alcohol often flooded the village after successful commercial fish periods.

In 1960 commercialization of salmon was a statewide concern. The history of salmon harvest concerns in southeast Alaska created a need for industry fishing regulations and proper management guidelines. Before salmon became a commercial industry, Alaska Natives never practiced fish or wildlife harvests with intent to sell the harvest as a commodity, with the exception of the fur trade, for which a traditional system of bartering existed. But collecting large harvests with intent to exchange them for capital was never practiced. Traditional Natives recognized that all wild resources were seasonal and the seminomadic lifestyle enabled the harvest of these resources to meet food security needs.

The ADF&G Division of Commercial Fisheries is responsible for all fisheries. In response to a growing number of fishers trying to participate in any commercial Alaska salmon fishery, the state created the program to limit number of fishers who can participate. Residents had to show proof that they had previously fished for salmon to acquire a limited-entry permit and to then sell salmon to a catcher/seller in exchange for cash. This created the first market economy of a subsistence resource critical for Native food security. Over the years, development and salmon management efforts have been at times controversial with conservation concerns and at other times successful, providing cash infusions to the communities.

All Alaska commercial salmon fisheries use the limited-entry program. To sell salmon, fishers must have a valid state permit to legally participate. Each fishery is allowed a certain number of permanent permits to help maintain the number of fishers who can participate. The Yukon River so4y fishery has about six hundred permanent commercial fish permit holders, with fifty-four permit holders living in Pilot Station. Permit holders must renew their permit each season to be able to sell salmon.

Most Alaskans are familiar with the Bristol Bay or Copper River salmon industry, where serious money can be made. The value of each fishery depends on the market value of salmon, the condition of the fishery, logistics such as access to markets and transportation costs, and salmon quality. In addition to selling fish, the permit holder can also sell their permit to another fisher. A retail value of $100,000 for a Bristol Bay salmon permit is not unusual. During the 1980s, the most prolific period for Lower Yukon commercial fishing, the permit value exceeded $30,000. In 2022 the permit value is less than $6,000. These values fluctuate with the total amount of sales that can be made during a season.

To help manage the fisheries, ADF&G created fishing districts along the main stem of the Yukon River with different fishing methods, openings, and regulations. The coastal district includes the Bering Sea, and setnet gillnet fishing is only allowed in this area. The rest of the river is divided into six districts, and Pilot Station is in district Y2. Communities below Mountain Village are district Y1, and the Y2-Y3 border is above Marshall. Districts Y1 and Y2 are the main salmon commercial fishing areas. Communities above Russian Mission have some commercial fishery but depended on the availability of a buyer and a developed salmon market. District Y5 and Y6 are closer to Canada and include the Nenana and Tanana River drainage.

Every Yukon River community depends on salmon as a traditional resource. The task of managing salmon includes difficult collaboration between all users, including traditional First Nations of Canada. The fishing district system allows management to protect stocks of concern by closing fishing times to allow salmon to reach spawning sites.

The Yukon River has five salmon species: pink, sockeye, coho, chum, and king salmon. The pink salmon is the least significant, and there is no river-wide commercial fishery. Although Natives traditionally observe the salmon season as a single period, ADF&G has categorized it into two seasons: summer and fall. The summer chum and king salmon are fished during summer season, and fall chum and coho salmon in fall season. Of all the salmon species, the Yukon sockeye or red salmon is the least understood. The sockeye is mainly fished in the Copper, Kuskokwim, and Bristol Bay and is not as abundant or significant for the Yukon River. All Alaska's Pacific salmon are anadromous, which means they live, feed, and grow to adulthood in saltwater and swim upriver to freshwater streams to spawn and die. This is a major natural life cycle for salmon. Not as one fish or two fish, but as a school of fish, they travel together from smolt fingerling to adulthood to live, spawn, and die in all river tributaries of Alaska and Canadian side of the Yukon River.

The most abundant Yukon salmon, and thus the primary commercial harvest salmon, is the summer and fall Yukon chum. The coho fishery occurs at the same time as fall chum and is also a significant commercial resource. The average price for Yukon coho and chum salmon has never exceeded more than a dollar a pound.

The main commercial salmon moneymaker is the chinook or king salmon. The largest of all salmon, the wild Yukon king has had difficult conservation concerns with ADF&G as the only responsible manager. It is a prized commodity to subsistence, commercial, and sport fishers. In 2005 the commercial value of a Yukon king was $5.50 per pound, with the average salmon weight between twenty-five and thirty pounds. In 2005, according to *Alaska Fish Radio*'s Laine Welch, the value of a whole Alaska Yukon king was over $270 per fish at the Fiji Market in Japan.[2] Due to conservation concerns, commercial fishing for king salmon is not guaranteed every year.

At one time, traditional bulk harvest of salmon was cut, dried, and stored to feed sled dog teams. Although sled dogs played a significant role in the transportation and mobile history of the Eskimos, there are no sled dog kennels in Native Alaska. Snow machines are the main method of winter transportation. The care and maintenance of sled dogs is labor intensive and more economically demanding than most people tend to claim. The scrutiny for use of salmon as dog food has been controversial and as a result there are no dog teams in Lower Yukon communities. Cost and economic conditions such as lack of jobs are a leading cause of economic disparity. Before the salmon fisheries became controversial, Pilot Station hosted dog team races. Some remember a time when forty teams participated with a mass start. The last race occurred in 1985.

Drift gillnet and setnet fishing are the main methods of catching salmon. Traditional methods once include fishwheels, partial weirs with large fish traps, and homemade twine nets. Rod and reels or jigging for salmon is not common on the main river; the Yukon is full of silt and sand, so lures and baited jigs are invisible. Rod-and-reel fishers are familiar with a handheld dip net to scoop fish out of the water. Try to imagine use of a dip net to scoop salmon out of a river as big and wide as the Yukon. ADF&G now regulates dip-net commercial fishing, despite objections and controversial claims of inefficiency. The main argument against this new method is that the Yukon River is broad and deep, so a four-foot round dip net is a tiny hole in the water. There is so much room for fish to swim. Dip-net fishing is common on the Copper and Kenai Rivers and has been used for more than fifty years. Logically, it does not sound significant as a commercial fishery method for the Yukon River.

A dip net is not like a gillnet that can be set, hung in the water to do its work by catching fish by the gills, entangling them more the more they try to get free. The netting of a dip net is less than four inches and does not allow fish gills to get entangled or damaged, so if the fisher does not scoop the fish promptly, it will get away alive and free. With a gillnet a fisher can set and come back later to untangle the fish. A gillnet does not discriminate what is caught. Because of concerns about king salmon numbers, ADF&G recognizes that commercial fishery is important as an economic opportunity and that more sanctions only create hardships without guaranteed emergency assistance if a disaster is declared. The summer run for chum salmon is concurrent with that of king salmon, and the dip-net fishery allows fishers to keep chum salmon to sell. All Yukon kings are immediately released unharmed.

Dad, Norman Kelly, was a commercial fisherman and U.S. postmaster. Dad not only passed out mail and freight but also knew when alcohol orders arrived. Many recipients would invite Dad to have a sip or invite my parents for a drinking party. In 1978 the State of Alaska began to regulate alcohol, and rural Alaska villages voted to legalize or ban alcohol as wet or dry communities. As a result, the U.S. Postal Service no longer allows alcohol to be shipped. Alcohol is illegal in Pilot Station, and bootlegging is rampant after successful commercial fish periods, the only time Natives have a little spending money to splurge.

Native subsistence and commercial fishers are the same: innovative and resilient to new changes. As a result of the dip-net fishery, fishers have become proficient at catching fish. Many learned little tricks to catching more. When there is a commercial surplus for harvest, not only do fishers have an opportunity to help sustain king salmon for future harvests, but the limited income from chum salmon sales helps pay bills in a region characterized with poor economic conditions and high cost of living. Although dip nets became appealing for commercial fishing, the negative impact to subsistence families is that more time and higher economic costs are required for traditional drying and smoking salmon for winter use.

During a 2016 tribal climate summit conference in Washington, a conference member asked me what my little village is like. Pilot Station is located one hundred miles inland from the coast and Bering Sea. Imagine what the fishery and communities along the Columbia River were like one hundred years ago.

NOTES

1. Ron Somerville served as a State of Alaska Board of Game member from 2003 to 2008.
2. *Alaska Fish Radio*, July 19, 2005.

4 ≋ Subsistence

"We did not expect to get seals. Our freezers are full," my wife, Janice, told our daughter Caitlyn on the phone. Caitlyn was visiting Kotlik, where she caught four seals. She was planning to bring one home. "The seal is already cut up and the meat is ready to pass out," she said. Caitlyn had just turned eighteen and was a successful young seal hunter.

≋

In 2000 the ADF&G Subsistence Division collected and compiled an estimated community harvest of wild foods. The average annual harvest for Pilot Station is 714 pounds per person per year. For a family of five, this is more than 3,500 pounds per year. Statewide, the annual per-person harvest for rural communities is 375 pounds, compared to 22 pounds in urban Alaska, as in Anchorage and Fairbanks, where harvest of wild foods is often considered recreational.

For those who have never been to Alaska, the general perception is that subsistence-oriented families live in small rural communities, traditionally on small farming tracts, and that they are self-sufficient from mainstream society. Alaska reality TV shows depict the lifestyle as self-sufficient farmers or gatherers with gardens that provide supplemental produce. In Pilot Station, there are no family farms or gardens or reality TV shows for the Lower Yukon. No one grows their food. In summer 1995 our nonprofit Association of Village Council Presidents ran a pilot project to try to help Native families become self-sufficient. I was fortunate to work as an agricultural assistant, receiving income and able to live at home where jobs are otherwise scarce.

When I was a small child, I remember, Mom had a garden in downtown Pilot Station. In every Yukon community, "downtown" is located near the river, our main thoroughfare. In a twenty-by-thirty-foot patch, Mom grew carrots, cabbage, potatoes, onions, and radishes. Other families had similar garden tracts, though there was a poor crop during harvest season—keeping neighbor kids from picking vegetables before they were ripe was more labor intensive than pulling weeds. Once the local store started to stock fresh produce and canned vegetables, growing our own produce became too labor intensive for its meager success. Pilot Station is considered part of the semi-arctic or subarctic, where the summer growing season is shorter than 120 days and harvest is small. In the 1970s, as food distribution and transportation developed, family gardening efforts phased out.

As part of the pilot project to introduce a family practice, my job as an agricultural assistant was an exciting opportunity to help Natives become less dependent on government food assistance. In 1995 Natives had little interest in participating in family gardens. My main duty was to introduce gardening to provide healthy fresh food options. The Native perception of gardening is a dilemma between time management and tasks of preparing wild salmon as a traditional food source. My second duty was to teach a safe food preservation method of canning or pressure cooking. As a preservation method, pressure cooking was seen as a practice by non-Native teachers. The few Native families who practiced canning learned this process from working at fish canneries and usually had canning jars and a cooker.

Like the door-to-door Jehovah's Witnesses who once visited our community, from house to house I tried to convince families to participate in our program. With 120 homes in Pilot Station, I could help many families. My pitch: Grow a garden, be outside, and enjoy the fresh harvest when the crops are ready. It is all for you and your family. I will teach you how to garden and pressure-cook fresh food for safe storage. Even though some were reluctant, I was persistent, and I convinced a few to try it. Those who were reluctant gave me one response that was honest, which reiterated for me what subsistence means to the Yup'ik people and discouraged me as the short growing season progressed: "I don't have time for a garden." Quietly I repeated this phrase as I tilled virgin garden plots and though about what these Natives are trying to say.

How can you not have time for a garden? I could help get it started, and then we'd just let it grow. Nature would take care of it. I could help select the site; I knew how. Many didn't know that I worked two seasons with the U.S. Soil Conservation Service and farmers in Fairbanks. I would till the soil, shovel and heap the mounds, help plant seeds, and the residents just needed to water and weed the garden. I could teach how to fertilize the plants, with natural, organic material from our salmon. I told local people that they had given us a brand-new gas-powered rototiller to till the soil. In our community, "they" means someone or some organization from outside our village but who was kind to provide this opportunity.

Green manicured lawns and property fences do not exist in Native Alaska.

As in every remote culture, it was non-Native teachers in rural Alaska who introduced Western education doctrines to the Native community. Western education taught rigorously that there was a right and a wrong way of doing things. Teachers used a judicial system to discipline and punish Natives whenever something was not correct. Elders talk about how a ruler was not a measuring tool for success but a tool for punishing students for wrong answers or behavior considered uncivil by Western society. Children speaking their own language was also reason for punishment. Learning under such disciplinary action is not a good experience. Elders know that Mother Nature is a teacher of culture, and the elders' role is to educate everyone about lessons learned from her. As good as non-Native teachers were at dispensing discipline, Mother Nature is not as forgiving with a right or wrong answer.

Other than dogs used to pull and haul sleds or carry small packs, Native Alaskans never practiced domestication, ranching, or animal husbandry. Agricultural methods of growing plants, fruits, or roots were never practiced. The Natives lived a seminomadic lifestyle, following herds of caribou or seasonally relocating to fish camps to process large amounts of fish. There were no customary herding or husbandry practices; there are no horses, sheep, cattle, or farm animals in Native Alaska. Occasionally families raise chickens, with varying results. The Alaska

Native way is to pursue life in nature as a hunter, fisher, and gatherer. This is the way to be a successful and respected Yup'ik.

In addition to canning jars, the Association of Village Council Presidents provided a twenty-two-quart pressure cooker, which I lugged between homes. The cover of the cooker had a little dial to gauge the pressure as heat is applied. One traditional family was immediately suspicious. Speaking in Yup'ik, they told me how a similar pot had exploded when they tried to cook jarred fish on a prime stove. Everything inside was ruined with broken glass. They threw away the cooker and had never tried it since. I convinced them that I would monitor the cooking. When steam started to hiss and jitter, the family became nervous something bad was about to happen. After some coaxing I convinced them that this was normal, and I turned down the heat and tapped the dial on the pressure gauge. Several months later the family asked if I could help jar frozen wild resources from their freezer.

Every household wanted to participate in this food preservation method. I provided the cooker and jars for everyone to share, they provided what they wanted to pressure cook: fresh Yukon salmon. Participation was instant. I did not need to convince anyone as word spread between households, and all sixty cases of pint-size jars were quickly taken. The result was excellent. Many families learned to can salmon, purchased their own canning supplies, and began to annually jar salmon and other fresh wild foods, including tundra berries for jam and jellies and new recipes for other locally harvested products. The glass jars can be reused over and over.

The garden project did not turn out. Vegetarians do not live in Native communities.

Eighteen families participated in the garden project, but as summer season progressed, I found myself the only one tending to the gardens. Families who had no time for a garden were active participants in the annual harvesting and preparation of salmon, only possible this time of the year, and always a family affair. These were the real subsistence practices for real people who live on the river. Setting up fish camps for cutting, drying, and cold-smoking salmon is the most effective preservation method, passed down through the generations. The dried salmon preserved in bulk this way is a main food staple for winter use.

Tending to salmon is more beneficial and more of a nutritional staple than tending to a garden, where the likely rewards are not as important as food security.

As a college student, I read about Greenland Inuit seal hunters becoming fishers as a result of global environmental changes, and the impact of that mental and behavioral change. Fishers were non-successful hunters. As a hunter and fisherman, I cannot imagine myself as a Yup'ik farmer.

In Native Alaska paved roads and green manicured lawns are non-existent, though many cut grass to control insect populations. A little breeze can help keep swarms of mosquitos, gnats, and flies down to bearable levels, especially around fish camps, where families spend time together. Areas of cut grass are comforting and that comfort is more pleasing than trying to create something aesthetic. There are no cultivated fruit-bearing plants, ornamental trees, hedges, or practice of silviculture. As a central hub community of the Yukon Kuskokwim region, Bethel has flourished with a community garden project that could be seen from the air in the treeless tundra biome. The garden tracts look like farm tracts in rural America, and the organic vegetables provide fresh local-grown produce.

The ADF&G Division of Subsistence has collected data of how much wild subsistence harvests are used as a source of food for each Alaska community. When this division was created, gathering wild food harvest data from an economic perspective was largely based on guesses. What this division has learned has revealed that Native Alaskans use many wild resources not regulated by any agency management guidelines, such as fish and animals not listed individually in regulation booklets but lumped together and categorized as "other" fish species or game animals with liberal harvest methods. The management agencies have no idea of the condition of these populations and where these wild critters roam. The subsistence division was tasked with learning about these other critters and their significance to main food sources as salmon, moose, and caribou.

Early anthropologists and ethnographers were familiar with and documented Native wild harvests. Managers fixated on a single resource responsibility continue to observe and assume that these other resources are insignificant management concerns. Pilot Station's average annual wild food harvest is 714 pounds per person per year. Imagine how many large, medium, or small pizzas that's equivalent to.

≥

"I cannot make akutaq with canned tuna," my wife, Janice, tells me.

"It's not tuna. It's whitefish," I say, holding the jar of canned whitefish.

I'm an agricultural specialist, and the practice of teaching canning methods had also made me look around for other traditional foods to jar. Since canned foods have become a worldwide sensation, opening a can and eating without cooking is accepted as an unconscious virtue. Canned food is easy and readily available. Every culture has traditional foods that make its people proud of their heritage and that make each special in their own way. For Eskimo people, the Eskimo ice cream, or akutaq, is one specialty of ethnic pride, enjoyed as a delicacy any time of the day, before and after the main course or as the main course. Non-Natives who try it for the first time say it is an acquired taste, especially when they see Natives enjoying it with the eloquent praises of a food connoisseur. Just mentioning the word makes Natives start to salivate, and the craving becomes a hunger pang for Native foods. Seal oil, mangtak (whale), and dried fish create the same cravings.

Unlike processed, churned dairy ice cream, the Eskimo version is not as generic: the main ingredients are fish and tundra berries. There is no dairy in akutaq. When my son Kalen explained to his army friends how this dessert is made with Crisco and sugar, they commented on the amount of cholesterol packed in. If there is a Native energy power bar, frozen akutaq on a pilot bread cracker or homemade bread is it. Dried king salmon and mangtak are close behind, like a caffeine kick with cholesterol to generate heat and body warmth. In akutaq vegetable shortening has replaced the traditional seal oil or rendered fat. The shortening is whipped and mixed with the cook's favorite berries and sugar. Most akutaq desserts have a similar ratio of sugar and shortening per serving as pecan or apple pie. Packed with berries or any combination of fruits, akutaq will never be refused by any respectable Yup'ik.

Preparing akutaq is time consuming, since the fish must be cooked, boned, and flaked. Biting a fish bone in a dessert is not pleasant, but the taste is like none other. I have tried this delicacy made of chum salmon, pike, sheefish, and whitefish. Each of these fish has a mild flavor, unlike the rich flavor of king salmon. To shorten the preparation process for my wife, I jarred several broad and humpback whitefish. When Janice made the dessert, she felt like there were several steps missing. In one hour, she was done with everything, when it normally takes four hours to cool and bone the cooked fish. The results were excellent. Making akutaq is similar to the time-consuming process of making Eskimo salad. Every Native food flavor is packed into this carrot, lettuce, and cabbage salad, tossed with seal oil and garnished with herring eggs, dried chum salmon, mangtak, and smoked king salmon. A side of poke fish and frozen whitefish makes for a formal Eskimo banquet.[1]

Teaching others the jarring method brought me an exciting opportunity to try canning other appetizing Native alternatives. One was the moose stew, the moose version of beef stew, with chopped potatoes, carrots, onions, spices, and moose brisket. With crackers, dried fish, and a thermos of tea, the stew is an easy meal to stuff into a hunting bag. One fine spring after river ice breakup, my brother Abe asked if I could go logging. Abe asked a non-Native carpenter building the new Catholic church if he would like to take a break, go for a ride, and go logging. Curious and excited for a boat ride, the volunteer agreed after he asked how long we were planning to be out. "Today," said Abe. In Native talk "today" is a term for Yup'ik time. Time is relative when daylight extends to the wee hours of the morning. We left in the afternoon and returned well after midnight.

Logging is labor intensive, so we reenergized on crackers, snack bars, and the traditional dried fish. When we finally sat down to eat dinner, I took out two jars of moose stew. Abe and I could only laugh when the volunteer said that he was vegetarian, but we had already eaten all our fish. Several days later, the volunteer came to visit just as we were preparing dinner, and he could not get over the smell of the cooking. He commented on the aroma of homemade bread coming out of the oven. Being good Catholics, Janice and I invited him to eat after I told him what it was, and I reiterated that it is made of moose meat. I don't know what it is about Catholics, where they have a list of these mortal sins and if any are broken than they must see a priest and give a confession to be absolved. When we were logging the volunteer enjoyed the moose stew because that was all we had. But I had to call Abe as the volunteer helped himself to a second bowl of moose chili and complimented the serving, mixed with praise about the cultural diversity one must experience to appreciate small wonders of life. For vegetarians in rural Alaska, the rich and variety of traditional foods is a taste like no other. I've heard of an urban legend where they call vegetarians poor hunters.

Abe also went to St. Mary's Mission and knows the boarding school method of using student labor to help with daily chores. Students were assigned to clean bathrooms, sweep and mop, haul trash, wash dishes, clean laundry, shovel snow, and other simple chores. Our weekly assigned rotating duties helped us learn that taking responsibility was a serious task and that we all needed to work together. Each chore lasted about half an hour before morning class sessions.

During weekends students were assigned more time-consuming chores. One fall chore was to help harvest garden produce that was planted and maintained by the Catholic staff during summer. Each August about 120 students arrived at the mission. The produce from the garden help feed everyone. Gardening at the mission and other boarding schools in Alaska was introduced to the Natives as a self-sustaining practice. Brother Robert Benson was a baker, and many enjoyed helping him. In addition to enjoying bakery snacks, students learned to bake cookies, cakes, bread, and pies. Brother Benson was also in charge of the garden and informally taught gardening and growing crops. Although potatoes, cabbage, lettuce, and carrots were the main crops, he also grew turnips, onions, beets, peas, rhubarb, and cucumbers. The rich, well-developed garden soil was tucked between cleared patches of birch, willow, and spruce trees.

By boat, St. Mary's is twenty miles from Pilot Station. When attending the mission my sense of home was never misplaced. This part of Alaska is considered a temperate subarctic region with a boreal or taiga forest biome. Black spruce and white spruce are the two main conifers. The many deciduous plants, brush, and trees help replenish the nutrients in the thin soil with their falling leaves. The main deciduous trees include birch, aspen, alder, willow, and cottonwood. This boreal forest biome is contiguous throughout the Northern Hemisphere, where the rate of organic decay is a slow natural process of recycling. Conifers are trees that keep their needles all year; deciduous plants drop their leaves during the fall stay dormant in winter and blossom with spring.

Pilot Station has one odd tree found throughout the subarctic. This tree is the tamarack, which most know as larch or lodge pole pine. This tree also exists in high places of the Rocky Mountains. So it is not an unusual tree except for one feature: during the summer it looks like a Christmas tree or conifer, but when the birch, aspens, and other deciduous trees start dropping leaves, this tamarack follows and drops its needles. In the subarctic this is the only conifer that practices this seasonal change. Foresters question why and must ultimately accept the Native answer that this is Mother Nature's way and that Mother Nature does not need to be questioned.

One cousin of this tree has a neat personality and grew and flourished when the dinosaurs roamed. Most people are familiar with the redwood tree and its cousins, the giant sequoias of western America. Some are so huge they have been given Christian names, and one has a tunnel that a small car can drive through. There is one tree that is like no other. Did you ever hear the story of the dawn redwood?

NOTES

1. Poke fish is dried fish stored and preserved in seal oil and eaten just the way it is.

5 ⬿ Federal and State

"From far away, I saw it coming. At first it was a dark figure, but it was a person, it was holding something and I did not recognize the person. When it came closer, I started to get scared." We are in our hunting tent and the elder is telling a story.

I was fortunate to go on this hunting trip. Dad did not want to take me because it was cold, with early morning frost and ice formations on the riverbank. Snow could start soon. I didn't know if Dad was still mad at me and Donald for commercial fishing without permission earlier in August.

It was dark outside, and we were in a fourteen-by-sixteen-foot canvas tent. Prime stove hissing, Dad was cooking a fresh goose soup, rich with onions and rice. Everything smelled good. The fresh air from the boat ride was tiring. I closed my eyes and Donald shook me awake. saying the soup was ready.

Next morning, Dad and the men talked about the splashing water heard during the night. I had slept like a log and did not hear anything. Someone mentioned this time of the year was too cold for a bear to be in the water for any reason, so it must have been a moose. Beavers are quiet swimmers and the only noise they make is when they splash their tails to alarm others of intruders present.

That evening as Dad was cooking another goose, everything seemed surreal, like déjà vu. After hunting all day, I was trying hard not to doze when one of the men said there is nothing in nature, the land, or the wilderness to be afraid of. Respect the animals and predators and they will keep their distance. They will respect you. Dan Greene was a well-respected elder. Sipping tea and pausing to savor the flavor, he talked about the time he felt fear out in the wilderness. My interest piqued and I shook my sleepy thoughts away.

As a young man, Dan was alone in the tundra. Far off in the distance he saw a dark figure moving along the willows. At first, he thought it was a moose or caribou. When it got closer, he recognized a person, holding a gun. He did not recognize the way the person walked. It was a stranger; Dan became afraid.

In 2006 Alaska governor Sarah Palin was asked a question about the role of Alaska tribal governments. Palin replied that unlike foreign or national governments, she was not familiar with Alaska Native regional and village corporations. Palin was born in Idaho and raised Alaskan; the role of tribes and local self-government is not as evident as many non-Native Alaskans tend to believe. Since the creation of ANCSA Native corporations, many assume that Alaska Native sovereignty, aboriginal rights, and tribal status apply to Alaska Native corporation shareholders similar to Indian tribes of the Lower 48. Landownership is a precarious argument of tribal sovereignty, accepted and adjudicated as Indian Country. Many have accepted the fact that there is no Indian-owned land in Alaska. Palin's claim that she is not familiar with Alaska Native corporations or their shareholders is a generalization of tribes and tribal membership. Imagine if every federal and state government leader assumed that every Microsoft and Exxon corporation shareholder was an American and represented the livelihood and concerns of every U.S. citizen.

In mid-1990, as the role of tribes in Alaska began to be discussed after the state supreme court ruled that preferential harvests of subsistence users was unconstitutional, the state senate prompted the state attorney general to issue a legal disclaimer regarding the existence of tribes.[1] This was also the time that Katie John's court case decision was pending. In the post-ANCSA era, tribes were long assumed not to exist. As the state legislature began to address more active Native organizations—though not village governments or village corporations—the state legislature referred to these organizations as *racially defined groups* for lack of a better word, rather than "tribes." "Tribes" and "Indian Country" are phrases used carefully in state proceedings discussing or referencing Alaska Natives. It is a legislative belief that use of these words could imply that Alaska Natives have the same sovereign status as Natives living in the Lower 48.

Alaska's statehood settled the issue of landownership and jurisdiction. Alaska is the forty-ninth state, and the Lower 48 had already dealt with Indian self-determination regarding sovereignty and landownership. Eventually, many Indian tribes negotiated treaty agreements with the U.S. government over land claims, and the accepted solution was to create reservations to keep Indians separate from mainstream America. Although the idea of assimilating the Natives to Western civilization was the preferred alternative, the reservation system kept Natives separate and hidden. The treaty obligations subdued landownership claims, but Natives' growing need for assistance in the form of social service programs, food, education, housing, and basic amenities kept reminding the federal government of its fiduciary responsibilities. In time, the federal government signed no more treaty agreements and created no more reservations. Unfortunately, after Alaska's statehood, the Native identity and claims of Native landownership needed to be addressed.

The 1959 Statehood Act allow the state to select land, sea, and waters as property claims with discretionary use, development, and management. In land selections, the state was nonchalant about prior land titles, and this raised Native concerns. Many argued that Alaska was never conquered, bought, or sold by the Natives. Before 1971, a growing Native empowerment movement started an outcry that the state had no right to land identified as Native allotments according to the 1948 Alaska Native Allotment Act. This federal act allowed individual Natives to select 160 acres of land for ownership. U.S. Department of Interior Secretary Stewart Udall signed a land freeze against the State of Alaska until these Native claims could be settled. Significantly, state land selections included the North Slope, where oil reserves and exploration by large oil corporations raised Native concerns. The federal government also held lands as reserves, refuges, parks, and national forests, but the intent of complete discretionary management application and landownership entitlement toward Native harvests of fish and wildlife was not the same as the state.

No matter what your ethnic identity is, that identity is important to you. Native identity is addressed as a legal disclaimer in many congressional acts and legal documents. The colonial period during Russian American occupation and pre-statehood identified Alaska Natives as nothing more than aboriginal occupants. When the United States bought Alaska from Russia, provisions of the purchase agreement include the Natives as wards of the federal government with a clause that no intentional harm would come to them. Before statehood, the Natives were recognized as territorial U.S. citizens and after statehood as Alaska residents. Although this dual citizenship gave the Natives the same citizenship status as all Alaskans, the issue of land rights similar to those of Native Americans in the Lower 48 is a nagging identity of being a Native Alaskan. No matter how this ethnic identity is to be assimilated, the Natives are Native and can't help it. It was assumed as long as Natives recognized themselves as such, their potential claims to land, fish, wildlife and resources would preempt federal and state management responsibility over ownership claims. To address this, the ANCSA, signed by President Richard Nixon in 1971, extinguished aboriginal rights to hunting and fishing.

ANCSA lifted the land freeze and created Native corporations to select 44 million acres of land, with a settlement payment of $9.5 million. The act rescinded future land selections of the Alaska Native Allotment Act. The regional and village corporations now own and manage Native lands, including surface and subsurface rights to minerals, oil reserves, and forest products. The fish, birds, and animals Natives depend on as food sources were excluded as Native management responsibility and given to the state as wildlife management responsibility The corporation structure allows Natives to enroll as shareholder-owners with all the corporate benefits of future development and investments in the land and resources. Because of ANCSA, many non-Native residents and state representatives were pleased the Natives could now be treated as equals.

Unfortunately, the perception of Native corporations as service providers proved short-lived when the State of Alaska realized that the Native ethnic identity is a major part of the state government responsibility as Alaska residents. This identity is still a major influence. In 2018 under the administration of Governor Bill Walker, the Natives as first peoples continue to be a strong distinct ethnic group. Even as the state assumes we are all one as Alaska residents, the Native identity gets in the way and is addressed differently in every state department. It is a paradox. When ANCSA was passed, the state assumed Native identity was extinguished and that Natives were now corporation shareholders and Alaska residents.

In 1975 Congress passed the Indian Education and Self-Determination Assistance Act, allowing regional nonprofit organizations to provide Native services with federal funds and lighten the responsibility of the State of Alaska. The Native problem in Alaska has been unique, and every elected governor must deal with Native issues from health-care services to economics and development. No other issue has been as significant as the issue of hunting and fishing. Although the state will always claim management responsibility, conservation concerns about animals and fish result in differences of opinion over management guidelines, political oversight, and responsibility over Native food security. When the State of Alaska challenged the U.S. Supreme Court's Katie John decision, the rest of Alaska paid attention as the state tried to address this precarious situation regarding Alaska residency, ethnic identity, and harvest ethics. ANCSA misled everyone with this notion of extinguishing aboriginal rights. This paradox is a paradigm; "it would be nice if the state was to get a taste of its own medicine."

When Dan Greene did not recognize the man walking toward him, he felt fear because you can never learn the mind of a stranger or read their intentions. In the wilderness, nature dictates what the animal does or intends. When one spends time in the wilderness one learns to read the mind of an animal and to understand what it may or may not do. In other words, the mind of an animal is predictable and if given space, it will do what it must except when judging unforeseen circumstances. The mind of a human is unpredictable. When you meet a stranger for the first time, you can never know how that person thinks or what that person's intentions are. It takes time to build trust and to get to know a person once you find similarities you may have in common.

All Native hunters know this. A hunter told a story about Dad as a young hunter and their encounter with a bear. During spring geese hunt, a brown bear came walking along the sandbar toward their bird blind. With only shotguns and bird shot shells, the hunter said, Dad spoke to the bear in Yup'ik. After some conversation the bear went its own way. In such Native hunting stories, the message of respect is reciprocal.

ANCSA created 12 regional and 220 village corporations with shareholder enrollment eligibility for every Native born before 1971. Each regional corporation represents the Natives who lived in its geographical region of Alaska. Although ANCSA recognized the major landowners as the corporations, state or federal, the irony is that hunting and fishing seasons and regulations began to differ about who owned the land and who claimed jurisdiction on it. Corporation lands are non-reservations legally recognized as private property with fee-simple title and subject to state jurisdiction including hunting and fishing regulations.

Regardless of Alaska residency status, Native identity is a state and federal issue based on who owns the land and who is responsible for the wild fish and animals. After ANCSA was passed, Alaska was happy to include Natives as residents, but implications of fair share and preferential use of wild resources kept interfering with the Alaska constitution. According to the constitution no harvest preference is allowed for any ethnic or rural resident, regardless of preexisting claims.

The main wildlife resource that kept federal and state attention was not salmon, moose, caribou, or any large land animal, but sea mammals and migratory birds such as geese and ducks. The state was trying to claim and manage everything Native, but the migratory critters reminded the federal government about relations and stewardship obligations with neighboring countries and nation states that share the same resource. States are not allowed to have direct agreements with other countries.

Natives were concerned about the influence of non-Natives over all Alaska Board of Fish (BOF) and Board of Game (BOG) harvest regulations. The Natives voiced their concerns, but implications of landownership gave the state every right to manage all wild resources. With this disparity between rural Native and Alaska residents, the federal government realized that all federal lands needed to address what ANCSA meant as "extinguishment of aboriginal rights," especially on federal lands and waters and with regard to migratory animals. Then Congress stepped in, and the state tried to stem federal influence.

After 1971 the state was trying to address the hunting and fishing needs of Natives as Alaska residents, but the regulations implied otherwise and would later be ruled unconstitutional. In 1978 the state attempted to prioritize rural subsistence harvests including creating the Division of Subsistence, a branch of ADF&G to research and provide data and technical reports on rural harvests. Unfortunately, this was not enough, and both the state and federal government passed more laws regulating Native harvests, clarifying conflicts of interest and addressing Native identity.

In 1980 Congress passed ANILCA, allowing agencies within the Department of Interior to manage federal land and waters. This act created a new harvest user with a new legal identity. Every annual state hunt and fish regulation booklet identifies users as *residents* or *non-residents*. ANILCA recognizes harvesters as *subsistence* or *non-subsistence*. Every Alaska Native is now recognized as a resident subsistence user, depending on whether their harvest activity takes place on state and federal lands. ANILCA also created the Federal Subsistence Board to provide oversight and regulation guidelines similar to the state boards of fish and game. Although subsistence and non-subsistence uses are recognized, ANILCA also addresses *rural* and *non-rural* harvesting associated with this subsistence hunters and fishers. Where roads exist and urban Alaskans have access to wildlife, it is easy to recognize who has jurisdiction, regardless of who owns the land.

The controversial issue ANCSA extinguished and what ANILCA was intended to address is preferential use. In large population centers, preferential use of hunting or fishing is seen as competition of prowling sportsman skills. Many non-Natives are not hunters or fishers per se; for many these activities are an occasional thrill, and the grocery store is a more convenient option. Sporting activities are seen as a fun hobby of a select few; non-Natives can choose not to participate. Whether the game meat is eaten or not is irrelevant. Non-Natives who participate in these activities are referred to as "sportsmen." Given the history of hunting and fishing regulations toward Natives, many Native hunters and fishers refer to non-Natives who participate in the regulatory process as respectable sportsmen.

In Native Alaska, regardless of what "preferential use" is intended to mean, Natives have adopted unique practices under the current regulations. If you live in these communities, regardless of whether you choose to participate, you will most likely get a share of the catch, with no payment necessary. Being a subsistence hunter and fisher is part of being a respected Yup'ik.

After ANILCA the state did not sit idle. Before 1989 the state tried to grant Native harvesters special recognition. In 1982 BOG and BOF formally recognized rural subsistence priority, but in 1989 the state supreme court ruled that regulation unconstitutional. After this ruling, Alaska Native leaders discussed efforts to reauthorize ANCSA to amend hunting and fishing provisions to address rural subsistence needs as an alternative to a state constitutional convention. Meanwhile, the Department of Interior continued to develop the federal subsistence program, including the Office of Subsistence Management (OSM) to assist FSB. Using provisions of ANILCA, Katie John challenged the State of Alaska, claiming that subsistence salmon fishing on federal and state waters is eligible for federal management because of subsistence priority. In response, the state argued that all navigable waters in Alaska are managed by the state, similar to many U.S. states, and that preferential harvest is unconstitutional to any user, resident or otherwise.

When state and federal regulations are created, Native identity continues to be included with special provisions. Statehood created a new resident user, and ANCSA extinguished one to make everyone the same. Congress, with the 1976 Indian Education and Self-Determination Assistance Act, recognized Alaska Natives as tribal members, and ANILCA in 1981 recognized Natives as subsistence users. In turn the 1989 state supreme court decision reminded everyone that preferential subsistence use is unconstitutional. As a result, Native identity is always an issue to consider in legal proceedings, whether in regard to hunting and fishing or child custody and social welfare.

In 1980 a respected Yup'ik elder composed an Eskimo dance song addressing this very paradigm as a traditional historical footnote never to be forgotten. The dance moves showed opposite hand motions about how confusing the ethics of non-Native hunting and fishing regulations applied to all Native harvesters. As if Native identity had never been controversial, in 2014 and 2016 the U.S. Department of Interior and several Native organizations signed a co-management agreement and created a new Native identity, ignoring Alaska residency status. The state and Alaska residents were uninvolved. The co-management agreement supersedes state management authority, regardless of residency claims and constitutional guidelines.

The new identity outlined in the agreement is called a federally qualified user. Is this respect for the Native?

NOTES

1. Alaska Attorney General Bruce Botelho to Alaska Senate Judiciary Committee Chairman Robin Taylor, re: Tribal sovereignty questions, April 18, 1996.

6 ⪦ Roots and Moratoriums

"Nicholas and Caitlyn are going to stand," my brother Abe told Janice and I. "They've been coming to practice and I made a new song for Nicholas." Abe was excited. "You guys have to learn how to dance these songs."

⪦

February 1970. Over the CB radio one Sunday afternoon, an elder of the Eskimo dance group announced for certain elders and singers to come to his home. Messengers from St. Mary's were in Pilot Station and an Eskimo dance was announced for that evening. At the dance, the messenger invited attendees to a potlatch in St. Mary's the following weekend and listed some of the people and families who should attend.

Everyone was excited. Pilot Station residents helped coordinate travel arrangements, men from St. Mary's helped pick up residents, and flight arrangements were made for elders. With as many as three Natives on a snow machine pulling a wooden basket sled with family and sleeping gear, Friday was a day of travel. St. Mary's was seventeen miles away. Down the Yukon River through the snow machine portage, as many as five children sat in a ten-foot-long wooden basket sled bundled in blankets, with an older sibling standing on the sled rails. Cold and chilly, stopping now and then to warm up, Mom cautiously warmed cold cheeks with powdered snow. Many families stayed at the homes of relatives. Meals were a coordinated challenge, and sleeping arrangements were whatever floor space was available. My parents, brothers, and sisters stayed at Uncle John Thompson Sr.'s three-bedroom home, and they had a similar large family. John's home was packed. Many St. Mary's homes were in a similar state of happy disarray.

That evening at the community hall, the St. Mary's dance group greeted the invited guests and ushered them to their seats, with elders and men in the front row. Guests sat on one side of the dance hall, with an open dance floor as the stage. On the other side, St. Mary's dancers would sit behind the singers and drummers, but at the beginning of the ceremony these seats were empty and would fill as the procession started. A St. Mary's dance-group leader gave a welcome speech, presenting a special group of honored people who had initiated this ceremonial event. The first honoree was brought in, and a dried seal skin was laid on the floor for the person to stand on. An elder introduced the person, accompanied by parents: "Curious with the gathering of Natives and the drum beat and songs calling, this person came into our Eskimo dance hall and presented him- or herself. As this person dances, we see the likeness and character of who this person is named after and that he or she has indeed returned back to place of living."

Dressed in their finest regalia of fur garments—parka, boots, mittens, and fur hat—the person is presented with a gift of significance to be given to their namesake family or close friends during another lifetime. This person's Eskimo name or names tell whom they are named after. Eskimo names provide a long lineage of cultural significance of a person reincarnated for as long as time can be remembered.

Everything about this ceremonial event had cultural significance: the introduction, fur and ceremonial garments, song and dance, gift presenting and giving, and guest participation. After the honoree was introduced, their gifts were given to namesake family or friends of another lifetime as special guests of this event. The people receiving the gifts were happy for the return and hugged their mother, father, or lost loved one and were comforted in their grieving. Immediate St. Mary's family members presented bales of cloth tied end over end onto the sealskin. The cloth symbolizes the umbilical cord and birth of the namesake person. Gifts from family and relatives were placed next to the cloth.

After this, another honoree was presented in the same fashion. The people presented are known as the people standing. St. Mary's has stood as many as fifteen members in one ceremonial potlatch. After all those standing were presented, the local Catholic priest and Native Eucharistic minister shared a prayer and blessing. With a prayer in

Yup'ik, holy water, and a traditional blessing of feather wings fanning smoke from dried Labrador tea leaves, the event was christened. All gifts were set aside in another room, and the dance floor was prepared for the first song.

A St. Mary's elder beat a drum and quietly sang the first verse of a song. This was a key signal to people standing. They shed much of their heavy winter fur clothing, dressed in the traditional formal homemade *qaspeq*, or hooded dress shirt made of calico cloth. The men and boys kneeled and held dance fans made of wood and ptarmigan or owl feathers; these were shared by the dance group. The women and girls stood behind the men, dressed formally with beaded fur headdress, beaded necklace, designer qaspeq, and their own personal dance fans with bird feathers and animal fur that provide dance movements all their own. Traditional men's dance fans are made of woven wooden strands tied together in a circular form, while the women's dance fans are made of a carved wooden piece with two small holes and are held with fingers tipped. The traditional Yukon River women's dance fan is intricately designed with geese feathers and delicate to hold. Today, most women's dance fans are made of caribou fur, a traditional coastal Yup'ik design.

The person standing took center stage with immediate family around them, family members' positions depending on whether they were a child or adult. Families used similar qaspeq colors, with that of the person standing having more elaborate designs.

After everyone was positioned, the song and drumbeat started, slow and formal. The song was sung to its first repertoire with little dance movement; open dance fans provided traditional reverence and appreciation of the guests. In unison, the beat of the drum told dance fans what to do; each movement told a story. Each song had several verses, a chorus, and an *apalluk*, best described as a verse of a verse between choruses. The apalluk was repeated after several repetitions of a song, and the tempo slowed the drum and song. The dance started with immediate family, and then, after the first apalluk, relatives joined, followed by the rest of St. Mary's, all showing their support of the person standing. Everyone was dressed in their finest garments; colors helped to differentiate families. The dance was repeated for guests to enjoy, as they called out praises of "again," *calii*, or "encore," *pamyua*.

Each person standing had a special song and dance. Some danced to old songs, traditional storytelling for as long as time can be remembered, and some were new and special. Some were recognized as significant for certain families and villages, some were humorous and characteristic of the person standing, and some were thought provoking and methodical. Every song is a story. The first night, every person standing danced their song and introduced the guests to their namesakes. At the close, leaders announce for guests to return the next morning for passing of the gifts.

In the morning, guests were greeted and ushered to their seats. Family and relatives helped pass out the gifts of the person standing, with significant gifts given to namesake friends and relatives. Many of the gifts were food items, such as flour, sugar, pilot bread crackers, tea, and coffee. Women received cooking utensils, dishes, pots, pans, and sewing equipment and supplies, and cut and shared the cloth. The men received tools, work gloves, and hunting and fishing supplies. Children received candy, gum, hats, socks, and gloves. It's like another Christmas. After the gift giving, leaders announced that men and widowed women should return that afternoon for another gift-giving event and that the second night of dances would continue that evening.

The afternoon gift event was coordinated by the hunters and fishermen, the providers of the community. Everything given to the guests was the bounty harvested from land, air, river, and sea: meat from moose, caribou, rabbits, beaver, birds, fish, seals, whale, and berries. The widows recognized in this sharing of gifts understood the loss of their loved ones would never be forgotten. Christian prayers and traditional blessings are also a part of this event. Grandmothers and mothers of the people who stood passed out dried fish and akutaq for guests to enjoy.

The Saturday dance, the final event, was filled with ceremonial significance. St. Mary's performed the first song honoring the community and a significant elder who had passed. Unlike the first night, guests were invited to join the dance. St. Mary's performed the same dances as the first night, and, following the tradition of respect centered on the elders, singers from St. Mary's approach elder guests to ask what song and dance they would like to hear. With these requests, the singer drummed and sang quietly, and dancers listened and prepared in case their song and dance were requested. Similar to the first dance performance, the first verse and dance belonged to immediate family. After several verses, relatives and community joined, then guests were welcome to dance with their namesake relative. Immediate relatives and friends danced close to their reincarnated lost loved one, happy for their return. Some tried to make a mistake dance move to confuse others. The mood was humorous, serious, and ecstatic, and teasing cousins and relatives was open entertainment for everyone to enjoy the significant ceremony.

The floor was filled with dancers. Spiritually every song came alive. Guests called *calii* and *pamyua* many times. The apalluk allowed everyone to recompose: the tempo slowed down to let everyone to catch their breath, the drumbeat allowed the heart to pace itself, and then the tempo picked up where it had left off. The first night was formal and serious, recognizing the dance and songs of St. Mary's as special to the namesake person standing with deep traditional ties of respect among our people. At the first night guests were discouraged from dancing; the second night we shared the namesakes' joy.

Several hours later, St. Mary's invited the Pilot Station guests to trade seats. Pilot Station had hosted a potlatch a week before with St. Mary's as guests. The potlatch ceremony is a reciprocal event that follows similar traditions between the two communities. After trading seats, Pilot Station performed dance songs recognizing the people who had stood the week before. Although every song is significant, two standup songs were sung the second night. The St. Mary's hosts sang one as an invitation for everyone to dance and share this event, and the other as a farewell song at the close of the event. In the standup songs, men and women danced standing, wearing or holding gloves, without dance fans. Traditionally, holding or wearing gloves is a recognition of the difference between the spiritual and physical world we share with the afterlife; a dancer should not perform without an offering, symbolized by showing empty hands.

St. Mary's has had a strong influence from the Catholic church. Traditional potlatches were seen as unchristian dance and song activities honoring a demigod. In 1969 Pilot Station and St. Mary's elders revived this practice, working with St. Mary's Mission church leaders not to offend one another. One Catholic priest, Father Rene Astruc, was instrumental in helping the Natives with this revival. Father Astruc learned the Yup'ik language, participated in the Eskimo song and dance, and learned the significance of potlatch as a cultural activity. His influence with the Jesuit diocese helped clarify that the potlatch, though traditionally significant, has no implications to Christian faith. If anything, the two can coexist and provide comfort in the mysteries and convictions of each faith. To help this revival, Pilot Station elders completed a qasgiq project in which Natives paid homage to the Yup'ik worldview and the respect among Natives as a society. In time, as this niche developed and grew to its current annual potlatch hosted between the two communities, the tension created by early church leaders eased.

"Hmm, it tastes like seal," my Native guest told his friend as I cut raw meat to cook into a traditional dish. The two are Siberian Yupik from the St. Lawrence Island community of Savoonga. Siberian and Central Yup'ik are Yup'ik language dialects, but speakers of both are still Eskimo—eaters of raw meat. They asked for more and I was concerned when they enjoyed the frozen delicacy a little too much for my comfort as a Central Yup'ik descendant. I know the taste of raw seal but this was not seal; these two Natives are seal hunters.

I told a story about when my brother Abe was invited to travel to the coast to hunt moose. My brother teased his friend that their moose meat tasted like beaver, thus beginning a teasing trend about how Native food tastes better near home. Several years later, Abe caught a seal near Pilot Station and his friend told him upriver seals taste like beaver.

St. Lawrence Island is in middle of the Bering Sea. No beavers exist on the island. I was skinning and gutting a large beaver, but the young Siberian guests thought I was cutting a seal. Even after I told them what it was, they wanted to sample more, and I told them that we Natives in this part of Alaska eat this meat raw only if we have no other choice. Excitedly I told them they should try fresh moose liver and kidney; it is a delicacy every respected hunter should try.

In 1982 St. Mary's elders hosted a three-day dance festival with nine Yup'ik dance groups from Yukon Kuskokwim villages. This event helped revive Eskimo dancing as a region-wide cultural practice. Several years later, the Calista Corporation created a Calista Elders Council to help coordinate a region-wide dance festival, including the annual Camai event in Bethel. Camai is similar to the Quyana Festival of the Alaska Federation of Natives (AFN) Convention hosted between Anchorage and Fairbanks. Camai and AFN Quyana are the largest gatherings of Alaska Natives and host performances of many traditional dances.

In November 2008 Pilot Station had the honor to host Yupiit Yuraryarait, a festival of Yup'ik song and dance that originated after the 1982 St. Mary's gathering. This festival, though not an annual event, is the largest gathering of Yup'ik dancers and singers. In 2008 seventeen dance groups performed, and many estimate the number of people in Pilot Station was five times its typical population of seven hundred. In our three-bedroom home, we had fifteen guests from St. Mary's, Nightmute, and Savoonga.

The dance event took place in the Pilot Station school gym. Each group performed and told stories into early morning hours. Many of the songs and dances are similar; everyone speaks Yup'ik, and the difference in dialects is reflected in the songs sung from Central Yup'ik, Siberian Yupik, to Cup'ik, and from coastal to inland. Slight differences in dress, drums, and dance fans reflect the natural diversity of the traditional ancestors of each community. Of all groups present, the Siberian Yupik is the most distinct from mainland Yup'ik. The Savoonga women's traditional qaspeq length is longer and dress-like. Their song and dance reflect the Inuit Eskimos of northern Alaska in style and rhythm. Yupiit and Inuits are considered Eskimo with different ethnographic, cultural, and demographic characteristics, but the Siberian Yupik ancestral language is Yup'ik. The Inuit cultural influence reflects people who depend on the sea for food security and have limited resources for traditional artifacts, tools, and material.

The Eskimo drum is an example. The traditional Eskimo drum material is a large bladder of a sea mammal, tied with sinew on steam-treated, round driftwood. Throughout the song and dance, the drum material is pulled and tightened to the drummer's desired tone. Round and similar in size, the Siberian Yupik drum is made of walrus intestine, and constant care is necessary to maintain its flexibility and strength. The drummers moisten and rub the drum with freshwater to prevent the skin from drying and ripping. Mainland Yup'ik drums are made of plastic material readily available, and the care is not as necessary as it used to be, except for occasional tightening of the drum to change the tone. A new favorite among dance groups is airplane wing material, which is stronger and provides a percussion with a soft, resonating, aerodynamic sound, especially when the song reaches maximum crescendo.

The drumstick is also different; most are two feet in length and round in shape with a slightly tapered end for finger holding. The mainland drummer hits the top of the drum for a throbbing beating sound. The Siberian Yupik stick is tapered wide rather than round, and the drummer hits the bottom of the drum to create a hollow, deep resonating sound. Accompanied by the song, the drumbeat and dance tell a story. The Siberian Yupik song and dance performance is similar to the Inuits', and they dance each song once, unlike mainland Yupiit, who perform the same song and dance to their hearts' content. The drum is the beating heart of all traditions.

After 1969 the Pilot Station and St. Mary potlatch became an annual event in January and February and accepted as culturally significant rather than an unchristian ritual ceremony. St. Mary's also began a new tradition during the Sunday morning Catholic mass on the third day of potlatch: a christening ritual recognizing the people who stand and their Yup'ik namesakes. With parents or immediate guardians as hosts, the Catholic priest christens their Yup'ik names, similar to the Christian baptismal and confirmation rites. Unlike the Christian tradition of keeping birth names as to mark family relations, Yup'ik newborns receive the names of people who have recently passed. Many newborns are given more than one Yup'ik name, after people who pass at about the same time. Elders may also give a name after a vision or dream of a relative or friend. These names are recognized when a person stands at potlatch.

Jesuit priest Rene Astruc arrived at the St. Mary's Mission in 1964. Father Astruc was open-minded and apostle-like and learned to speak Yup'ik. Astruc attended and participated in Eskimo dances and became accepted into the Native community. His participation helped reconcile the tensions created by early Jesuits about Christianity and traditional potlatches. In 1984 Father Astruc stood at the St. Mary's potlatch and was recognized with a Yup'ik name, and his name was reincarnated with Native children born at the time of his passing. One of my cousins has his name, and it is apparent when Father Astruc's true character surfaces to reveal who my cousin is truly named after. During several church services, my cousin, as a young teen, volunteered to be a eucharistic minister to help with services, though he had never received confirmation or been ordained. The first time my brothers and I saw this, we could not get over his namesake characteristic. Many parents and elders have stories of reincarnated lost loved ones and the joy, irony, and comfort of these experiences. Simple facial expressions, social interactions, and likes and dislikes are similar to the person they are named after. We could only shrug our shoulders when as a young boy my son Kalen talked about so-and-so owing him some money from another lifetime.

Native traditions such as this namesake birth rite imply a reincarnated afterlife, so the stories of purgatory, heaven, and hell were a challenge for early Christian denominations with their message that there is a right and wrong way of reverence to the mysteries of life and that the soul of these Natives needed to be saved. Throughout Alaska, Christian denominations banned traditional activities such as Eskimo dancing and potlatch ceremonies at about the same time ethnographic documentation of the Natives was being collected. Anthropologists universally recorded Native people living happily in their world despite the hardship and desolation the barren land and environment implied.

Nicholas and Caitlyn were ten and eleven years old during their potlatch ceremony, and their standup songs were characteristic of their personalities. Caitlyn's was an old song about sledding down a hill and enjoying the winter snow outdoors carefree and full of fun; the dance moves mimicked holding onto a sled as one slid down a hill. The new song Abe made for Nicholas was about hunting and providing for community and family. It was a song about when Nicholas caught his first moose. This potlatch event was in 2009 and followed much of the traditions revived in 1969. Every potlatch has ceremonial significance. On the first night of the 2009 Pilot Station potlatch, an old formal song was performed, a favorite children's fable story. All children standing that year danced this song in addition to their own standup songs. The children started this dance by themselves for the first apalluk before elders, parents, and community joined. With events and performances such as this, it is heartwarming to know that traditions shared with children are difficult to set aside, ignore, or replace as a historical footnote. The children's song is similar to "Mary Had a Little Lamb" or "Itsy-Bitsy Spider."

In 1969 Pilot Station elders completed a traditional qasgiq to help revive the potlatch. A large qasgiq, a dome shaped of logs and a mud-covered roof, was built with apprehension to host guests from St. Mary's. Once, wooden masks and shamans were rumored to have been part of potlatch storytelling festivals. With Christian influence, the traditional ways no longer incorporate these practices. It is often accepted that what people fear the most is what they do not understand. With this as a tool, early Christian leaders instilled fear into the hearts and minds of the Natives with stories of an afterlife that depended on how we live and worship as a living people. In the same way, early Christians feared the Natives and their traditional ceremonial ways as worshipping an ancient demigod and forbade these practices. As a humble people, the Natives had no option but to oblige.

7 ≷ Alliance Seekers

"Ready," we all whispered.

We readied our guns with clear sights. Domonic sat in the boat with his gun propped on sleeping gear; Bruce and Nathan sat on the beach with guns shouldered; I stood with my gun resting on a tree limb.

As a Native, I've always had a notion that PETA is willing to support Native hunters who do not get any thrills from the ethics of hunting for food. Being proud is one thing, but we will never see support to justify cultural integrity. Many law-abiding hunters attest to the ethics of fair chase, the significance of the trophy, and the thrill of pulling the trigger. Many agree that there is a sense of excitement. Subsistence hunters don't have a choice. The economic reality of living in Native Alaska, where supermarkets do not exist, means there are few other options. The idea of a law-abiding subsistence hunter is silly. Natives going hunting and fishing for fun can create serious food problems.

The Atchuelinguk River drainage is a favorite for hunters. Annual moose numbers are consistent in this area, although not every trip is a guarantee.

Native hunters siding with PETA will raise ethical questions and laughter from respectable sport hunters and state managers. I can only imagine the outrage and reiterated questions of ethical issues and "conflicts of interest" from PETA members standing to justify their convictions. Conflicts of interest from special interest groups are a pale shade of white, not as clear as sunlight.

Sitting on the Atchuelinguk riverbank, prime stove hissing, eating dried fish, crackers, and tea, looking out for our winter supply of meat, conflict of interest was far from my mind. Nathan nodded his head with a mouth full of crackers and pointed with his teacup across the river. A hundred yards away a young bull moose stuck his head over the riverbank. Quickly, quietly, we decided what to do. We aimed and whispered *ready*; someone whispered *fire*.

It sounded like a twenty-one-gun salute. Such were many successful hunts, fresh meat next to the boat, winter's quick supply.

The ethics of fair chase and the sport hunter mentality do not exist for Native subsistence hunters. The value of that fresh meat is so critical that the Native notion of fair chase is to knock the moose down quickly beside the boat, making it easy to load. Unfortunately, the ethics of subsistence regulations mirror the fair chase ethics of the sportsman who created the regulations. Actually, why am I trying to say something worded carefully when I can say it directly? There are no legal state hunting and fishing seasons for any subsistence harvester. Every harvest effort has a binding regulation with special provisions that must be followed. Whether I purchase a current license is beside the point. The special management provisions attest to the fact that the state's role in all subsistence resources is not arbitrary.

The Alaska constitution mirrors the public trust doctrine of every U.S. state. Unfortunately, the state's public trust fails to recognize the Native way of life and its food security concerns. This is an issue especially for cultures that have no notion of farming and growing crops, and it is the reason USFWS and ADF&G apologized to Alaska Natives for the hardships created by the early hunting and fishing regulations. These same regulations continue to impact the Native way of life.

In 1968 two iconic leaders visited Pilot Station. In addition to learning about rural village conditions, the two brought national political influence. Ted Kennedy and a young Ted Stevens visited and reported on local housing conditions, lack of health-care facilities, transportation access, education, and condition of the U.S. post office. As the only federal employee, Dad was the host, language interpreter, and visitor guide. Dad had a picture taken with the two leaders and this is something he never talked about. At the time of the visit, everyone was getting ready for the salmon fishing season, and the federal presence in our small Yukon River salmon fishery was insignificant. In 1993 Alaska congressman Ted Stevens created and passed an act that impacted the fishery in Pilot Station in such a way that created economic hardships and brought into question the fishery's viability as a local commodity.

Boreal Fisheries Inc. had been a major fish-buying company for my part of Alaska since 1971 and had weathered challenging salmon fishery issues. Randy and Edna Crawford first visited St. Mary's as schoolteachers and created Boreal Fisheries as a family-owned business. The wild Yukon salmon is a prized worldwide commodity, and one unique characteristic of this fishery is that all commercial fishers are Natives of this area. In rural Alaska, fish-buying companies have historically provided economic incentives that would otherwise be unavailable. Many commercial fishers in Alaska have a permit that legally allows them to sell the fish they catch, giving them a chance to earn income. Similarly, permit holder catcher-sellers can legally purchase salmon from commercial fishers and resell the salmon on the domestic market. For a fee, anyone can apply for an Alaska catcher-seller permit.

In 1993 Congress passed the Magnuson-Stevens Act and created the Community Development Quota (CDQ) program for the Bering Sea trawl fisheries. Although the two-hundred-mile exclusive economic zone gives the United States and Alaska ownership of the coastal zone, foreign fish-processing vessels operating in Alaska waters pose a pillage issue for all offshore fisheries. The CDQ program created regional fish corporations with quota shares for Bering Sea fish resources. Communities within a fifty-mile radius are eligible to be members of this program. Pilot Station is not eligible to join this collective. The Yukon Delta Fisheries Development Association created the enterprise fish-buying company Kwik'Pak Ltd., which directly impacted Pilot Station. The Magnuson-Stevens Act was never meant to apply to a salmon fishery on a river system; the act was intended for the offshore fisheries, and not specifically for Alaska salmon. With millions of federal startup funds, these corporations became conglomerates of the Bering Sea fisheries and non-associated businesses were set in jeopardy. In fact, many small fish-buying companies ceased to exist. As conglomerates these CDQ corporations were able to set the price on raw fish and have the funds necessary to weather corporate losses. There have been rumors of these corporations purchasing small fish buying companies for pennies on the dollar.

Although Boreal Fisheries was a major Yukon River fish-buying company, other companies had existed with varying degrees of business success. Any business's success is evident by its growth, the services it provides, and its increase in clients. Boreal Fisheries' existence as a family business and the services it provided can never be quantified on a spreadsheet. Throughout these years, Boreal Fisheries faced the challenges of its aging fishing vessels and facilities. When fish-buying boats have mechanical issues, fishers from as far away as Russian Mission must travel the eight-hour boat ride to Boreal Fisheries to sell their salmon.

In 2001 Kwik'Pak Fisheries became a major Yukon salmon corporation. The conglomerate mindset of taking over the Bering Sea trawl fisheries became evident as the fleets became community based and helped corporations grow into monopoly organizations. With this mindset, Kwik'Pak infringed on the Yukon salmon fisheries and put the existence of Boreal Fisheries in jeopardy. As Kwik'Pak was a CDQ corporation under the Magnuson-Stevens Act, the State of Alaska was required to monitor it and to set the seasons for offshore and Alaska river salmon fisheries. The relationship between Kwik'Pak and Boreal as competing businesses was not cordial. With competitive buyers, the retail market for Yukon salmon provides incentives to Native fishers. Wild Yukon salmon is an important Alaska commodity and provides critical support to communities who participate in fishing. In 2004 the existence and role of Boreal Fisheries was put to the test.

As community planner for the Pilot Station tribal government, I sent a letter to Governor Frank Murkowski with a report on the impact of the CDQ program on Yukon salmon fisheries and non-CDQ communities. The report included statistics of the salmon fisheries and income earned, including the fact that Native families depend on the fishery as their only viable income source. According to the Magnuson-Stevens Act, regardless of the two-hundred-mile exclusive economic zone, communities within a fifty-mile radius of the Bering Sea are eligible to join the CDQ program and receive benefits and services such as heating fuel assistance, community infrastructure developments, and student scholarships. The Yukon River villages of Pitkas Point, St. Mary's, Pilot Station, Marshall, and Russian Mission directly depend on Yukon salmon and do not receive any incentives. As these communities raised concern, Kwik'Pak signed an operation agreement with Boreal Fisheries to continue to buy fish from these non-CDQ villages. In 2017 Kwik'Pak did not renew this agreement.

Boreal Fisheries closed in 2017. After the summer salmon season, another West Coast fish-buying company participated in the fall season and purchased salmon at the dock in St. Mary's. Fishers had a choice to continue selling salmon to Kwik'Pak or to the new fish company, FishPeople Seafood. In 2018 Kwik'Pak, FishPeople, and a Kodiak-based corporation, International Seafoods of Alaska, all purchased Yukon salmon, allowing Native fishers an opportunity to earn income. In 2019 Fish People and International Seafoods of Alaska closed. Kwik'Pak is now the only fish buyer.

Perhaps this is a good time for Congress to create a quota share program for Yukon salmon similar to the Bering Sea pollock and crab quota share program. Although I can only tell the story of the fisheries from my part of Alaska, fish companies farther up the Yukon River have another story to tell about the impact of the CDQ program.

Like many Alaska Natives, I don't remember the last time I bought a legal State of Alaska hunting license. Similarly, I have never bought a duck or bird hunting stamp. Every year my family harvests wild salmon, moose, and birds. Many rural families face serious food shortages if we do not participate in subsistence hunting and fishing. Next to salmon and whitefish, moose meat is the main staple in Pilot Station. These resources will always be a concern.

The renewable and nonrenewable natural resources of Alaska are recognized as public trust resources that belong to every Alaska resident and U.S. citizen. Nonrenewable resources include oil, coal, gold, and many geologic minerals Alaska is famous for. Renewable resources include the forest and plants, wildlife, and fish and birds that also call Alaska home. Together these resources are part of the public trust domain, where every citizen has a voice in management responsibility, including use and access.

After ANCSA the land settlement gave the state full discretion to develop large oil and gas reserves as a major nonrenewable resource. As the Alaska oil pipeline was built, Native hunting and fishing concerns became nonsignificant issues for the state. But the use and management of wild fish and animals are the real public trust domain for Alaska Natives. The Alaska state constitution recognizes both Natives and non-Natives as Alaska residents. According to the claim that ANCSA extinguished aboriginal rights, Alaska Natives have no more preexisting claims to manage these resources. Before 1971, no legal claims recognized Native rights to hunting and fishing.

Before ANCSA was passed, there were several Alaska organizations that monitored the treatment and livelihood of Alaska Natives as advocates, including the Alaska Native Brotherhood and Sisterhood of Southeast Alaska promoting Native solidarity. These organizations are based on traditional ethnic groups recognized between neighboring cultures that live in and share Alaska. ANCSA also created nonprofit corporations such as the Association of Village Council Presidents and Tanana Chiefs Council to address social service programs. After Congress passed the Indian Education and Self-Determination Assistance Act of 1976, AVCP was formally incorporated as a 501(c)(3) nonprofit corporation.

Before AVCP was incorporated, a similar Native movement advocated for hunting and fishing concerns. It was often associated with AVCP—some say it was usurped into this organization. Nunam Kitlutsisti was the name of this movement. In Yup'ik the name translates to "protectors" or "guardians of the land." The original theme recognized that the Natives are the forefront, the eyes and ears of the land and resources, so if Natives are concerned about a natural resource issue then management agencies should recognize these concerns. It is easy to speculate that the creation of this organization stemmed from the Alaska Territorial Guard during the last world war, when Alaska Natives were enlisted to be the eyes and ears of the U.S. military. Invasion of the Japanese army into the Aleutian Islands triggered a need for this.

After AVCP was created, Nunam Kitlutsisti went quiet and no longer exists. In 2014 Tanana Chiefs Council and AVCP began talks of creating a Yukon River Intertribal Fish Commission to address Native empowerment. In 2017 Natives began to discuss forming a statewide tribal government: Nunavut. Translated it means "Our Land."

8 ≶ Whitefish Fishing

"You have to be like those fishermen. You have to be *pe'tungyuq*," I told John and Nancy how to spearfish.

It was midnight. I set down the kerosene lantern and sat on the gravel beach. I was cold and one side of my hip boots was damp. In the dark I watched a group of Asians speaking excitedly in their language. The one holding a kerosene lantern speared another fish. Still wiggling, into their five-gallon bucket it went. Their bucket looked heavy.

I was a student at UAF. It was late fall, and John and Nancy had talked me into spearfishing for whitefish on the Chatanika River. It sounded like fun to catch fish on a spear. The idea is to wade the shallow river during dark of night holding a lantern and spear the fish. The lantern gives an even light, reflecting the shiny fish movements. Flashlights do not give the same surface refraction and make it hard to see the fish, the same way sunlight makes it impossible to see anything below the surface. For the three of us, it was our first time.

John and Nancy retreated to the truck to warm up. Although we had one spear and lantern between the three of us, we had no luck. We tried everything from trying to surround and corral the fish to kicking and shooing it to the spear holder or to the beach, two of us laughing and holding arms out. We even tried throwing the three-pronged five-and-a-half-foot spear like a harpoon.

I stared into my empty bucket, then looked around to see how many fishers were having any luck. Earlier in the darkness, there had been at least ten fishers; now there were just two groups of Asians. I was not ready to quit. Another group's chatter grew excited with commotion as another fish went into their bucket. Were they working together? This time I watched, pretending to fiddle with my spear. No one at home in

Pilot Station speared for fish. The other group spotted another fish and without hesitation the lantern holder ran and caught the fish on the second jab. Rejuvenated, I realized our mistake; their method actually worked. All this time like a predator to its prey, we were trying to be sneaky and quiet. To catch fish, I have to be *pe'tungyuq*.

I smiled when John and Nancy found me. Our bucket was not empty. "You have to be like those fishermen. You have to be greedy."

≈

Every Native culture has stories and oral traditions that teach respect for animals and reiterate the existence of a deeper spiritual realm that shares our world. It is my custom to respect and learn from my elders. As long as I can remember I've helped someone harvest fresh whitefish from the frozen Yukon River. Setting and maintaining gillnet under the ice is no easy chore. A fresh whitefish is a Native delicacy.

Of all Native ingenuities, I've always taken for granted that once you've seen the method of setting and maintaining a net under the ice there is no need for an explanation of how it works. The method is tried and true. These gillnets are twenty feet long, and one long hole to set, maintain, and check the net is not required. Although this may sound simple and logical, don't let my enthusiasm fool you. I've had to help ice chip the frozen river as thick as four and a half feet to set and maintain a net. I've also watched many elders check their nets barehanded in freezing conditions and use snow to clean the fish slime and warm their hands.

Robert Greene was an elder who enjoyed checking his fishnet under the ice.

Bill Nye the Science Guy would have been impressed with Robert's Native ways. One standing method of modern science is that once an experimental process is developed, other scientists should be able to do a similar experiment and come up with similar results. Robert Greene has maintained a whitefish net under the ice for as long as everyone can remember. Robert was the son of Dan Greene. Dan passed much of his teachings to Robert and his younger brother, James. Along the way, these men learned practical methods of maintaining a net under the ice and collecting simple observations of Mother Nature via the worldview of Yup'ik ecology. In simple essence, this information is cataloged as Native science or Yup'ik science.

After an observation is made and discussed with others who see similar observations, it is accepted that this is the way it is, and an explanation of why it is so becomes unnecessary. "That is the way it is" is an acceptable Native answer, and if it pertains to the mysteries of Mother Nature, no in-depth explanation is necessary. This is how traditional cultures collect ecological observations of harvest methods and make corrections to avoid unforeseen circumstances via experience taught over the years. An example is preventing the net from freezing steadfast onto the ice and being lost to the river as a ghost net. These whitefish nets have no buoys or floats for bobbing. Another ancient Native tradition is the use of snow to warm cold cheeks and prevent frostbite.

If I were to explain the ethics and teachings of Bill Nye the Science Guy to Robert Greene, about how science can help explain the natural world and our traditional ways and methods, Robert would agree, nod his head, smile, and compliment Bill Nye the Science Guy as eccentric. A fresh fish is always delicious. Be very careful when the river ice is thin.

Most Alaska Natives have heard rumors of using snow to warm and prevent frostbite on the face and hands. The Bethel regional hospital and non-Native physicians distributed winter safety information discouraging use of snow to prevent frostbite. Checking whitefish nets barehanded in winter, when Mother Nature is not kind, Robert has accepted the use of snow to warm his hands and prevent frostbite. Factor in the wind chill and instant freezing conditions of water on exposed skin, but those who advocate against Native traditions have never been there and done that.

The insulation quality of snow shelters and Eskimo igloos are accepted as traditional survival techniques. But the use of snow to prevent frostbite is like using fire to fight fire. In any freezing condition, the physics of water is constantly changing from snow, slush, and ice, but the thermodynamics of snow will always remain the same. Snowpacks and snow crystals will always be near the freezing point of water or near 32 degrees Fahrenheit; science refers to this as latent heat. Compared to wind chills of -40 degrees and exposed facial skin surface temperatures of -10 degrees, the latent heat of snow is warmer. Exposed gloves or mittens have the same surface temperature as the wind chill. Experienced Natives will use dry snow on exposed cheeks and keep skin surface dry to prevent serious icing or frostbite and warm the skin temperature to near 32 degrees with less energy expenditure. Caution is the key to using this method.

After a long run in the cold, Alaska sled dogs will roll in the snow to wick moisture away from their inner fine fur and warm their outer fur by shaking away the excess before it melts.

Genetic traits like small moose antler size, spiked antlers, and jack kings are usually not prized characteristics of our sense of nature and theory of evolution. Recessive genes are not prized characteristics of sportsmen who actively catch these animals. For Natives, recessive characteristics are not an important factor in determining whether to catch any fish or animal. Wetting your lips and imagining the taste is an excellent reason to catch that critter. The Yukon king salmon is recognized as prized in Native heritage. Tradition speaks loudly when the first kings are shared with elders and as many families possible. The first kings of the season feed many families.

Pilot Station Natives have fished for salmon since the Yukon River has been there. Many have learned from elders not only the methods of catching fish but also observations of the fish caught. Most people often assume that a king salmon is a king and a chum salmon is a chum. But Natives have observed differences in not only whether the king salmon is male or female, big or small, but in what kind of salmon it is. One prized Yukon king arrives midseason of the summer salmon run, two to three weeks after any first salmon are caught. Many refer to this salmon as the white-nose or blue-nose king. This salmon is larger in size and an aggressive fighter when caught. It has an excellent taste; the meat melts when properly cooked, and the fish oils are rich and sublime.

Natives will let others know when they have caught a white-nose king and others will try to catch some for their own personal use. Although Western science has a nomenclature for every known species and subspecies of living creature, in Alaska subspecies are not integrated into current management. Information from the Natives was anecdotal and generally ignored because of lack of scientific information. Over time, as managers heard rumors about the blue-nose or white-nose Yukon king, they realized the Natives were probably talking about a subspecies king salmon. It is hard to verify this without current scientific information. General physical traits are not as convincing as genetic information that could be used to verify this. DNA data could verify this claim. Perhaps a blue-nose king is from a certain Yukon River tributary.

Everything about the way managers think about Yukon salmon management is chronological. A linear thought process in which time and order follow a sequence with a beginning and an end. This is an attempt to simplify complicated aspects of Mother Nature. In comparison, Natives see Mother Nature as a simple existence amid all our needs, providing opportunities that define our tradition and culture: to hunt and fish for food. In a sense it is what many non-Natives call harmony with nature. Singing out of tune, the managers are trying to keep everyone happy: subsistence, sport, and commercial users and non-users. The managers listen to the loudest voice. With this linear thought process, one statewide salmon management tool aggressively used is mid-point salmon passage estimates. After this passage estimate, commercial fishing was allowed when white- and blue-nose kings were observed. As a result, ADF&G has no idea of how much of an impact this management method has caused in Yukon king salmon size and numbers.

Many families who have a whitefish net under the ice have elders to share and enjoy the catch with. When there is more than a surplus, fishers will share this fresh delicacy with many families. It is something immediately available, fresh, prepared in many ways, or eaten just the way it is. Winter whitefish nets also catch sheefish, pike, or salmon. The practice of catching fresh fish with a winter setnet is unique and successful for many who live on the river.

We also have other fishing methods. We use fish traps made of baling wire for burbot and blackfish. Traditional fish traps were made of willow, birch, and spruce driftwood. Flexible in design, these traps were tied together with roots, braided grass, and animal skin twine.

Blackfish traps are less than five feet in length, two feet wide, and are set in certain shallow sloughs that usually do not freeze during the winter. In one trap, a thousand blackfish can be caught. Six to eight inches in length, these small freshwater fish have a sweet delicate taste that is as unique as the fish itself—almost similar to the taste of crayfish. Soaked in seal oil, elders savor the taste and tell young kids to be quiet to keep from swallowing pin-size bones. The burbot or lush fish is similar to blackfish. Burbot can reach salmon size and are caught in large fish traps and partial weir in the main Yukon River under the ice. As many as fifty burbot can be caught in a trap. Burbot fish traps are big and bulky: five feet high, six feet wide, and seven feet deep. It takes at least four men to check these traps.

Another local delicacy is lamprey eels, caught before the Yukon River freezes in late October. Most Yukon communities do not harvest eels, but the communities that do will try to catch eels as they migrate to spawn in freshwater. Natives designed a barbed stick to sweep eels out of the river as they swim as a large mass. Similarly, there are other fish and methods of catching recognized as unique and special. Small critters like smelts, tom cods, cisco, and freshwater clams are recognized by the state as significant resources for subsistence and as nonsignificant to other users, with no regulatory provisions for harvest seasons or bag limits. Management has no idea about the general condition of these fisheries, and no current numbers to provide acceptable population estimates. Natives know if there are lots, some, or not enough.

These fisheries help supplement food security needs. Wintertime weather conditions are cold, harsh, and difficult, and patience and respect for Mother Nature is critical for safety. Rushing to make decisions is a risk; being greedy is not a good thing.

The Native perception is that greediness in a hunter or fisher is not acceptable; the image can be used to ridicule another Native. Recognizing patience and sound logical decision-making is a sign of respect. There is nothing more humiliating than to tease another Native as being greedy or *pe'tungyuq*, especially if they miss the opportunity to catch a critter without patience and Yup'ik logic. Spearing for Chatanika River whitefish is an exception. Recognizing a new skill, learning to adapt, and teaching others are subconscious virtues that come natural to Natives who hunt and fish.

In 1995 there was rumor of a new wildlife trooper asking Natives who were checking their whitefish nets under the ice if they had a current state fishing license. It's logical for the trooper to ask this, with evidence of a fishnet in the water. The trooper had surely grown up with the colonial concept that all wildlife belongs to the government and was doing his job as a state enforcement officer. As the rumor had it, respected elders and the state court magistrate told the trooper to quit asking for a current fishing license.

These local harvest methods are unique, and the State of Alaska does not have clearly defined open or closed seasons or bag limits for non-salmon species such as whitefish, not intended to give amnesty to Natives for exclusive wildlife harvests, regardless if regulations apply to all residents. When these Native harvest methods are ignored where precedent to purchase a state fishing license is not questioned and the population is not a concern, this behavior is a preemptive strike that all Native ways of harvest are the status quo. If a non-Native was caught with these same harvest methods without a valid license and was issued a citation, there would be a public outcry that the state cannot allow Natives to harvest wildlife without purchasing a valid state fishing, trapping, or hunting license.

The Alaska state constitution claims preferential harvesting is not allowed. If state troopers enforced this legislation uniformly, every Native would be guilty and the troopers would have more than sufficient evidence to prove it. There is no special sunset clause that allows Natives to practice these activities until such time as Alaska is developed as the rest of America. Because of this discrepancy, it is not unusual for Alaska voters to recommend a constitutional convention to address Native harvests as an alternative to amending ANCSA and aboriginal rights. Every ten years, a provision of the Alaska constitution allows voters to decide whether the state should host a constitutional convention to address and change any language of this living document.

Since the Federal Subsistence Board was created to help with subsistence management, the board tries to be cordial in the federal regulation booklets and emphasizes that harvest documents and legal licenses are required. But when one Native is cited, all Natives tend to stick together and create dissension. The relationship between federal and state agencies and their sense of Native responsibility depends on who is making the call, whether it is on my land or your land, my problem or your problem. One side will not require a legal document while the other includes a legal disclaimer to allow wildlife harvest. Natives are treated as if they live in a mixed society with a sense that these requirements and management process need to be addressed rationally, rather than seen as a mixed message about the Native problem and traditional ways. This is the reason Katie John shared her story.

Existing roads between communities indicate that mainstream development is in progress. There are no roads in rural Alaska where any enforcement officer has an obligation to stop a moving vehicle and ask for a valid state driver's license. The license to drive is a privilege; a hunting or fishing license is an obligation.

I am an Alaska Native. It is time for the legal system to address and accept a final decision whether Alaska Natives can harvest wildlife without a valid state license. Ignore civil obedience and issue wildlife violation charges of fishing or hunting without a license and let the courts decide—as in *Sturgeon v. Frost* case in 2019.[1] Whether you live in Montana, Texas, or Tennessee, Alaska is part of the United States and Alaskans are recognized as U.S. citizens, the use and access to wildlife by Alaska Natives gives every U.S. citizen as much right to these activities. I am a U.S. Citizen and Alaska resident. The U.S. Constitution does not make people special because of where they live. The fish and wildlife trooper presence is a benefit to the people and the services they provide guarantee perseverance of wild resources for future generations.

Although I have a legal State of Alaska driver's license, I am different—I am a member of a federally recognized tribe. Like and unlike Alaska Natives, I am a special trust of the federal government. *Tribal members* are not mentioned in any federal or state harvest regulations or Title V of the Alaska State Statues. The U.S. Constitution mentions American Indians and Native Americans, including Alaska Natives.

As a tribal member, how am I different?

NOTES

1. John Sturgeon is a non-Native hunter who sued the National Park Service, claiming that management authority of Alaska's navigable waterways belongs to the State of Alaska. In 2019 the U.S. Supreme Court agreed. John Sturgeon is allowed to use a hovercraft to hunt moose on the Nation River located on park service land in the Yukon Charlie National Wildlife Preserve.

9 🖈 Yup'ik Economics

"You call that a speed boat?" I asked the elder as I nodded to a young man driving a seventy-horsepower seaworthy skiff that looked like a traditional Eskimo *umiat*.

I enjoyed listening to the elder and encouraged him to tell his story. I've never heard anyone speak with an accent so entertaining and pleasant in some indescribable way. His drawl sounded like many Canadians, but I had to strain to understand his heavy French accent. As U.S. students attending school in Vermont, our small class was visiting Red Bay Labrador on a road trip. Two of us were Alaska Native, and our accent was entertaining and difficult to understand. It was not until I attended school in Vermont and visited people from the East Coast that I realized that I also had an Alaska Native accent. I could only laugh when a classmate asked me to keep talking even though I had nothing to say. Rural Native children are open and honest when they comment on non-Native teachers' accents and say they cannot understand them: *heh, you talk funny.*

After enjoying the brilliant fall colors driving through Vermont, New Hampshire, and Maine, our class road-tripped to Nova Scotia, Labrador, and Newfoundland as part of the school curriculum to learn about glacial moraines, Norse archaeology, treeless tundra, Arctic plants, wildlife, and fisheries and to visit local people. Our small school in Wolcott, Vermont, was the Center for Northern Studies. The other Alaska Native was Phillip Kuzgruk, an Inupiat from Teller.

Locals in Labrador and Newfoundland told stories of their plights, hardship, and challenges for the future. To these Canadians, subsistence means a practice completely different from what I grew up with in

Alaska. I was a young adult, and this was 1986; passports between the United States and Canada were not required.

When I heard about Red Bay, I imagined this place was named after a bloody battle between the Natives, French Canadians, and British. Visiting homes and sightseeing in the protected cove, we learned Red Bay was named after a fierce nor'easter storm that sunk a wooden ship carrying a load of red roofing tiles. The red tiles move with the currents and pepper the bay. This place is void of trees. Many homes maintain gardens. Several of us helped one family harvest small and abundant red potatoes, and the family was happy. Using hands to dig into the soil, we pulled up two rocks for every potato and set them aside. The garden soil was rocky and sandier than humus. One homeowner talked of a time when every potato was hit with an Irish blight during a fishing disaster season and how this created a community hardship.

The bay is in the center of town. The speedboat was bigger than the boats used on the Yukon River. To the elder, this boat was just a recreational vehicle to the young man. The elder talked about using the boat and seining for Atlantic cod as an important commercial industry. This place used to be a busy fishing community. When the elder talked about the decline and crash of the cod fisheries, I looked toward Alaska and realized that when I saw home from far away, the similarities in the issues we address did not seem redundant. The Atlantic cod fishery was not as vibrant as it once was.

Visiting Newfoundland, unlike eastern Labrador, I was pleased to see trees and spruce boreal forests that remind me of home. The only piece missing was the Yukon River. Newfoundland is south of Greenland, and the economies of both areas are similar. Greenland has a long history, with stories of early non-Native contacts with Inuits, whaling ships, and searches for the Arctic Northwest Passage. At the Center for Northern Studies, a large collection of *Arctic* and *Arctic Anthropology* magazines told many stories about this region. One intriguing story is about the Greenland Inuit seal hunters before the turn of the century. Every early written record of the Inuits describes their existence thriving in the cold and barren icy conditions of the Arctic as successful seal hunters. The first non-Native contacts gave the Inuits the English name of Eskimo, meaning "eaters of raw meat."

In the 1800s the European search for an Arctic Northwest Passage formed the basis for the major contact period between the white man and Inuit Natives. During this period, many non-Natives perished as a result of inexperienced, unprepared expeditions to the cold and barren Arctic. The most famous of these ventures is the Franklin Expedition, in which both sailing ships and their entire crew perished due to extreme climate and food starvation. In the midst of this cold realm, the Inuits live and thrive. Not all early explorers perished; some successful explorers survived and recorded the geology and geography of the Arctic and lives of the Inuits. With the exception of early whalers who lived in their ships, those most successful adopted and used Native survival methods, clothing customs, transportation means, and hunting techniques. One successful explorer was Robert Peary and his search for the North Pole nearly succeeded because of its use of Native methods.

Many people have a notion that global warming or climate change is a new concept. For these people, reading the history of the Arctic and its peoples should be required. There is tons of historical information on this circumpolar world. One curious historical anecdote is of the southern Greenland Inuit men and an identity crisis that altered how they viewed themselves and their traditional hunting methods. At the turn of the century, Inuit men who had thrived as seal hunters were forced to find new subsistence methods as a result of receding sea ice. The seals retreated north and moved farther away as the sea ice melted and enticed non-Native explorers that the Northwest Passage could be found this way. The Inuits were then living in permanent communities with a less nomadic seasonal lifestyle.

As the environment changed, Inuit men become sea fishermen. In the traditional hierarchy of a Greenland Inuit hunter world, the fisherman or fish provider held the lowest social status. Mother Nature created a hierarchical system of how primitive Natives perceived themselves socially. The retreating sea ice demoralized Inuit men's seal hunter identity and role in their society. The Inuit women, tasked with gathering, had developed an identity resilient to the changing environment, and survival became more dependent on their harvest success.

Inuit seal hunters viewed fishermen as unsuccessful hunters who did not know how to brandish a seal harpoon or practice patience well enough to be skillful providers. Fishermen were poor hunters. As a result of the harsh Arctic conditions and limited options for food survival, all Native hunter-gatherer societies share a division of roles in which the father figure is provider of the main food staple and the mother figure and young are main gatherers. In temperate regions of the world, diverse and abundant options for food provided mixed cultural chores as shared responsibility between traditional hunters, fishermen, and farmers.

These cultures flourished without requiring that any one gender take the primary harvest responsibility of providing a single food source necessary for survival. Still cultural idiosyncrasies developed and hindered the success of cultural survival. In Yup'ik culture, the father figure as hunter-fisher is provider of the main food source, and the mother, as the main gatherer, manages chores as responsibilities the family all shares, chores that became practical traditional management doctrines. In retrospect, it is natural for Native women to adapt to the cultural changes of a modern world and successful professional careers more so than Native men.

As a Yup'ik man I fear loss of my identity as a hunter and fisherman as a result of a changing environment. Trying to change my people into farmers will only disenfranchise our cultural identity. The attempt to introduce gardening was not successful in Pilot Station. There are still no gardens in the community. For those people raised in a mixed society as urban residents, what is the element of identity they are most afraid of losing as a result of a changing global environment and food security?

≳

The public trust doctrine is the base of our state constitution. If the state recognizes Native subsistence as preferential harvesting, subsistence hunting and fishing regulations would not be necessary. When any criminal charges are filed according to the U.S. justice system, the criminal is assumed not guilty until proven otherwise. Since 1989 Alaska Native hunting and fishing regulations have included a curious disclaimer to avoid constitutional procedural issues. The state allows subsistence harvests with an emergency order issued from the ADF&G commissioner. This emergency order is necessary to make it legal without conscientious objections from other users who also participate in harvests for personal use and sport activities.

Unlike in any other state, under Alaska's dual management system with the federal government, the Secretary of the Interior can step in and help Alaska Natives to address subsistence harvest needs, disregarding any state regulations that may apply. The intertribal fish commissions are an example of this fiduciary responsibility.

In 2007 my nephew was charged with wanton waste of several moose legs left in his boat for a day too long. At his court hearing, I try to reason with him to plead "not guilty," to argue that moose hunting season was about to close, and to tell the court about his freezer situation. They do not live in our village; they do not know how we live and what we have to go through. They are *outsiders*. We have nothing to say when they make all rules and regulations.

I told my nephew about Katie John and the ADF&G commissioner's use of emergency orders. Like the John Sturgeon case of using non-Native laws to his advantage, Natives can use the Katie John story to ours. Whether she was fishing out of season, on federal or state waters, or without a state license is irrelevant. The use of a traditional fishwheel is legal and recognized in the state constitution, which also abolishes fishwheels for commercial fishing. When the U.S. Supreme Court sided with Katie John, the burden of proof became the state's responsibility, that with impartiality the justice system would uphold the public trust doctrines of the constitution. There is one phrase never used in her Supreme Court documents—Katie John is a *tribal member*.

There is sufficient documentation that Alaska Natives practiced subsistence long before the state constitution was ratified. In a legal situation where common law prevails, the final decision is a challenge; ANCSA extinguished aboriginal rights but did not extinguish, recognize, or create Alaska tribes. Questions about tribal sovereignty and autonomy of tribal self-government remained unanswered. Instead, the courts declared that Alaska tribes do not own the land required to be sovereign. Self-governing tribes in the Lower 48 states are recognized under federal Indian laws and are usually respected with jurisprudence in their respective jurisdictions. In 2017 the state attorney general issued a legal opinion that Alaska tribes are sovereign.[1] This opens endless possibilities for the future of Alaska tribes to address economic development, tribal justice, and food security needs.

For example, many can argue that tribal members' subsistence hunting and fishing was never addressed in any pact or agreement with the state or federal government. I admit I am not an aboriginal member of any Alaska Native culture ... I am a *tribal member*. If Katie John had used these words in her legal proceedings, she would have been speaking the truth. This argument is different from the *Venetie* case, in which claims of Indian Country implied property rights rather than citizenship rights. In 1986 the Native Village of Venetie tried to collect property tax on a non-tribal entity for building a school in the village. The State of Alaska challenged (*Alaska v. Native Village of Venetie Tribal Government*), claiming that ANCSA lands are not Indian Country, and the U.S. Supreme Court agreed. The *Venetie* decision was adamant that Alaska tribes do not own land on which to claim and exercise sovereignty.

The Katie John case provided a confusing time period for everything subsistence, particularly the state's efforts to properly manage it. When the commissioner's office issues emergency orders, it helps to ensure that no person will be deprived of life, liberty, and due process, recognizing no special privileges. There is no recognition of status quo. Unlike addressing Native harvests as an economic necessity, this same emergency order procedure should apply to every resident and nonresident for all wildlife and fish harvests.

In Native Alaska, the concept of cash infusion is not as foreign as it once was for my ancestors. The U.S. dollar is accepted everywhere, and for many there is never enough. During his presidential term Ronald Reagan was ridiculed for his management of the U.S. economy. Although I do not remember anything ridiculous about Reagan's approach to the economy, it was regarded as voodoo economics by certain prominent politicians and economists who understood the mechanics and investments of the digital corporate world. For many, economics is a complicated subject.

In a 2008 AFN Alaska Marketplace competition, one contestant won grant money with a project titled "Another Man's Trash, One Man's Treasure." The goal was to gather broken, unused snow machine parts and rebuild a usable rig to resell. This was a resourceful attempt to earn money and provide someone with transportation. Using free broken parts to create a usable machine is not unusual in rural Alaska. This is a basic virtue of Yup'ik economics.

The original Western definition of *economics* was "the science of the household." Yup'ik economics is the study of the environment. In the sciences, Yup'ik economics is like elective courses for an environmental science degree, but in the humanities, Yup'ik economics is subsistence. The unique characteristic of Alaska Native subsistence is the sharing of resources among many community members; academics call this "socioeconomics."

Pilot Station Natives have a special collection of observations of the salmon fisheries. Every year the returns of Yukon king salmon are a concern. For the Natives it is an issue because state regulations continue to enforce fishing gear restrictions and closers. For the managers, conservation concerns, preservation measures, and treaty obligations with Canada are issues to address. Although Native people from the Lower Yukon voice their concerns, managers have no obligation to provide special services, and stringent measures are necessary because returns and king salmon are getting smaller in all Alaska waters.

In April 2015 the Pilot Station Traditional Council sent a letter to the ADF&G summer season manager, with a traditional projection that Yukon king salmon returns for the next several years was promising and a request for lenient subsistence salmon harvests.

ADF&G biologists use quantitative and qualitative data to make statistical population projections, but the management decisions follows a state regulatory process. Unlike use of theory and science, Yup'ik economics is best described as academic language between philosophy and theology. Yup'ik economics includes a collection of environmental observations on the weather, climate, habitat, wildlife, and fisheries, and communication with other Natives observing the same collection of information. The conclusion of all this gathered information is the kicker: how can we explain the outcome without being ridiculed that this information is nonsense? There is no qualitative proof, but all this traditional information is telling us this is going to happen. Western science calls this process an ad-hoc hypothesis and difficult to prove. Although the 2015 traditional projection promised more king salmon returns, the 2003 projection predicted the king salmon crash. Because of a language barrier and the intimidating authority presence of previous managers, Natives could not explain this traditional information adequately. The manager's way of thinking follows a set order of qualitative principles and doctrines.

The problem with managers in 2000 was not only a linguistic issue. Natives have had to deal with a language barrier since statehood. The barrier of confusion was the power of authority that came with management. All Yukon managers since the inception of the program have been non-Native. Perhaps the easiest way to describe the role and ideology of the managers is that they are educated as "old school" and believed the decisions they made alone made a difference. What was good for all Alaskans was also good for all Native people who depend on the resource. This is a colonial self-imposed mindset that the people are not stewards of their resource, but instead that the managers are the stewards and people are to do what the manager decides, nothing more and nothing less. The old school managers were the earl and dukes of the Middle Ages and the fish and wildlife was owned by the crown. The non-Native people were an imagined hierarchy of servants, and the Native people were the peasants and cared for the leadership.

In 2000, when Natives tried to explain the concerns they had observed on the river, managers considered this information trivial compared to other issues of that time. Managers were busy addressing other fishery issues and were incapable of corroborating this Native traditional information. Statewide challenging issues Alaskans were concerned about included bycatch of king salmon by Bering Sea pollock fisheries, that salmon size was assumed to be smaller, and that test fish and sonar data contradicted Native harvests and passage estimates into Canada were higher. In response to all these concerns, subsistence Yukon salmon harvests were further restricted, making it difficult for Native families to meet food security. Gray whales stuck in the Arctic Sea ice were a nationwide news event with news crews following efforts of Native people from Barrow to cut breathing holes and lead the whales to safety. For the Yukon River, no one understood the Native information of unusual Yukon sightings and premonitions. Instead, more harvest regulations and gear restrictions were proposed and passed by BOF in

2010. The challenge was the translation of this Native information for non-Native managers. Natives have a good understanding of English, unlike the language spoken by the biologist or the hushed whispers of the respectable sportsman to BOF members of measures that need to be taken. The year 2010 became a significant year for the Pilot Station Traditional Council.

Many elders saw and experienced these same dismal salmon returns. Although this observation was an integral part of Yup'ik economics, people in Alaska heard and read these wildlife mammal sightings and dismissed them as nothing more than information reported in the statewide news. Elders talked of a crash of king salmon after these sea mammal sightings and higher-than-average returns several years later when there are no recent sightings. As a Native I understood this information as part of oral history. After what Natives saw in mid-2000 and later after 2014, Pilot Station tribe told the recently hired ADF&G manager that Yukon king salmon returns looked promising for 2015. Elders spoke about history and their observations of weather, fish, wildlife, and events in the environment will repeat each other. Like our seasons, what has happened before will happen again. Perhaps the managers will listen if we explain this information logically. We want to help manage subsistence salmon harvests. We want to work together.

Because of elders' experience with the ego of previous managers, many are reluctant to share traditional management methods. Many don't trust Fish and Game. Because of this, in the years between 2010 and 2016, five ADF&G Yukon River managers quit the department. In 1969, when elders told the old school manager about what was seen on the Yukon and projection of salmon returns, the manager laughed at Native ways.

If this traditional observation brings change in wildlife numbers, what can we learn from these Natives?

NOTES

1. Alaska Attorney General Jahna Lindemuth to Governor Bill Walker, re: Legal status of tribal governments in Alaska, October 19, 2017.

PART II

You should remember this day and what is being talked about. We were not brought up to depend on assistance. Healthy young people were taught to be responsible and be out hunting and [caring] for their family. Able-bodied men would be [ashamed] to have others support them.

—IRVIN BRINK JR., Kasigluk Yup'ik hunter and fisherman, *Tundra Drums*, March 27, 1997

10 ≋ Social Morals and Obligations

"You caught three seals and this is your first time seal hunting?" Lillian asked my daughter. Caitlyn was visiting Kotlik and caught three seals with a spear. This was not her first time hunting seals, but she had finally caught not only one, but three: a ringed seal, a mukluk, and an isuguuin. Different seals we value for different uses: ringed seal for the fur, mukluk for the meat, and isuguuin for seal oil. Lillian could not get over the fact that Caitlyn had done this as a young woman. Many women have caught seals, but Lillian grew up respecting our traditional ways and customs; Caitlyn was more than seven months pregnant.

During one winter ice spell, a traditional friend came to visit. She did not have an extra sweater and got chilled, even with our woodstove roaring. My wife's clothing was too small, so I grabbed my thick warm wool shirt off the clothes rack. After a while, warm and comfortable, she dug into the pockets and pulled out a book of matches in a small Ziploc bag. Laughing, she showed it and asked if I smoke. I told her they are only for emergency and she was wearing the shirt I use when I go hunting. Immediately she took it off, commenting something about taboo, bad luck to hunters, and women touching hunters' tools and clothing. I had forgotten that and did not realize she took it seriously. That I use that shirt for working outside was no longer an acceptable excuse; we laughed when we realized that I use all my clothes for hunting and fishing.

I told a similar story about Mom. One winter, as I was preparing to go out into the cold, Mom recognized my gray wool pants and commented that Dad used to have the same kind. We laughed when Mom said that they had to give them away after they shrunk when she washed them in hot water, and she reminded me not to wash mine in hot water. Dad had gotten mad at Mom for ruining the pants, but Mom reminded Dad about gender roles and how women are not supposed to touch hunters' clothes and such. Dad agreed. "Yes, and see what happens?" Mom got back, saying, "Well, you told me to wash it."

Lillian is the wife of Reynold Okitkun. Both are Yup'ik Eskimos who grew up in Kotlik, a small village located at the northernmost slough of the Yukon River. The Bering Sea was outside their doorstep. When the weather was clear they could squint and see Russia's skyline to the northeast. The idea of women hunting and using men's hunting tools in the old days was a serious social issue.

"We thought you guys went home."

My brother Abe and cousin Leonard unzipped the fly and peeked into our tent and laughed. Abe and Leonard had thought we were on our way home and did not expect to see us so soon. They were not laughing at the thought of seeing us again; they were laughing at the spot of our tent and the way we looked in our sleeping bags. Getting out of our sleeping bags, our muscles ached everywhere. It seemed like we had just closed our eyes and lain down. We were still tired. There is absolutely nothing more uncomfortable than sleeping on grassy, hummocky tussock moss. If you think it is hard and difficult to walk on, try sleeping on it. There was no such thing as a comfortable spot. We were glad to see them.

We couldn't help the tent spot. Of the spots we had checked in the dark, this was best, and it was close to the beach and our boat. On our way home from the Innoko River, we waved at Abe and his hunting party at their camp site.

Checking a small slough as an excursion, we beached and quietly walked into the thicket looking for any meadow, clearing, or pond where moose might be moseying. This place was new and unfamiliar, so there was no sense but to scout the area. Every hunting trip the main caution is to be quiet and listen. Holding our guns ready, walking cautiously, we crept into the thick patch of willow and alder. The grass was over five feet tall, and the tussock made it difficult to walk. Not far into the thicket, Bruce whistled to get my attention and nodded his head for us to return to the boat. This place was like many places we checked to try our luck. The brush was thick and the grass was tall. No open meadows to call out the moose. This place was ideal for moose, not ideal for moose hunters.

Bruce whistled and scurried forward, spotting a bull moose near the river's edge. With instinct, we chambered a load into our rifles. We had one moose all cut and covered; one more would give us reason to head straight home, an eight-hour nonstop boat ride.

We decided this was a chance for Nathan's first moose kill. We whispered to Nathan to keep shooting until the moose fell. The moose was seventy yards away and close to the beach. Packing the meat would be easy. We were Native hunters; none of us had scope rifles.

Guns are a natural traveling companion and household item in Alaska. It is natural to see guns on snow machines and skiff boats. Many are banged up, rusted, missing trigger guards, duct taped onto homemade wooden stocks with string shoulder straps. These are not collector's items. Passed from one generation to the next, these are prized heirlooms used to provide food. For young hunters, possession of guns like these is reason to smile and go for a ride.

Young Natives with small rifles learn to shoot at large animals by shooting at the same time as hunters with larger-caliber guns. It is exhilarating for youngsters to know they helped in making the catch. These youngsters look forward to the next hunt, to go for a ride, to go camping and build excitement for the next season. Thoughts of plucking feathers, skinning fur, and cleaning out the guts and innards of the birds, fish, and animals grow with the mind of our young. They learn early in life that the animals provide food. They learn respect and gratefulness of the natural world of the animals, fish, and birds and how nature provides more than serenity and beauty.

Our tradition grows when young hunters and fishers learn the taste of what we catch is exhilarating and subconsciously grown to appreciate. Goose soup, moose stews, dried chum salmon, beaver chili, garlic roast seal, and king salmon strips are a few delicacies. Alaska Natives created festivals, potlatches, and celebrations of our customs recognizing our way of life with the food we catch. Special celebrations many of us look forward to hosting and sharing with our youngsters, recognizing a first catch or first kill, honoring the skill learned. We want to share this with everyone.

Nathan shot and put his gun down to look. Bruce and I immediately started talking: "Keep shooting, don't stop!" We knew what a first shot means. The moose was spooked. The first shot was a miss. The moose jumped and looked behind as the bullet whizzed and rattled through the trees. Nathan shot several more times and we heard the thud of good hit. The adrenaline of the moose kicked in, and the muscles were taut and tense. The moose ran injured into the trees, leaving tall willows waving for us to follow. The bright crimson blood trail was hard to miss; tiny air bubbles showed that it was shot through the lungs. In a small clearing the moose staggered and fell.

The moose was a mile from the boat. Packing out the meat would require an extra day, which could ruin the other meat in the boat. It was late evening, and we were losing daylight fast. Bruce and I agreed that we needed help. After we gutted and quartered the animal, we boated upriver to Abe's camp six miles away. They were gone taking an evening ride, so we left a note about our camp and the moose, that we needed help. In the morning Abe and Leonard awoke us we were happy to see them. They helped pack out the meat and we left for home later that afternoon.

One of the neat things about Native hunters is that there are no commercial guides. Natives will help other Natives from other communities as a courtesy of being Native. This custom is embodied in the way we grew up and how we saw our elders and parents offer this courtesy to others. Registered commercial guides are more likely to be organized as a unit, contrary to subsistence users, who are concerned with needs of the home and food security. Subsistence users tend to work together to make a successful harvest. There are no registered Native guides in my part of Alaska.

Game management units in Alaska are associated with residents of the immediate area. GMU 18 includes a good portion of the Lower Yukon and Kuskokwim River. There is no road system and access for non-Natives has been limited. One issue the state continues to address is whether the harvesting of wild resources should only be allowed for residents of the immediate area. Differentiating between Native and non-Native residents within the regulations is not the same as resident or non-resident. Making changes to address this would require careful consideration because the consequences can impose more serious and complicated disparities. A recent example addressed by the BOG is for winter moose hunts for *non-residents* and use of snow machines. Should this be allowed for western Alaska?

There is belief among Native hunters that payment for services is not necessary. The need for help is reciprocal and part of Native Samaritanship is that when a hunter should need help, help will be provided. Abe and Leonard had three young hunters the same age as Nathan.

Pilot Station School is one of ten schools within the Lower Yukon School District. At over twenty-two thousand square miles this district is huge, but the school district has a youth program unlike any other. Every school enlists a group of high school students to help address risk behaviors and school and community issues. Each school has about one hundred kindergarteners to twelfth-grade students and every student knows every other student. The high school students who participate in this program provide a pivotal civic role as community members and student leaders. The student group has no government function or student council responsibilities. Any high school student is eligible to join this program; there are no grade-point-average requirements. There is one unique leadership skill used to select leaders with no campaign requirements. This program is the Natural Helpers and leaders are selected according to one characteristic: if you were to turn to someone for help, who would you ask?

In April 2010 Pilot Station School hosted a student retreat gathering of Natural Helper students from the district. An evening entertainment skit contest was required for each school site. Students from Mountain Village performed a skit about a successful traditional moose hunt with cardboard caricatures and homemade costumes. In the skit the young hunter travels a river in a kayak, beaches near an open meadow and calls to the moose. A young bull moose sticks its head out of a sapling grove of willows played by younger students and the hunter makes a successful catch. The meat is brought back to the community and shared in a feast. The student who played the hunter was a girl and the story was about a young woman providing and sharing the food with the community as a hunter. Traditionally, Yup'ik women working as hunters was a social issue. This perception has changed significantly in Native communities.

Pilot Station School includes cultural activities as part of the school curriculum. In September 2016, fifty students boated upriver to hunt, fish, gather wild resources, and camp for three nights. The Atchuelinguk River includes many lakes, sloughs, tributaries, and channels; it is a huge drainage. I boated a group to the headwaters of the Chuelinguk. Many were amazed at the river current, water ripples, and small whitewater on the river. Everything below this river is calm, and the only way whitewater is made is with gusts of wind. Sitting on the gravel beach one adult commented, "It feels like we are still in a moving boat." Many were amazed when I told them that I had boated up this river another six hours and described some of the sights, and that I knew of other Natives who had gone farther and had heard their stories of what they had seen.

Heading back to camp, we met Paul and Cindy Fancyboy. They were happy to see us. We talked of our adventures of the day, animals we had seen, fish we had caught and places we had visited. Paul and Cindy were the eldest couple and had several grandkids participating in this cultural event. They were waiting for someone with additional rope. About 150 yards from the beach, Cindy had caught her first bull moose. The moose was feeding in a shallow pond when shot. With additional rope, Paul used his boat to pull the critter closer to the riverbank. Several months later Cindy and her son Logan would stand at the Eskimo Dance Potlatch in Pilot Station.

As an additional lesson I helped teach students rope and knot-tying skills. I offered a ten-dollar bill to any student who could replicate and tie a simple knot without assistance. The knot was available for all to view, handle, and examine to their heart's content, with the exception that no one untie the knot to copy it. Many boys were enthusiastic and quickly tied a similar knot until I told them to look closely. Many gave up after the tenth time or so. The girls continued to tackle this because it was a challenge. One girl commented, "This knot looks so simple, but it isn't . . ." Overhearing this, a schoolteacher saw the knot and tried to replicate it. The teacher also gave up. Many students were discouraged, but I taught a safety waist rescue knot with a one-hand motion. Fifteen minutes later, the seventh-grade girl who had made the comment tied the secret knot. I gave her the ten dollars and told her that this knot should be kept as a secret used to puzzle others of what we know.

The Mountain Village students and their moose hunting story placed third in the school skit contest. Kotlik Natural Helper students won the skit contest with a choreographed mime performance accompanied by a musical repertory that all students could relate to. Stereotyping people who listen to different music genres, from rap to easy listening to hard rock, the students mimed performing the influence of drugs and alcohol over education, sports, and friendship and how drugs and alcohol impact families, parenting, and community. The student mime was a high school senior about to graduate that year. Two years later, at the 2012 Natural Helper retreat in Russian Mission School, the coordinators invited the same Kotlik student to perform the skit to a new audience of young students. At every performance, the Eskimo dance song reminds everyone of Native culture and tradition.

11 ≋ Calendar Cycles

"This light is strange," my mom said. Hmm, the sunlight looked all the same to me.

I reminded myself that other elders had made the same comment. It was midafternoon, clear and chilly early March. Trying to be logical, this was not an observation of one spring season but an observation based on other successive seasons. Many Native cultures accept that change in Mother Nature is common. Like Yup'ik science, this observation does not need to be explained. It is unusual, but the question of why is left unanswered because the cause is often not obvious.

The strange sunlight Mom was talking about was the albedo. Many prominent environmental leaders have a strong notion that change in the Arctic environment will create drastic global warming events. Examples of climate change catastrophes include sea ice melting, increase in inclement temperature, rise of sea level, and drastic changes to the food chain. Pilot Station is considered part of the subarctic. It is a region of the world in which the majority of communities and people live in the circumpolar North.

≋

To watch moving parts is fascinating to humans. But to sit and watch Mother Nature requires patience. When we look at the clock to get a sense of time, we create a small, fixed subconscious period for that moment. If we have a sense that the time is wrong, we look for another time machine to comfort our subconscious; our sense of time is precious to the meaning of life. It is easier and far more comforting to forget this nonsense and accept Einstein's proven theory that time is relative. To sit sublime and enjoy the moment—don't bother me with this nonsense. Most everyone accepts the saying "I'm not getting paid to think."

Until we suspect the clock is broken, something's got to be done, and that serenity in my place in time has to be adjusted to reassure my comfort. We can either try to fix it, replace the part broken, change the batteries, take it the shop, or throw it away and accept the fact that time is not important. If this time machine is no longer important, another new one can replace it, like an upgrade, a digital one, or better yet, a smart one.

Most Natives will tinker with it, try to fix it, or try and find another use for broken parts. Between different cultures, this extension to objects is the same as the extension to the natural environment. Take, for example, global climate change. The news media and many documentaries often discuss climate change with regard to its negative impacts to the creature comforts we have grown accustomed to. In general people are afraid of change.

Many Alaska Natives are skeptical, asking how this is global warming if it is not happening in my little world. Compared to rural Alaska, large metropolitan areas create micro-environments that influence their own climate patterns, then turn around and impose on smaller communities to accept these as facts. If they have to make changes to their way of life, everyone has to make changes. To think green and reduce carbon emissions and other elements that are not good to a healthy environment and come up with nonsense that a carbon footprint is relative to Mother Nature's aesthetic image.

Children love to play with water or better yet to play in water. Most everyone accepts the image of Alaska as a cold place. Although it is hard to imagine children in cool Alaska swimming in lakes and rivers for fun, it is common during the short summer season. A local favorite swim hole is seven miles from Pilot Station in a clear water lake inside Blueberry Slough. It is not uncommon to see ten boats with families swimming and enjoy a little outing.

Although the temperature might reach a balmy 90 degrees Fahrenheit during the midafternoon sun, the water temperature will vary between 57 and 65 degrees. These swimmers are not advocates for those polar bear clubs whose members jump into the water and jump out because they could. They jump into the water to have a good time. It is a little cool and children with chattering teeth will say it is easier to get used to the cool water once you jump in. Small campfires warm the swimmers and roast hotdogs, fresh Yukon salmon, and marshmallows. Although most families allow their kids to play in the water for most of the day, they head home about nine or ten in the evening, before the summer sun sets. They head home before the weather temperature is chilly from boating in an open skiff. After they leave, it is common to see another group of swimmers finally heading out to go swimming—families who have perhaps grown acclimatized and more resistant to the cool environment, usually with a larger number of teens and young adults who really enjoy swimming. Wetsuits are unheard-of luxuries; no one locally is aware of their insulating ability and comfort.

In every village, kids, teens, and young adults often stay up late into the wee hours of the morning just hanging out. Teens' sleeping all day is a village trend. It is not uncommon to hear people teasing and most times complaining about young adults finally getting out of bed late in the day, or to see kids walking in early in the morning to comment that they have not slept yet. How families deal with this varies between parents and households. During summer, daylight all night is common, which influences the weather and temperature variations. Most people are accustomed to the fact that the warmest air temperature of the day is midafternoon to late afternoon. Weather conditions during this part of the day are fairly comfortable and a good time to enjoy the outdoors and leisure activities such as swimming.

In Pilot Station, the most experienced swimmers know the best time to be in the water is not during warmest part of the day, when the air temperature is the hottest, but between the hours of 10 p.m. to 2 a.m. The best time to swim is usually close to midnight. Although the level of daylight during this part of the day is fairly bright, the air temperature is cool and below 60 degrees Fahrenheit, especially if there is a light breeze. In Alaska, cool evening temperatures are a norm. The water temperature on the other hand is as warm as it is going to be at any part of the day, whether the sun is shining or not. Swimming this late in the day, it is warmer to be in the water than to try to warm up close to the campfire, where the air temperature is cooler. After a hot afternoon sun, it is not unusual for the evening water temperature to be a comfortable 70 to 75 degrees. Swimmers toweling dry and trying to warm up by the fire may shiver, but they've got to admit that the water temperature is nice and comfortable, and sometimes swimmers jump back into the water to warm. This same variation also applies to the coldest part of the day.

It is natural for rivers in Alaska to freeze. Similar to ambient temperature variations, the same conditions also apply to frozen water. The people in Nenana, Alaska, have been around for a long time. Since 1917 they have documented significant periods of time, monitoring and recording dates and times of river ice breakup. Simple data collected by simple people who often fail to question climatologists about science and scientific data for simple people to observe and collect. Nenana, like most of Alaska, is located at a geographic place that is considered subarctic: really cold during winter and really warm during summer. It is a place where temperature extremes are accepted. Ice breakup records from this place can prove a cooling or warming trend as a result of global climate change. If early ice breakup is proof of global warming, what does the Nenana River ice data say?

Temperature is an accepted scientific measurement observation that can monitor daily variations of our climate conditions. Every elementary textbook has temperature information as a simple introductory topic. Elementary students are taught that air temperature is warm during the day and cool at night. The temperature is warm when the sun is out because sunlight warms the earth. When the sun is not shining, the temperature is cool, and we lose the earth's heat out to the atmosphere or out to space. But in all lessons about temperature, many students will not retain the fact that the coldest part of the day is just before sunrise.

In 1990 three of us were hunting in a small river tributary. We had a jet lower unit that allowed our boat to travel in shallow water. Five miles from the gravel shallows, we set up camp and lightened our boat load of gear and excess fuel. With a lighter boat we traveled farther upriver than we intended. It is easy to get fixated and push to see what is on the other side of just one more bend. Three hours from camp we caught a big moose. By the time we loaded the meat it was twilight. Since we had several spotlights, we should have been able to return to camp in the darkest of night. But with the spotlights we could not tell the deeper channels, and every time the boat was up on step, we ran aground and the boat got stuck on gravel. Seeing the river with a lantern for whitefish spearfishing is not the same. After several hours we were exhausted and started to get the chills after sweating to push the boat to the deeper river channel. We knew camp was two hours away during daylight. At night it would be twice as long, so we decided to build a fire and get some rest in a spruce grove. At 2 a.m. in the middle of September, the temperature was hovering near freezing and the stars were out.

Our camp and warm sleeping bags were ready and waiting. We were dressed warm with lots of firewood, but we used our tarps to cover our meat. Watching the stars, feeding the fire, and trying to sleep was not comforting as some may think. It was the coldest night I have ever spent and it got colder as the night progressed. Colder than spring bird hunts and winter camping and snow shelters. At 6:30 a.m. the warmth of the fire did not help, even as we fed it more wood. Sunrise heat was four hours away.

The warmest evening water temperature and coldest morning air temperature are examples of latent heat. This is a natural, everyday occurrence. If we take this example to our current global situation, these observations can help explain many of the changes we are experiencing. This process may also help explain why the effects are not instantaneous as many advocates of global warming may think. Regardless, global climate change is often seen as negative manmade catastrophe, and we must do everything to prevent it from happening.

The strange sunlight Mom was referring to was the intensity of sunlight or level of albedo. Mom does not speak English, and she described the sunlight as if it became alive with motions to the eye. We have taken for granted that the level of daylight we see is always there as part of the sun and extension of the universe. We've accepted the seasons as the cycle of the earth's orbit around the sun and influence of earth's tilt on its orbital axis. Unlike albedo, when people see a lunar eclipse for the first time, we have a general reference for how the level or intensity of light/sunlight changes with the shadow of the moon. This is a cause and effect we understand and take for granted; when the moon is between sun and earth, our level of light will change. The change in sunlight Mom was referring to was based on collection of observations in reference to other seasons at this time of the year. Every spring, about the time of the spring equinox, the length of day gets longer, and for people in Alaska, this is the time of the year when we look forward to the start of another season and cycle of a major period of weather conditions. It is the time when we look forward to another new year of life.

Observation of bird behavior during lunar eclipses is interesting as a cause-and-effect scenario. Birds are natural at observing albedo. In 2014 these two young boys were geese hunting during a full lunar eclipse, and they talked about how all the animals became quiet as the level of light darkened. After the eclipse, flying bird activity increased, unsure of what was going on, and the boys returned home with several geese, saying the birds were easy to catch.

According to Mom's observation, the intensity of sunlight was brighter than previous seasons. Although the snow-covered landscape intensified the brightness, the level of sunlight was intensified with a blue neon glow. As an elder Mom noticed this, as did others who made similar comments. Some young adults also commented that this level of sunlight seemed unusual.

≋

Global warming and global climate change are two different things. One is a change in temperature variation, a warming trend in the system, and the other is a natural event for Mother Nature. For example, it is natural for Mother Nature to cause earthquakes, volcanic eruptions, storms, floods, and river erosions. As we collect and monitor the volume and magnitude of these events, we create a base log of data comparing each event to the last major event and highlight changes in intensity and rate of occurrence. The most devastating events occur near where people live.

As a result, we have created a fear of change. This fear of change in the environment has created a subconscious guilt that we must all do our part to keep it from changing. A warming environment will create impending drastic disaster to the creature comforts we've grown accustomed to. If we were to create a list of changes that are positive for the people, the animals, and human environment, people would be more likely to view climate change as a natural event. For example, a warmer temperate Alaska sounds more appealing than a cold frozen Arctic.

When we have extensive periods of cold weather, advocates of global warming are absent from the media. If these advocates were to rationalize their observations to say warmer temperatures will cause colder snaps and longer warmer periods will cause longer colder snaps, this is a weather pattern where the extremes and extent of temperature take turns with each other and one will override the other to try and reach an equilibrium. This reasoning is rational according to simple laws of physics. Man has no idea about Mother Nature's sense of global climate equilibrium.

In major periods of earth's history, the fossil record indicates long forgotten periods of ice ages when the earth was covered with large continental ice sheets and cold chilly temperatures were normal. Weather and temperature conditions were not pleasant or what we know as comfortable. The period of global warming events is not as evident, and man's effort to prevent this from happening will infringe on national and global effort of support and empathy. If we were sure that global data suggested a major cooling period in our near future as another ice age, the cause of this natural event as result of man would be difficult to accept. Global soothsayers would warn of ice and cold disaster and unpleasant environmental conditions. Many would provide alternatives to convince others how to prevent this from happening. No matter how much man has influenced environmental changes, Mother Nature often reminds us of her global weather patterns and natural disasters that wreak havoc on man's claim of dominance.

As people who live on our planet, we measure time in relation to a fixed point in space within our universe. Time has a meaning with every revolution of the earth as it rotates around the sun. We measure twenty-four hours, one earth revolution, as one day, and we accept a year as a complete circle of the earth as it revolves around the sun. The earth's orbit around the sun is not a perfect circle, and we use the odd Gregorian calendar year to compensate, with number of days in February changing in a leap year. Because the earth's orbit is not a perfect circle, we add one day in February every other year to match the number of days relative to the earth's rate of rotation. The earth's rotation and tilt influence global climate conditions, creating ice ages and major periods of global warming as part of earth's history. Man has a difficult challenge to convince Mother Nature to prevent another global warming or cooling cycle.

The odd light illusion Mom observed is a result of the orbital circle shape and tilt axis of the earth, influenced by the distance of the sun. If the earth orbit around the sun were a perfect circle, our weather patterns would be geo-synchronized daily and seasonally. Unfortunately, the earth rotation influences the horizontal and vertical position of the polar regions, and the polar hemispheres experience more environmental influences. One influence is artic haze. I have heard rumors that this Arctic haze is a collection of manmade waste particles accumulating in the polar extremes, creating changes in visual perception within the visible light spectrum. Without a doubt man has influenced global climate conditions with the waste products of human evolution. The ice ages occurred during times when the earth was the furthest distance from the sun influenced by the tilt axis of the polar regions.

Using magnetic tools as a navigation aid is instrumental in exploration and discovery of the far reaches of the earth. Traditional Alaska Natives have never used any magnetic instruments as navigation tools. The use of stars, landmarks, and topography such as treelines and plant species aid in navigation. During heavy winter storms, snowpack hardness, texture, and direction of grass in certain areas provide a reference, all depending on how familiar the Native is with the area. In geology, the theory of magnetic reversals in earth's history applied some interesting academic discussions about earth's changing rotation.

During a classroom session when I explained magnetic declination and the difference between true north and magnetic north, one student stumped me with a question: Is the magnetic north alive? In the last decade the geographic location of the magnetic North Pole has moved significantly. The Gaia hypothesis incorporates ancient Greek mythology to posit that the earth is a living, breathing organism.

12 ≋ Environmental Realms

"Eeggigi . . ."

I opened my eyes, hearing Mom say this word over and over.

"Eeggigi. Chawa'taq." I heard my auntie. "Now that is a sight . . ." in awe.

After putting on his boots and stepping over the coffee brewing on the prime stove, Dad went out of the canvas tent to see why the two ladies were excited. My brother Donald jumped up from the sleeping bag, following barefoot.

"Eeggigi, Eeggigi . . . nutanatam." I heard Dad. "Alright, alright."

"Holy cow! Holy cow!" Donald yelled. My brother Dayboy and I jumped up to see what the commotion was about.

Yesterday we traveled more than eight hours with an eighteen-foot Lund aluminum skiff after Dad got off work at the post office and arrived at Owl Village in the dark. As Dayboy and I exited the tent into the bright clear sunshine, we could not believe what we saw. I had never seen the tundra like this before.

Salmonberries carpeted the tundra. Red was everywhere, and the berries were big. Salmonberries or cloudberries are normally seen as yellow berries in pictures. As they mature, they turn red in color. As they ripen, they turn yellow and later into the season the berries are pale yellow. The riper berries are softer, squishier and sweeter or punchy sour. Families prefer berries just before they are too ripe, when the petals of the leaves open and the berries are easily picked, fairly firm and clean of leaves and stems, ready to be stored. A state when the berries are just turning from red to shades of yellow.

Like many families, my parents would load the boat, choose which of us ten kids to take, and travel with a relative or two. With my own family I have returned many times to this part of Alaska to pick salmonberries. The spectacular tundra carpet of that morning surprise was the only time I've seen berry numbers of that magnitude. Every time we sat for a meal, my parents and auntie could not stop talking about the berries; it was and is a rare sight. Everywhere we walked it was hard not to step on berries.

≈

Albert and Agnes Beans were the parents of Janice. My parents were Norman and Mary Kelly. At the time of our wedding I had five sisters and five brothers, and Janice had five brothers and six sisters. With numerous nieces, nephews, aunts, uncles, and cousins, it is hard to keep track of family relations. Nonetheless, the family size reflects our dependence on subsistence activities for everyone's well-being.

In the early 1970s, when television was introduced to Pilot Station, my fondest memory is watching a Saturday morning cartoon with Grandma Anna Alick. Curious why Dad was on the roof of our home, Grandma Alick came to visit as everyone was fixated on the brand-new TV. As the reception cleared, Bill Cosby and the Fat Albert gang appeared onscreen. Grandma sat fascinated over the real cartoons and wondered how they had learned to talk. Every Yup'ik was familiar with cartoon books, but the cartoons on TV looked creepy, like tricks of vision; the movement of these characters was a cultural mirage of shamanism and witchcraft. Grandma wondered where these cartoons lived and if Bill Crosby was a liaison and cultural interpreter.

Grandma Alick was familiar with 8mm projector reel shows at the community hall with the cartoon previews before the actual start of the movie, but a human talking with cartoon characters was alien to Yup'ik worldview. Grandma Alick kept looking behind the black box and touching the screen to see if someone was there and commenting about how cartoon people are real. Although the cartoons of Fat Albert and his gang were interesting caricatures, it was the color of Bill Cosby that was more of interest. My older sisters Agnes and Melgie tried to explain the cartoons to Grandma. But for me and my brothers this was no fascination, this was entertainment. Mom and Grandma Alick spoke no English, so when they were interested in a particular show my sisters would interpret and explain what was going on. To enjoy the show perhaps it is easy to keep a blank, clear mind, free of all convictions.

Grandma Alick is originally from Chakaktolik. Although early non-Natives often describe the Yup'ik Eskimo as friendly and gregarious, the Yupiit of Pilot Station have a dark history. Stories of bow-and-arrow wars with another group of Yupiit living in Chevak are told by elders from both villages. Pilot Station is inland, while Chevak is west and closer to the Bering Sea. The Kashunuk River connects the two villages. In the middle of this river is the old village of Chakaktolik, where many of my relatives are originally from.

≋

"Did you see that? It was bright as day!" my brother Abe said excitedly. We were boating home in an open skiff in late September. We passed Blueberry Slough under a dark moon full of stars and saw the lights of our village when all of a sudden, all around us, it was bright as day. For a second this explosion of light was everywhere.

In 1986 the St. Mary's Mission graduated its last high school graduates before closing for good. At the mission the student quarters included three main dorms: one for girls, one for boys, and teacher housing. Although boarding school students share many stories and experiences, from social to cultural and socioeconomic to behavioral, there was one ecological experience of the St. Mary's boy's dorm that was unique. All the boys were Alaska Native and knew this similar experience from their own hometowns. Late at night during cold winters before the 11 p.m. lights out curfew, we heard loud whistling throughout the dorm, a signal of an natural light show like no other. The highest piercing whistling provided the most response, but when a group of boys whistled a crescendo as a team, the volume of the dancing northern lights was an ecological show of amazement and wonder. With open windows, many boys huddled in the cold to watch the northern lights dance.

In Pilot Station the sound of the 9 p.m. curfew was a hand-cranked fire department horn. The low wailing caused the northern lights to dance with changes in visible color variations from dark green to bright deep red. When the night sky is calm and quiet, the northern lights were a familiar green color, but when a loud whistling sound is made, there is a disturbance created with kinetic energy of sound waves bombarding the magnetic waves that create the aurora borealis.

Most everyone is familiar with rainbows and how moisture refracts sunlight to show colors of the visible light spectrum. In the Northern Hemisphere, there is another phenomenon similar to the rainbow called a sundog. During cold winter spells the dense cold air freezes a particle layer in the atmosphere as crystal-like ice. With sunlight the refraction is visible as a prism of rainbow colors. The sundogs appear like balls of rainbow on either side of the sun. All rainbows are made with the same color variation, but unlike northern lights, rainbows need moisture and sunlight to create the light refraction. Unlike rainbows, the northern lights are burning earthly gases caused by solar magnetic influence.

That northern lights make sound is another rumor. During cold clear nights when the northern lights are active and alive, I have heard a crisping sound as the lights dance—almost like the sound of crickets. If the light refraction is a visible rainbow, the sound of northern lights is the result of igniting burning gas. When we heard the wailing curfew sound, we ran home to keep our parents from paying the twenty-five-cent curfew fee. Folk stories of northern lights coming down to take children were common among Natives. Some of the most entertaining stories were of lights chasing dog team travelers late at night with a loud cackling sound.

In Pilot Station the concern for global climate change is not evident. Other than what is reported in the news, it is hard to support any cause without immediate results. During cold spells and freezing inclement weather, it is easy for Natives to ridicule and ask, "Where is this global warming everyone is talking about?" It is freezing here in Alaska. It seems like yesterday when words like "nuclear winter," "acid rain," and "CFCS" were issues of global concern and magic keywords for news media to recognize as newsworthy. "Global warming" and "climate change" are catchphrases for guaranteed funding for environmental projects, especially if used with adjective fear words: "decimated," "declining," "melting," "warming," "rising."

There are berry picking sites used exclusively by certain Native families where berry abundance is noted from year to year and compared with other seasons. Many have noticed that salmonberries are not as plentiful, that more grass and sedges are growing in areas that used to be predominantly tundra. Willow, alder, and birch trees are growing thicker and taller near the high banks of the Kashunuk River where tundra used to be visible along many parts of the river.

Similar to seasonal folklore observation of groundhogs, Yup'ik elders have similar traditional forecasts. One is the amount and growth of grass during summer and fall. Tall grass is a forecast of lots of snow and precipitation the next winter, and lots of snow provides several forecasts of its own. One is that more snow and ice will provide cooler spring and summer season temperatures and more tundra berries the next season.

What is it about tall grass that can explain the amount of precipitation? Many science classroom walls and textbooks have diagrams of the water cycle. Cloud creation, precipitation, sunlight, and evaporation are key concepts. Central to this system is the battle between heat and cold. The low-lying land mass creates the heat source for evaporation, while the water mass provides water molecules and higher elevations provide the cooling source for precipitation. This is a system. Water bodies and plants are the main source for evaporation and as more sunlight heat is applied, evaporation rates quicken and the system thickens with cloud formations and cooler elevations create precipitation such as rain and snow.

Tall grass and more plants create more surface area for evaporation and moisture collection. This is the same influence as in the Amazon rainforest, the Pacific states of Oregon and Washington, and southeast Alaska, where much of the state's rainforest exists. Early sodbusters in the prairie Midwest learned this lesson the hard way. All the prairie grass was cut and tilled to plant seeds and crop, and bare of plants with no surface for evaporation to match sunlight heat, the soils dried and created dust storms like never before. Salmonberry abundance favors mild summers with consistent rainfall during the growing season, keeping the tundra moist; dry tundra provides no moisture for berries. On the other hand, as a main food source for caribou, lichen prefers dry conditions and caribou tend to be found on hilly terrain and the high Arctic, where the tundra is well drained and conditions are dry.

In 2014 my brother Martin and I were logging to stock up on firewood not long after ice breakup. In Pilot Station spring breakup and ice had been flowing steady for several days. In the Atchuelinguk River there was something unusual: there was no ice, logs, or wood debris. For the last several years this river had some unusual ice breakup. The normal river characteristic was high water during spring, and through the summer the water level would taper depending on the amount of rain interior Alaska experienced. During the fall, the water level would drop. What was unusual was that we were getting high water during fall season and the water level quickly dropped before ice freeze up. During winter the water level continued to drop and cause the ice to buckle.

As part of the Yukon Kuskokwim Delta, the Lower Yukon is a huge fluvial tributary, and satellite aerial photos show it as a huge delta estuary. If terraforming is an indicator of global change, the topographic features of this delta are a keystone indicator as irrefutable proof. As Martin and I were boating up the Atchuelinguk we saw no drifting ice, logs or wood. We assumed that this river was done with spring breakup. At the entrance of Anqercak we could not believe what we saw. Anqercak Slough is one of several rivers that feed the Atchuelinguk from the Yukon River. Floating ice, logs, and wood debris were bank to bank and flowing upriver into Atchuelinguk. This was the first time we had seen this. Several years later the same thing happened again.

There is another unusual spring ice event. Alaskans are familiar with the Nenana River Ice Classic, where participants can win money for predicting the day and time of breakup. Before 2000, Pilot Station ice breakup occurred ten days to two weeks after the Nenana River, and this was what we expected. In the last several years the lapse of time between the two ice breakups has been shorter. In 2016 the river ice broke only days after Nenana. In the last several years the ice broke almost the same time. Nenana River is a thousand miles inland from Pilot Station.

Another Native ecological observation is the abundance of salmon entering the Yukon River. During midsummer it is not unusual for the Yukon water level to drop after the main king salmon and summer chum salmon pass Pilot Station. After the salmon reach their spawning tributaries, the water level will drop by as much as fifteen feet. As fall salmon enter the river the water level rises to springtime conditions. Imagine a million salmon entering the river and the amount of water they displace as they swim upriver. In a large school of fish, they leave a trail of fish slime that creates white frothy trails on the surface. Before the Pilot Station Sonar Site became operational, elders tried to convince ADF&G managers of this relationship between water level and froth trails, arguing that with the number of salmon, subsistence harvest restrictions were not necessary.

When Abe and I were boating home in the dark and saw a flash of bright light, the reasonable explanation was a reflection of sunlight off a solar panel of a manmade satellite as it whizzed along its orbit. The flash of light was only a second or two and, in that instant, we could see all around. Startled, Abe and I looked to the clear cloudless starlit sky to see if we were about to be beamed aboard. Other late-night travelers have experienced this same phenomenon.

In 2009 a small village near the edge of the Bering Sea once called Sheldon Point was able to get its community name changed to its traditional Yup'ik name of Nunam Iqua. In 2017 Barrow, Alaska, also changed to its traditional Inupiaq name Utqiagvik.

In April 2015 AVCP president Myron Naneng was instrumental to convince the State of Alaska to change the name for the Wade Hampton Census Area. This is my part of Alaska. The Wade Hampton Census Area is 99 percent Yup'ik. In the midst of the 2016 U.S. presidential election frenzy, Inuit Kotzebue resident and former Alaska state legislator Reggie Joule told Native leaders at the Tribal Leaders Summit on Climate Change in Ferndale, Washington: "Alaska is the northernmost southern state of the union." As a Native, I did not realize how formidable it is to be recognized as a Republican or Democratic citizen. It seems like one party is more intimidating than the other.

Like early European mysteries of Davy Jones's Locker, I did not know Wade Hampton was the name of a former Confederate general during the last American Civil War. Alaska has no counties and the local census area was named after an iconic fearless Southern leader who never visited Alaska or met with any Natives. Alaska was never involved in the Civil War. When the regional *Delta Discovery* newspaper reported about changing the name of this census area, it was appealing to some local Natives to change the name to Nunam Iqua Census Area. Instead, the name was changed to Kusilvak Census Area. This is the same name change situation of Alaska's famous mountain of Mount McKinley to the traditional Athabascan name of Denali. Instead of a name of a previous U.S. President, Denali means "Great One" in Athabascan. Kusilvak is the name of the highest mountain in this part of Alaska. It is not as formidable as mountains in the Alaska or Brooks Range, but all alone in this vast flat part of Alaska, Kusilvak is formidable in its own way and provides a reference point surrounded by treeless flat land in middle of nowhere.

In Yup'ik, Nunam Iqua means "edge of the land" or "the end of the land." Wade Hampton Census Area is no more. We are residents of Kusilvak Census Area. Kusilvak means to "stand on the shoulders of one and look around."

13 Spiritual Realms

"No, we don't want to sue the State of Alaska," we told the Indian Child Welfare Act case lawyer.

In 2014 AVCP helped Pilot Station tribe with a two-year child custody case. The families who had been involved were relieved the State of Alaska had agreed with the tribal recommendation for adoptive parents. After the decision, the lawyer asked if we would like to sue the state for not following the Indian Child Welfare Act; two years for a decision was two years too long. The child was in state custody in a non-Native foster home in Anchorage.

In previous child custody cases for the Native Village of Venetie, the Minto Traditional Council and Tanana Traditional Council had filed suit against the State of Alaska for not following the act. Yet the state was continuing to treat each Indian child custody case without regard to the act. Our tribal council did not want to sue the state. The lawyer and Indian child welfare supervisor were discouraged and wanted to make sure our decision was final. They reminded us that the state needs to be reprimanded and laws need to be followed. They both repeated that we could win.

"No, we don't want to file a lawsuit, but we are interested in a class-action suit with other tribes." This was in 2014. In October 2017 the State of Alaska signed a compact agreement recognizing the Indian Child Welfare Act, which Congress had passed in 1978, and recognizing tribal responsibility over all tribal child custody cases.[1] The state wanted to work with tribes in all Indian child welfare cases.

"What?" I held up my arms and looked to my co-worker. I felt awkward because he was just staring at me. We were both foresters working in the middle of this boreal forest near Fairbanks. Mike was big and burly and breathing heavily; the hot humid weather made him sweat profusely. The mosquitos had been menacing, and the agitation had finally gotten to him. "You never put on mosquito dope, how come the damn bugs are not bothering you!" Hmm, try thinking Native?

My favorite job was working in the Tongass National Forest of southeast Alaska. Based out of Juneau, I traveled as a forest pest technician with the U.S. Forest Service's Forest Science Lab (FSL). We monitored forest pests from the spruce bark beetle to the hemlock sawfly, including the Alaska yellow cedar decline and spruce tree rusts. To be honest, one redundant forest tree pest was the hemlock mistletoe.

On Prince of Wales Island, FSL had several mixed conifer plots to determine the growth rate and impact of mistletoe on young spruce, hemlock, and cedar trees. Prince of Wales Island has a major logging history, and clearcutting is the most economic industrywide practice for harvesting trees. As a result, the regrowth of forest trees provides an even-age forest stand. The trees in the mistletoe plots were about twenty-five years old. The unique characteristic of these forests is that they are natural revegetation plots, with no seeding planted by hand. In a lush maritime forest, revegetation is natural and competitive among all plants. The only silvicultural application was thinning of trees when the stand was fifteen years old, like weeding a garden. When undesired plants are pulled the remaining plants have more access to soil nutrients, sunlight, and a chance for a quicker rate of growth. In any agricultural or forest biome a productive crop is always appreciated.

As a forest disease the mistletoe is a parasite; it needs a host species to live. The unique size of this parasite is that it is small and not visible from the ground or from great distance. In every tree, the only way to find mistletoe is to climb and inspect every limb for growth defects, like small burls. As mistletoe grows and steals nutrients from the tree, it causes the tree to deform. One deformity is a witch broom that can be visible from a distance. For a research project, every tree is climbed and combed, and every specimen found is measured and mapped on the tree. The next year we return and measure growth rate, inspect for new infections, and determine rate of spread. How this disease spreads and propagates is as interesting as its physical form. Mistletoe has several fleshy tentacles. As mistletoe matures, seeds develop at the end of each tentacle, similar to a pomegranate seed encased in a gel-like substance. It does not depend on wind, insects, or any critters for seed dispersal. Instead, the seed builds up hydrostatic pressure within this casing and pops and spits out the seed to neighboring tree limbs. The gel is sticky, and the seed starts to grow roots implanted through the bark to steal nutrients from the sap. The mistletoe offers no symbiotic relationship or benefits. By itself the mistletoe does not necessarily harm the tree.

Trees already infected tend to spread more infections, and neighboring trees get infected because of their proximity. The rate of spread becomes constant at an exponential rate, where one propagates one, the next year two to four, and so on. Eventually, the growth rate of infected trees becomes stunted and susceptible to other forest insect and disease attacks. The other unusual characteristic about mistletoe is that it does not need pollen to propagate, and whether it is actually a plant is questionable.

In my area of Alaska there are no hemlock trees or mistletoe. Many forest diseases are host specific and create similar tree deformities. The spruce and cedar trees have natural resistances that prevent mistletoe infections, but there are other forest diseases that infect these trees, and most create burls as a physical deformity. Many know mistletoe as a Christmas ornament, but mistletoes are not native in my part of Alaska, and hemlock trees are not native to forests north of the Kenai Peninsula.

The first time I saw mistletoe it looked like the plastic ones used for Christmas ornaments, but this mistletoe was a living specimen. I was amazed. There are similar forest diseases that create witch brooms on birch, and this is common in Pilot Station. The Natives collect this birch tree fungus and use it as like tobacco. People use tobacco products for different reasons, but most use it to get a sense of euphoria and spiritual experience. This fungus is highly addictive and can give a spiritual sense of euphoria. This Native tobacco is called *iqmik*.

≥

In 1980 the City of Pilot Station constructed a city municipal building with a unique Eskimo design. UAF hosts an annual Alaska Native Arts Festival at the Davis Concert Hall. The back of the auditorium stage is uniquely designed, with a strange boxy-shaped wall to amplify sound for the audience to appreciate live concerts. Without use of a microphone, the sound from the stage permeates out to the audience like in an amphitheater, and it is clean, rich, and crisp. Compared to dance events at the AFN Quyana or Camai festivals, the sound is not as hollow, where the bass and tenor tends to get lost in the corners of a large square building. Although microphones attempt to collect and gather all this sound into a vibrant collection as music, the increased volume also creates a reverberation, diminishing the acoustic performance of the singing and beat of the drum, making the performance just another live event.

For large gatherings there is no choice but to host the event wherever there is space. In many Alaska villages large community gatherings are hosted at the school gym. Every gym building is designed for sports, and the square corners help provide structural integrity. To try and enhance Eskimo singing at the school gym, the Pilot Station dance group hangs large plastic sheeting at the back and over the drummers and singers to heighten the sound experience for the audience. Although the sound still seems hollow, sitting in front of the singers and drummers provides a better sound experience than without these alterations. The real experience is in the traditional qasgiq. In 1969 Pilot Station elders completed a large qasgiq, and the music enlightened the elders' memories of when they were young and rejuvenated the significance of many local Eskimo dance customs.

Every traditional qasgiq is dome shaped and made of earthen material. When the drumbeat and singing are experienced in this earthen atmosphere, the acoustics of the higher and lower decibel tones are absorbed by the heavy logs, mud material, and hollow dry plant cells. As a result, there is no sound reverberation, especially when the drumbeat reaches crescendo. There is no echo. When I first experienced this as a child, it seemed like the sound was coming from everywhere. What was eerie was that the sounds seemed to be coming from the dancers, and I was completely mesmerized by the dance fans. With grant funds elders encouraged the City of Pilot Station to construct a dome-shaped building with a single igloo interior. Without structural corners, the dome shape and sound dynamics provide an Eskimo song and dance experience like no other.

In 2008, when Pilot Station hosted Yupiit Yuraryarait dance festival, the gym was packed and crowded with audience members who had come to enjoy this cultural event. Due to weather and passenger numbers, every flight out of Pilot Station was booked for several days. Although the majority of visitors flew out the day after the event, several dance groups had no choice but to spend more time in Pilot Station. As hosts, Pilot Station continued dance events at the dome with a smaller audience. My houseguests from Newtok were weathered in, and they could not stop talking about the acoustics of the dome as a mini-amphitheater. Every dance came alive with the crisp lyrics of the singers as the story was told.

When we hear sound, an echo location helps point the direction the sound is coming from. In the dome this is not the case; the sound comes from everywhere and the Eskimo drumming and singing experience comes alive. The acoustics are clean and vibrant, and the lyrics to any song are rich. I am not a singer or drummer; the lead singers talk about how listening to the acoustics helps feedback on pronunciation and tone. As a result, I have heard many compliments about Pilot Station dance group singers having crisp and clean vocals. Although the dome is fifty feet in diameter, there is another sound phenomenon unique about its design. In any building when someone is fifty feet away it is difficult to hear what they say without yelling, but in the dome when one whispers to the wall, a conversation can be had between two people at opposite ends of the building. This is similar to a string and paper cup telemachine. In February 2007 Pilot Station had the honor to host the Yukon River Drainage Fisheries Association annual meeting in this dome. Sitting on opposite ends, several of us listened to the excited whispering of upriver association members' talk of proposing BOF net restrictions on the perceived size decline of Yukon kings and about how to apply for funding to set up a fishwheel to monitor salmon.

For safety concerns, in 2020 the City of Pilot Station demolished the old dome building.

≥

"No, tell him how they make this and who made this," I told Rex to tell the non-Native about what he had in his mouth.

In 1990 I chaperoned two young high school students to an inhalant abuse conference in Phoenix, Arizona. Rex Nick and Harry George were young boys from Pilot Station. This was my first trip to Phoenix, and for the boys this was their first trip out of Alaska.

In June the Phoenix shade temperature was 105 degrees Fahrenheit. The coolest place was the air-conditioned buildings. As we stood in the cool safety of our room, the desert heat emanating and creating a mirage of the faraway hills scared the two Natives about going for a walk around the block. I finally convinced the boys that we could visit the Phoenix Suns building where the NBA teams play. Basketball is big in Native Alaska. Although the building and season were closed, just touching the sunbaked building provided a little spiritual experience that we've been there and done that. The boys returned home with stories to tell. The conference covered the impact and abuse of sniffing inhalants and behavioral side effects. In rural Alaska the most common inhalant abused is gasoline; it is used in every vehicle and readily available.

Unlike inhalant products, tobacco nicotine is a common Native addiction. As a major agricultural industry, cigarettes and chewing tobacco will continue to be made as long as consumers are willing to buy them. The company will provide the product and reap the cost despite the risks. Although nicotine is the addictive ingredient, Yup'ik Natives have another natural product used with chewing tobacco leaf. Growing up, for my generation this addictive product was only used by elder women, but now it is readily available and used by most everyone including tweens and ten-year-old kids. The traditional product is a socially accepted family habit with many household members addicted. The Bethel Yukon Kuskokwim Health Corporation tobacco coalition helps educate about the risks of all tobacco products, including iqmik. The tobacco coalition has a challenge.

Any tree is susceptible to forest disease, and many common infections cause trees to rot or create physical deformities. One common forest disease is in the mushroom and fungus family. Many mushrooms provide an excellent food ingredient and are accepted worldwide as produce. Some are poisonous and some can create sensations of euphoria. Mushrooms and fungus can infect all tree species and all forest organic material. One fungus in Alaska used by the Natives is the conk infecting birch trees. Natives call it a punk, and going out to collect punk is taken seriously. Young entrepreneurs will collect this product and sell for spending money. This Native product is not an industry product. Twenty dollars for an eight-ounce jar sound like a potential investment return but it is not a regulated product. Anyone can go into the woods and collect it.

One conk most everyone has probably heard of is chicken-of-the-woods, an edible fungus of the mushroom family. The iqmik punk is not an edible product. The punk is collected from the birch trees, dried, burned to ash, and mixed with tobacco leaves. People who are not familiar with this product will see Natives take out a small container or baggie and take a pinch of iqmik between the gum and cheeks, same as any chewing tobacco. Some real chewers will chew it. Most will spit out excess juice, but at its potency, chewers will put it back into the container and later chew it again. Chewers will reuse iqmik over and over until it loses its kick, whatever that is. I have never tried iqmik, so I can only speculate based on what I see, and whatever euphoria these chewers experience is something that is all in your head. Mom, Grandma, and many elder relatives were avid chewers, and from what I have seen, making this product is not for the meek. Perhaps making this product is like stories of psychedelic experience of peyote and Native Americans in Arizona. I have heard stories of young novice Natives trying to make iqmik for the first time and quitting tobacco for good after the experience.

Rex Nick is a successful commercial fisherman. During a busy salmon season, Rex and I were visiting the Pilot Station Sonar Site checking on the run strength and location of the main salmon pulse. Rex had just taken a pinch out of a generic tobacco container when a non-Native Fish and Game employee asked Rex for some chew. Rex commented that he did not have any. Out of tobacco and in need of a fix, the non-Native called Rex "stingy." Offended, Rex told the guy that what he had was not chew, it was iqmik. Curious, the employee asked to try it because he had seen other Natives use it, and if everyone was doing it, it should have been okay to try.

With a nicotine fix, the non-Native chewed with glee and sparkling eyes. Rex talked about iqmik and the birch punk and I told Rex to tell how Natives make it. For its potency there is a natural enzyme required to make iqmik. Elders call making iqmik as *cuyaq*. Sometimes Mom dreads making cuyaq but is pleased when someone makes it. The punk ash is rolled inside the tobacco leaf, and together this plug is mixed and chewed with saliva. This is where the potency is at its extreme, and the euphoria can knock the meek senseless. Elders who use this product have developed a resistance to this euphoria and taste. Like any drug, it is true that more is needed to get the same sensation as the first time. Elders are able to bite and mix the ingredients together with natural enzymes from the mouth juices to help break down the properties of punk ash as a fungus. The result of cuyaq is iqmik.

Satisfied, the non-Native was nonchalant and cool and I asked, "Who made the iqmik?" When Rex answered, "My grandma," the Fish and Game employee ran out of the tent retching and spitting out the iqmik. Many Natives cannot afford escalating costs of chewing tobacco or cigarettes.

Cancer is also a leading cause of death among Alaska Natives.

NOTES

1. Lisa Demer, "Alaska Tribes and State Sign Historic Document on Tribal Child Welfare," *Anchorage Daily News*, October 19, 2017.

14 ⋛ Is It Too Big?

"Alaska is so big it has a half-hour weather report," I heard one of my co-workers as he called relatives living in the Lower 48.

⋛

As large as Alaska is, the U.S. government is revered as a democratic system representing all people and guided by the principles and doctrines of the U.S. Constitution. Within this system, the U.S. House and Senate oversee the Code of Federal Regulations where all laws of the land are written. To be impartial and represent people equally, the number of state house and senate representatives is determined according to the population of the decennial population survey.

Since statehood Alaska has had one U.S. House and two U.S. Senate representatives voicing all statewide concerns, compared to a state like California, where the number of representatives is significant based on the number of people living there. If the Alaska population changes significantly, we are likely to get an additional seat in the House or Senate, and Alaskans may not be pleased with more government oversight. Should we give in to this system and request more government power with the assumption that it is good for Alaska? If anything, here is a lesson for tribes. Just like at the state level, the federal House and Senate leaders represent a district that changes with population dynamics. They do not represent an enclosed land base like a reservation; the districts are treated as a living entity that changes when people move or as families grow and build homes.

When ANCSA first created the small village corporations, the Native Village of Venetie and Arctic Village took steps to dissolve all corporate existence and continue to exist as traditional Native entities. Tribal members voiced opposition to the Land Claim Act with a notion that they would rather be recognized as a sovereign tribal entity. Following ANCSA guidelines, Venetie and Arctic Village created a village corporation with shareholders, selected land holdings, transferred the land together, and created one entity. After this creation, the corporate existence was dissolved, with no ties to any village or regional corporation shares. Venetie and Arctic Village were no longer a Native corporation and recognized as one tribe: the Native Village of Venetie.

ANCSA lands are not Indian Country, despite any preexisting recognition Natives may try to claim. All corporation lands are conveyed as unrestricted fee-simple title subject to state regulations that supersede tribal jurisdiction. The Venetie and Arctic Village actions were taken after 1971. With several court cases against the State of Alaska, the Native Village of Venetie claimed reservation recognition gave them tribal sovereignty. Regardless of these court decisions, many Alaska tribes provide economic development opportunities and critical services in many small communities, despite the existence and function of local village corporation or municipal governments.

Since 1989 the Alaska region BIA has hosted an annual clearinghouse conference for Alaska tribal members without emphasis on Alaska Native corporation issues or concerns. The BIA conference addresses tribal issues including realty, transportation, housing, trust resources, child custody, wildlife, fisheries, and gaming. It is the largest gathering of tribal members, many of whom are still learning about the role of tribes. Each conference session emphasizes encouraging Alaska tribes to be self-sufficient, with lessons of what other tribes are accomplishing for their communities.

Native empowerment is evolving and growing. Although there have been several attempts to meet and create a statewide tribal unity, Alaska tribes continue to be fragmented, addressing their own issues.

Alaska tribal sovereignty is not self-evident. Questions of self-government and tribal sovereignty are difficult to answer. This point of view continues to develop with the administration of every new Alaska governor. Unlike the federal administrative procedure of tribal recognition and recommendation for consultation, many prominent Alaska leaders continue to ignore the role of tribes with the preexisting notion that tribes have no sovereignty rights. Many remind Natives that ANCSA extinguished this claim. It is taken for granted that ANCSA recognized the major landowners and that tribal existence is irrelevant. Because of the preexisting ethic of Indian Country, does a tribe need to own land to be a tribe?

≋

The role of state governors is to uphold the state constitution. Like the power of veto used to amend legislative decisions, the governor has administrative powers that come with holding office. Governor Frank Murkowski was quietly disappointed when he realized he could never make any changes to the existence of tribes in Alaska and the way tribal existence was addressed and settled by the three previous governors, Knowles, Hickel, and Cowper. Despite claims of extinguishment of aboriginal rights, the 1989 state supreme court rural preference decision started a process of addressing tribal existence as an ethnic issue, not as an ethic issue. This ruling began the process of tribal recognition that is still evolving today.

The last fleeting administrative order Governor Steve Cowper signed in 1990 recognized that *tribes exist in Alaska*. After one term Cowper did not run for reelection. In fall 1990 Walter Hickel was elected, and his first administrative order superseded Cooper's claim. Hickel stated that there are *no tribes in Alaska* and we are *one country, one people*. The general consensus of the state government was that tribes do not exist and that Governor Cowper had misled the people. After one term Hickel lost his reelection to Tony Knowles. Knowles served two terms as governor.

Alaska resources are not only about big oil and gas reserves. The state supreme court decision allowing no preferential harvests for subsistence also started discussions of wildlife harvest management concerns with emphasis on Native customary and traditional ecological knowledge. It is taken for granted that as *one country, one people*, we are the same, or at least we should be. We are equal, and this concept dovetails with the trust doctrine of the Alaska state constitution—not recognizing any one person as special. The notion of *one country, one people* emphatically denied preferential harvesting of resources that belong to everyone, regardless of which part of Alaska one lived in. It was at about this time the U.S. Supreme Court addressed Katie John's story of harvesting salmon with a traditional fishwheel on a state river system. As she was an Athabascan elder, fishing for salmon was not a violation of any rules or regulations. This was subsistence—heart and mind.

At this time there were several organizations created to deal with our fishery resources. Senator Ted Stevens successfully created the Community Development Quota Program for fishery harvests and economic opportunities for communities along the rim of the Bering Sea. The Yukon River Drainage Fisheries Association, Yukon River Panel, and Yukon River Inter-Tribal Watershed Council were organized to address Alaska and Canadian communities that depend on wild resources of the Yukon River.

During his second term, Governor Knowles dealt with the issue of tribes and quieted the state responsibility over controversies that stemmed around subsistence. In one stroke of a pen, Knowles superseded Hickel's administrative order and made it impossible for any future governor to argue or deny tribal existence. Knowles's administrative order implied that if the federal government says tribes exist in Alaska, then tribes exist in Alaska. This is recognition of a government hierarchy system in which the federal government supersedes the state. It is a fiduciary system supporting the fact that the federal and state governments are in agreement about the existence of Alaska tribes.

Governor Knowles also signed the 2001 Millennium Agreement. This agreement not only reiterated tribal existence but recognized that the state was willing to work with Alaska tribes by requiring each state department to create tribal consultation procedures, similar to those of the Department of Interior. Tribes will always be in a position to be reckoned with.

Alaska has 229 tribes, and membership is determined by each tribal constitution and elected council leaders. Unlike ANCSA Native corporations, every shareholder is a tribal member, but not every tribal member is a corporation shareholder. Being able to own or buy shares is not an obligation of choice; it is a privilege of investment. How federal taxpayers spend or invest their earned money is up to each individual. Instead of allowing Alaska Natives a choice, ANCSA gave corporation shares only to privileged Natives born before 1971. Afterward, any non-shareholder, whether Alaska Native or not, who can receive corporation shares must have the last will and testament or proof of direct ancestral lineage of the deceased shareholder based on the decision of a court magistrate. Each Native corporation continues to address this provision with the notion that any descendants should not be left behind. This is a virtue of Native cultures, which foster a social obligation to try to help everyone. Natives born after 1971 are addressed in every corporation meeting.

When the Native corporations were created, there was excitement and emphasis on how much money these businesses could generate. The regional corporations were given a huge amount of startup funds to provide economic opportunities to help develop and maintain rural Alaska with jobs, community infrastructures, training opportunities, and other economic possibilities. High expectations of how much money these corporations could generate with promising shareholder dividends created disappointments. Heated discussion of dividend payment was often a topic in corporation meetings. For a time attending corporation meetings was not pleasant. Fueled by comparisons of dividend payments of other successful corporations including CEO salaries, it was hard to feel gratified, realizing that all this was in exchange for a land claim settlement and loss of wildlife responsibility.

Unlike in the Lower 48 states, there are no counties in Alaska. Similarly, in my part of Alaska there are no boroughs. There are many small city governments that provide municipal services and receive shares of state revenue funds, depending on the whim of the current governor— conditions in rural Alaska are often not recognized as priorities of statewide concern. Governor Murkowski cut the community revenue sharing program between local municipal organizations. Governor Sarah Palin later reinstated the local revenue sharing. This show of support of rural communities is only a whim based on the notion of *one country, one people*. The rural communities have nowhere else to turn; perhaps Alaska is too big for our state government. The current governor continues to address serious fiscal concerns as a result of declining oil revenue and services that need to be provided.

As a result of tribal recognition, despite the guidelines of the Millennium Agreement, one nagging attribute of Lower 48 tribes has become a quiet issue of concern: are the tribes in Alaska sovereign? In 2007, as a guest speaker at the annual AFN convention, Senator Ted Stevens addressed the Native shareholders and reassured everyone that tribes in Alaska can never be sovereign because they do not own the land. Although leaders like Ted Stevens and Walter Hickel were involved with the inception of ANCSA, the perception of tribes has been an ethnic time lapse comparison of Native empowerment movement that initiated ANCSA and the current identity situation. Many Alaska leaders of this generation believed that tribes do not exist in Alaska without a reservation or landownership to claim sovereignty and that the corporation concept had extinguished aboriginal rights. To clarify this issue, in 2017 Governor Bill Walker asked the state attorney general for a legal disclaimer regarding Alaska Native tribal sovereignty.

The lapse of time between ANCSA and Ted Stevens's speech created a statewide mindset that Alaska tribes have no power of authority. During this time, to avoid any potential power struggle, some state departments included tribal sovereignty as a disclaimer before any state services can be provided. The Department of Transportation included contract provisions to waiver tribal sovereignty immunity for any state projects in areas where roads and tribes exist. Tribal organizations who were asked to waive this condition quietly ask: How can we give you something when we don't know if we have it? Perhaps if the state says that tribes in Alaska have sovereignty, then the tribes must really have the power to govern themselves to waive as a contract provision.

Then the state realized the Department of Transportation was treading water in the deep end of the pool. There are no alternatives if the state claims responsibility of communities where tribes live and refuses to provide department projects until tribal immunity is given. The only option is cessation of all state responsibility or no services until these tribes sign this waiver. This does not sound like a democratic government process.

As a result of tribal recognition from the Millennium Agreement, there are several examples where the state successfully negated further conflict by consulting with the tribe before carrying out tasks that used to be simple government responsibilities. One example is an airport runway expansion project in southeast Alaska where several tribal members were buried in a small ancestral cemetery. The proposed airport expansion overlapped a traditional burial ground. The state consulted with the tribe, and the tribe recognized the limited options and agreed to move the cemetery to another similar historic site. This is one example of a government offering respect as an extension of customary diplomacy embedded in all cultural traditions. It is comforting that the state was willing to consult with the tribe and avoid further conflict by working together.

Another cooperative issue is non-tribal and tribal child custody cases. Native identity is prevalent in every child custody case where ethics is a leading decision-maker to address child safety concerns. Traditionally, the state government claimed full responsibility for all custody and adoption issues; the tribal side of the story was never addressed. Stories from the Office of Children's Services are difficult to listen to. It is a somber realization that we all care for our children and the protection we extend is recognition that we are all human. All child custody cases are sensitive issues and like the State of Alaska, tribes and tribal court do not discuss these issues openly.

The tribal courts consider elder recommendations in local civic cases and restorative justice options. Tribal courts are part of a judicial court system addressing the responsibilities and actions of tribal members. With declining oil revenue, the state continues to address difficult funding obligations. As tribal courts develop the existence of tribes cannot be ignored, set aside, or acknowledged only when issues become critical for services. Tribal courts do not reside over city ordinances, state regulations, or federal codes, but they can help address many local issues, aside from state fiscal and judicial obligations.

Before Knowles signed the administrative order about tribal existence, Knowles visited with Katie John and listened to her stories about fishing on the Copper River. Afterward, the State of Alaska stopped challenging the U.S. Supreme Court decision and signed the 2001 Millennium Agreement. In 2017 the state attorney general issued the legal opinion that Alaska tribes are sovereign.

The big issue is subsistence. I admit I don't remember the last time I bought a state license to legally participate in securing meat for my family. The more Natives I confer with, the more I become convinced my reason for dissension from state regulations supports tribal solidarity. Although I can purchase a five-dollar state subsistence license to legally participate, how much time and money is the state willing to spend to justify my reasoning if I refuse to buy a license? A five-dollar subsistence license would make me a respectable participant to Fish and Game board members. If a fish and wildlife trooper cites me for hunting or fishing without a state license and I plead not guilty, someone has to be willing to buy a five-dollar license to settle the issue. The more I learn about subsistence, the less I find reason to be afraid. The State of Alaska has no options to challenge Katie John's story; we Natives have nothing to hide.

In July 2022 Alaska governor Mike Dunleavy signed House Bill 123, forever changing the state's role and the status of Alaska tribal recognition.

15 ⬳ More Native Teachers

"Alcohol . . . ," one bingo player said. He sat quiet when I asked, "Too much, or not enough?" My response caused the bingo player to stutter. As community planner for the Pilot Station tribal council, I was collecting a list of issues and constraints for our first community plan.

In 1970 discussions at local community Fish and Game meetings with federal and state representatives were often lost in translation. At these meetings someone local was assigned to translate the Yup'ik language. The dialog about Native concerns depended on the translator's knowledge. Education and knowledge of the issues created another challenge. A difficult example is BOF or BOG proposals with goals and objectives written in elaborate words. In these meetings it was not unusual for someone to interrupt the language translator and retranslate the point with a completely different meaning. As a curious child, I remember visiting Dad during these meetings and seeing lost looks of confusion from the elders. As a result of this confusing time period, Thomas Berger began his collection of Native voices written in the book *Village Journey* addressing the fear of 1991.[1] Why were Natives afraid of 1991?[2]

While collecting information on issues and constraints, I balked when a bingo player mentioned community freezers as an issue. In village Alaska, conducting community meetings during bingo is common. Community freezers have nothing to do with community development, but I reminded myself to be impartial and that there was no right or wrong answer. I left the bingo hall thinking about community freezers. It seemed like my family's two freezers had always been more than sufficient for our needs.

Another need mentioned was for "more Native teachers."

My brother Donald and I went to look for our younger brother James. While returning from Bethel by snow machine, James ran out of fuel about fifteen miles from Pilot Station. Before his cell phone battery died the previous day, James called during the heavy snowstorm. Since his call, it had been snowing nonstop for twelve hours. It was not the light fluffy snow. The weather was near freezing, and the snow was heavy and wet. On our snow machine the snow was plaster and molded into snowballs inside our undercarriage.

This area is less than an hour's ride away. After four hours we neared the spot where James was supposed to be. It was overcast and misty. On the highest peak of the low-lying hills, we could not see more than a mile in any direction. The spruce trees and willows were covered with wet heavy snow. We listened and everything was silent and quiet. No fresh tracks. We saw no sign and smelled no woodsmoke. The high humidity and foggy weather easily precipitated any woodsmoke. Low on fuel, we headed home on an alternate route where the trail was protected from the wind and the snow drifts were not as deep. Near home we met three searchers heading out to check on us and to see if James had been found. We updated them on the trail conditions and our route.

An hour later the searchers found James. Donald and I had stopped less than half a mile above him. James had a campfire blazing and had heard our snow machines. With a fire inside a heavy wooded spruce grove, the amount of snow on the trees gave the illusion that our engine sounds were coming from the Bethel side of the trail and that we would come around the bend and see him, when in fact we were above and behind his fire. James thought we would come into view and spot the bonfire. Ten minutes later, when James heard our engines start and became faint, he realized we were somewhere behind and above him and that he should have yelled, hollered, or shot into the air to make noise. As our engine noises quieted, James shot his high-power rifle into the air, but we did not hear the sound. We were already too far. James walked up the hill to our snow machine trail, and this is how the searchers found his snowshoe tracks.

Because of heavy snow sticking to snow machine tracks, Donald and I took turns leading and breaking trail. When one snow machine got stuck the other would pass and keep breaking trail. At times both machines became stuck and more time was spent trying to compact the snow to free it. The snow was over waist deep, and the one-hand shovel was small and more labor intensive than using our boots to push and compact the snow. The snow stuck to the shovel and made that much more work. James had carried enough gas to get home, but because of wet snow conditions he had burned more fuel. The sticky wet snow became extra weight on his snow machine and sled load of caribou.

Years later, as part of winter survival training sessions, Reynold Okitkun and I told students about search-and-rescue stories and rescue efforts when emergency responses are necessary. We often hear about people who get into emergency situations and never make it home. These become body recovery efforts. Listening to stories from people who have been there and done this or that is useful if one should be in a similar situation. During several sessions elders tell stories of similar search-and-rescue efforts. This firsthand lesson is priceless and holds the attention of the youth occupied. These story sessions help build trust between elders and youth, embodying the traditional social structure of Native education methods. Hearing a rumor is not the same as listening to someone who was there and who can answer questions from experience.

In October 2010 I visited staff at the UAF Rural Student Service to talk about the Lower Yukon Natural Helpers Program. Every college in Alaska has a mentor program to help rural students adjust to college life. RSS is a place to visit with other Natives and seek tutoring services, counseling, and peer support.

There are ten schools in the Lower Yukon School District. "Helpers of Today, Leaders of Tomorrow" was the Natural Helper motto. In each school there is at least one Native who grew up in the village and became a certified teacher in the same school where he or she was a student. My sister Louise was the first Native elementary school teacher from Pilot Station. For many years she taught in Pilot Station, Bethel, Fairbanks, and Anchorage before retiring.

In 2011 the Lower Yukon Natural Helper program provided a work session at the annual AFN Elders and Youth Anchorage Convention. Although I am not a teacher, every teacher conference focuses on education success and programs that are working for children in public schools. Many teachers learn of programs providing positive results and encourage others to try them as well. Although there are many teaching methods, many rarely focus on classroom weaknesses to address as reverse psychology. Reynold educated students on the Natural Helper program, peer success, and ways to seek help during times of duress. I, on the other hand, focused on the technical side of the program and helped educate students on other risk behavioral influences. Unfortunately, one statistic we cannot ignore is the number of students who drop out of high school, never to return. As parents we easily accepted every teacher training focused on success. Perhaps we could help educate all new Alaska teachers with a required class: *How to make successful students into high school dropouts*, and require teachers to address this in every parent conference.

The unique attributes of the Natural Helper program emphasize student peer support and how it can be used to help the school and community. For example, Natural Helper students work with and assist elders. As part of an elder service mentor program, students perform weekly chores from chopping firewood and washing dishes to simple household chores and visiting with elders. The program works not only for the benefit of the elders; the students learn more about our community. During a recent Christmas break, a student who participated in this program gathered firewood logs for an elder without being told to do so. Chris Beans was a young man working a construction job in Anchorage and had no relation to the elder. Chris provided several sled loads of firewood to elders he had visited as a Natural Helper student.

As a UAF student, my first dorm roommate was an Athabascan from Minto, Alaska. After graduating from Mt. Edgecumbe High School the same year I graduated from St. Mary's Mission, Rondell Jimmie was also a first-time college student. Although Rondell did not declare any college major, as a Native the natural world was also an interest, and we had many informal discussions on hunting and fishing. After I got expelled, I lost track of Rondell as my work and education travels continued my own journey. After I returned home and became involved with the Pilot Station tribal council, I traveled to statewide fish and wildlife conferences and was pleased to run into Rondell at every conference. Rondell worked with the Nenana tribal council supervising the Indian General Assistance Program's environmental program. Rondell was vocal and active in several fish and wildlife organizations, including the Yukon River Drainage Fisheries Association and Yukon River Inter-Tribal Fish Commission.

The last time I saw Rondell was at the 2015 co-management fish and wildlife conference hosted by the UAF Tribal Management Program. As we discussed our understanding of the statewide regulatory process, the role of tribal governments, and concept of co-management, we questioned the reason why Alaska Natives have two sets of hunting and fishing regulations. Rondell was an avid hunter and fisherman and familiar with many Native challenges. Nenana is not as rural as Pilot Station, but many issues are similar. Rondell said it best that "sometimes as a Native, I don't know if all these regulations are good or bad." In fall 2016 Rondell passed as a result of sudden health complications.

True or false: Teachers can be bullies.

"Yes!" the junior high students yelled in unison. One raised a hand to ask a question. Instead, the student talked of a particular group of teachers who seemed like bullies except for one favorite, and all the other students nodded in agreement. We got into a discussion, and the students were eager to talk about their teachers. I clicked to the next slide.

True or false: Parents can be bullies.

The students looked to each other and did not know how to respond. The most vocal of the students talked of so-and-so's mom, and the students got into an argument. I reminded myself that these were seventh and eighth graders. I clicked to the next slide.

True or false: Elders can be bullies.

Is this blasphemy?

"Bully, Bullies, and Bullying" was the theme of my presentation. Reynold Okitkun and I traveled to district schools and addressed issues local instructional leaders were concerned about. Most presentations focused on youth risk behaviors, adolescents, and village life. During the school year, Reynold's main focus was on inhalant abuse, such as sniffing gas or aerosol inhalants, and the associated risks. In every school, the elementary students were the main group for this inhalant behavior. Each of us is familiar with someone who has permanent physical and mental damage and someone who passed away as a result of sniffing gasoline or inhalants. Those who lost their lives as a result of inhalants first experienced a loss of consciousness and overdose. One child was found sitting on an ATV face down over an open gas tank. Other topics we discussed included emergency survival skills, safe winter travel, thin ice, boating, swimming, flotation vests, and alcohol, tobacco, and drugs.

Although most themes focus on risk behaviors, the main theme we enjoyed with all students was peer leadership skills. As much as we can, we trained upper-class high school students to give presentations to elementary and junior high students. The most successful presentations were tag-teams, with students providing classroom sessions for younger students. With a little training every student has a story to tell. Storytelling is always interesting for every child in a classroom. When students visit younger students, their stories about village life are similar, and how one relates to another sends a message an adult may never be able to portray. Students become role models. One third-grade elementary student phrased it best when he told one high school presenter: "I want to be like you when I'm in high school." The most difficult issue is the loss of loved ones.

The main district event is the biannual Natural Helpers Retreat. One retreat is held during the fall and introduces students to the core values of the program, including selecting student leaders for each site. The fall retreat provides incentives for a positive school year and teaches students how this program can help them work together to address any school or community issue. The second retreat is in late spring before students convene for summer break, reminding everyone that this peer support network is part of our community even when school is not in session.

The most difficult issue everyone talks about is suicide. Reynold is familiar with this topic. As Natives, many students relate to stories and questions that Reynold asks. Once a student talks about it, many learn that this is a subject that should not be kept quiet. As a peer support network, students working with other students help educate each other about the impact of the loss of loved ones. The St. Mary's Mission closed as a result of a youth suicide in 1985. This was the time Reynold graduated from the mission.

NOTES

1. Thomas R. Berger, *Village Journey: The Report of the Alaska Native Review Commission* (Hill & Wang, 1985).
2. The twenty-year provisions of ANCSA 1971 ruled corporation stocks could be sold or traded, and corporation lands could be sold or taxed. This raised fear of loss of Native control. The 1991 congressional amendments to ANCSA eliminated these twenty-year provisions, allowing Native corporation shareholders to decide membership eligibility, and lands are not eligible to be taxed unless developed.

16 ⋚ Educational Endeavors— *Poaching for Dummies*

"If we need to, we can stop here and pick up the antlers," Bruce told the three of us as we looked over the young bull moose that had been killed by a pack of wolves.

⋛

When the state BOG or BOF create subsistence regulations, they do not consider the social economics of Native way of life. What Natives do is not a choice. Harvesting animals and birds, drying and storing fish is part of establishing our food security.

Large extended families depend on individuals to supply the bulk cash or income to help harvest wild food. Most successful families have the resources to preserve or cache food for later use and in times of need. If there is one rural fact that should be recognized for its uniqueness: Alaska, the coldest state in the United States, has the highest average number of freezers per household.

In fall 2007 my nephew was cited and fined for wanton waste of several moose legs left in his boat for a day too long. My nephew's family has a thirteen-cubic-foot freezer. During the fall hunt, when moose harvest is legal, freezers are filled with Yukon salmon and wild berries stored for winter use. My nephew was cited toward the end of the hunting season. After season close, charges of wanton waste are not as serious as charges of hunting out of season, where hunting equipment can be taken away if the person is unable to pay a fine as a lesson that such actions are unacceptable. If the animal had been caught earlier in the hunt season, most of the meat would have been given away or dried if weather conditions were favorable. In jeopardy, the family needed meat, had no means to preserve it, and the season was about to close. Any animal caught after the season is poaching.

In late fall the normal weather condition is rainy, wet, and damp. Easy for meat to ruin, smell funny, become green with mold, and rot. Households are inundated with hunter catches, their freezers filled with the other wild resources harvested, bartered, and stored at this time of the year. There is no room in freezers for the bulk moose legs, rump, and neck.

Charged with wanton waste, my nephew was given a date to plead his case. Before the day of the hearing, anticipation and concern built with the assumption that he had done something wrong. At the dilapidated police station, like many similar State of Alaska proceedings, the judge spoke in a static telephone voice. If the village police officer position is filled, the officer listens to the proceedings as a formality. Although the city police have no authority over state hunting regulations, in addition to being a witness, the police presence is meant to show that the hearing is fair and impartial. Many village police are hired because they need income to pay immediate bills; state laws and regulations are a scratch on the head. This is not a local city ordinance concern. After receiving a paycheck, the village police will often quit and wait for another job opportunity.

Natives don't know if legal representation is necessary for hunting and fishing misdemeanor cases. Native ways of life centered on hunt and fish practices are simple and easy. The laws and regulations are confusing and difficult to understand. Mention the word "perjury" and many smile trying to recall what the definition might be. Natives smile when hard-to-understand words are used. This word has no local significance and is irrelevant to the immediate charges. Someone got careless and caught with evidence in plain sight of the wildlife trooper. Our way of life is at stake again. Charges and Alaska statutes are read. Penalties, fines, jail time, and possible probation periods are strongly reiterated. My nephew shrugged when the voice reminded him that he could lose all future hunting and fishing privileges. The real fear built when the voice mentions garnishment of hunting gear, boat, and motor. With his close friend and the current police officer for the City of Pilot Station as the only witnesses, moon-faced my nephew pleaded no contest.

It is ironic that poaching of large game is often associated with wanton waste. In the Alaska Native *Poaching for Dummies*, the main lesson is to do it quickly. Speed is of the essence, especially for those that have done it more than once and know that it can be easily mastered. I know of masters that have shot, skinned, gutted, and vacated the premises within fifteen minutes. Days later, we hear rumors of wildlife troopers peeking in porches of suspected poachers to look for evidence. Sometimes we hear rumors that the troopers were tipped by so-and-so. In small-knit communities, rumors as this can tarnish reputations and create tension in relationships, especially if fines or penalties are issued.

The most devastating penalty is garnishment, or taking away of hunt equipment as a lesson that illegal hunt activities are unacceptable. For rural families, these activities are the only means of food security. Lab rats tested to find food in mazes have it easy compared to the gauntlet of hunting regulations everyone must understand. According to the state, ignorance is no excuse. Every regulation booklet covers this liability and every hunter is responsible to know all current regulations and all changes, especially if emergency orders are issued for immediate changes.

Many Natives ask me about current regulations. I remind those I trust that no state or federal agents live in our village besides the U.S. postmaster. If you can get away with it, do it. Only if you are caught red-handed with evidence in plain sight will you be out of luck and have to defend yourself in the state courts. Otherwise, you can learn to speak a secret local language easily mastered. If there is no physical evidence and you have little understanding of laws and regulations, this special language tells the trooper that you have no reason to hunt or fish in Native Alaska.

With few economic opportunities, it is easy to master and hone poaching practices to provide food. With every successful practice, confidence comes easier. I know hunters who have mastered this practice then had to move to larger communities with mediocre jobs and meager income. These hunters had no choice but to move their families and live paycheck to paycheck. Albert Einstein would be proud of these Natives' trade and ability to feed their families where regulations and seasons are strictly enforced and the instinct to hunt will never be taken. They were born into it, they live with it, and they will never forget who they are. There is no record of how fast skilled Natives gut and quarter an animal. Fifteen minutes is not a record for large game like moose or caribou. Time is relative.

Like a two-way mirror, what many don't know is that many subsistence families qualify for food stamp assistance for groceries. Natives were once allowed to use food stamps to buy fuel for vehicles, shotgun shells, and rifle bullets—amenities used to gather wild foods that exist out in the wilderness. Because of strict harvest regulations, many Natives are not ashamed to cup their hands and their needs will be met. Many children see this way of life as the only option. State leaders should allow Natives to use food stamps to purchase hunting and fishing licenses and pay court fines as part of the state's vested responsibility to Native ways of life. Beginning in 2008 the U.S. Food and Drug Administration no longer allowed food stamps to purchase fuel, ammunition, or hunting and fishing supplies. It is not unusual for village grocery stores to run out of food items when monthly food stamps are issued, especially when the whole village qualifies for these services.

"Let me do all the talking," I yelled at Arlo and Nicholas as we watched the small blue floatplane circle. Every Native knows who these planes belong to. I had promised these two young boys I would take them bird hunting after I got our moose meat for the season. It was late September, and the geese were fat and plump.

The floatplane landed and coasted to a stop as I slowed down. The ADF&G trooper was out on the float pontoons and motioned for us to slow and approach. I looked around the boat and saw no evidence of any bird, critter, or fish that would give the trooper reason to doubt my excuse. The two boys were sitting with their guns displayed and ready for any critter for our evening dinner. About ten yards from the trooper, I talked loud enough to tell him that we were logging for driftwood. In response the trooper commented that he was pleased we were using our personal float vests. Before we could talk, the boys were excited to see a trooper in full uniform and sidearm and excited for the floatplane. We were in the middle of the wilderness. The boys were young students and asked questions young boys would ask, and the trooper immediately responded as a public information officer and smiled and talked to the boys. These boys had no fear of the trooper; they had not heard the same stories I heard as a young man. As they were talking another boat appeared, heading downriver loaded with fresh meat. The trooper waved his arm for the boat to slow and come over. I recognized the Native elder hunter driving the boat from Mountain Village. He looked apprehensive as the trooper thanked me and we were on our way. The trooper did not ask for my state ID or if I had a current hunting license.

That evening at camp, the boys lit up as I reminded them that we were there to bird hunt. Several days later, a Native family told me that the same trooper had issued a citation to their teenage son for hunting without a state license. As a family they were actually logging when the trooper saw a lone duck not moving in front of their boat, even though the duck is a migratory bird managed by USFWS.

Learning to speak the language is not hard for those who do not have a current hunting or fishing license. If you are ever approached by a wildlife trooper, there is no need for a license to legally scout for firewood, log, pick berries—salmon, blue, red, black, rosehips, raspberries, cranberries—harvest medicinal plants, "punk" for conks or punks, swim, look for diamond willow, or look for stove rocks for a steam house. Any excuse is better than "camping" or "picnicking," which bring immediate suspicion of trying to hunt or fish without a current license. If the wildlife trooper looks at all your guns and fishing supplies and ask about them, and only if they ask about them, remind them that this is Alaska, and this essential survival gear. Everywhere I travel I carry mine all the time. Legally, wildlife troopers are not supposed to ask about guns or fishing supplies; doing so is "leading the witness" to gather evidence. In very remote areas, this is somewhat arbitrary and left to the discretion of the trooper. As the trooper is mediator, judge, and jury, it is hard to believe a Native if it comes to a he said/she said situation. If the trooper issues a warning, it is not a question of whether you are guilty but an arbitrary show of authority.

Experienced poachers know the two words to avoid are "hunting" and "fishing" because troopers who hear those words will automatically ask for a current license. Don't talk about fish, animals, or sightseeing. If you have a license, you are fine. If you don't, do not say these words, and do not say you are going "out for a ride." These are incriminating words that can be used against you. Wildlife troopers know Natives do not just go out for a ride. If you say this as an excuse you are already a suspect with something to hide, whether catching fish or shooting a critter. If you have no physical evidence, you have no reason to be afraid—I think we are all protected by the Constitution.

Valid hunting and fishing licenses do not carry the same privilege as state-issued driver's licenses to drive vehicles on state roads. If Natives did not practice subsistence, families would face serious hardships if discretionary action were taken and troopers enforced the Constitution verbatim.

There is one state weakness: when Natives hunt seals, whales, or waterfowl, the state has no authority over these migratory animals. This is the reason the State of Alaska took an unusual action when it bestowed to the communities of Savoonga and Gambell, the two Native villages on St. Lawrence Island, complete management authority of their fish and wildlife in 2016.

For a time, fear of wildlife troopers created this notion that wanton waste was the only option for getting rid of evidence to avoid charges and stiff penalties. I know of Natives killing a large animal, taking a little piece of meat, and quickly vacating the area before that floatplane lands or wildlife trooper arrives. A little meat can go a long way. I know of Natives comfortable out in the wilderness practicing their activities without fear of nature and the animals that live in the woods. If there is one fear, it is fear of getting caught and charged with a hunting or fishing violation and branded as a criminal for life. It is a psychological premonition, being branded as a common criminal for breaking regulations. Many troopers and managers know that fear is an acceptable management tool for maintaining control of Native hunting and fishing activities. It made many elders doubt traditional practices when the state introduced a right and a wrong way of hunting and judged common activities as criminal according to non-Native judicial systems.

From what I have seen Natives learned from their mistakes. Not a lesson of what is good or bad, right or wrong, but a lesson in doing things differently. Learning from mistakes not to question traditional and cultural practice, but if we get caught and given a citation, how can we improvise? If I am caught the criminal charge is already with me so I have no more fear. We will try not to make the same mistake twice unintentionally. The state and federal government have taken away all my responsibility; I have no obligations to the fish and wildlife, and I trust my Native culture, my people, and my way of life. Young hunters and fishers see this lesson as the action of community. More are getting bold, like the culprits in Point Hope who shot one hundred caribou or the subsistence fishers in Marshall. We have grown unafraid when we practice against the regulations and dare the state to take action.

We can pretend to work with federal and state agencies in fish and wildlife resources, adhere to hunting and fishing regulations, and appreciate the Native corporations in exchange for wise resource management applications and settlement of landownership issues. But when government backs are turned it is easy to take freely that which was once ours. To become successful poachers to meet the needs in our homes. To keep secrets. In kindness, appreciate and hold cupped hands when assistance is offered; appreciate food stamps to buy groceries and energy assistance for heating fuel to keep homes warm. Appreciate going out to hunt and fish when permission is granted. This is our current way of life when corporations and prominent Alaska leaders make promises to protect subsistence.

It is easy to look to the state constitution and reassure ourselves that our legislative forefathers were sensitive to future issues of Alaska. But roads do not exist and communities not connected to the road system do not have same ethic values. The state continues to work on a statewide transportation plan to connect Native Alaska, to build roads and bridges and enable every community to be equal.

Some people in Alaska talk about a state constitutional convention to settle issues about status quo. Status quo is a special recognition that this is the way we do things, and a convention would readdress, rewrite, and reaffirm our trust of the state constitution as a living document. People who hunt and fish sometimes do not have the same ethics and needs as those who hunt and fish all the time. Those who hunt and fish for fun is the majority who will influence, rewrite, vote, and ratify the constitution. The needs of urban and rural, road and roadless Native and non-Native would be addressed. The hot topic the state is not willing to address is subsistence.

Federal recognized tribes exist in Alaska. The mixed message of tribal existence from state leaders created an identity crisis with status quo and role of tribes and tribal governments. Since statehood, Natives have talked about hunting and fishing. Our ancestors did it to survive and we do it for the same reason. We have not changed despite efforts to change our ways. We resent it when non-Natives give Natives permission to hunt and fish and remind us that ANCSA extinguished our hunting and fishing rights.

Perhaps we can teach everyone by allowing the state to manage grocery store hours. Many will learn that three hours a day, five days a week is not functional now, like stories of the Russians before and after the last world war. Seriously, more Natives are moving out of villages. Outmigration is a reality check. Natives move to Bethel, Nome, and cities like Anchorage and Fairbanks to get away from village life for economic opportunities, jobs, and homes. The cost of living in rural Alaska is exorbitant.

17 ⪦ Sustainable Management

"Get down from the tree and come to me!" I yelled to my nephew Kerry. A giant bull moose was thirty yards away and had not moved despite my yelling. Kerry and his friend Matt were fifty yards from me and a hundred feet up in a huge climbing tree. I was hidden from their view. I listened and heard no response; the wilderness was quiet. When we first saw this moose, we had heard it splashing in the water. I yelled the message again as loud as I could, and Kerry yelled, "What?"

They were surprised to hear me yelling. The moose was deaf but not dumb. Kerry yelled, excited about more moose movement, as I watched this one in front of me. The huge antlers started to move, and I yelled for Kerry to shut up. As our echoes quieted, the moose raised its head and looked right at me. I held my breath and stilled my heart; any noise or movement I made would spook it. It was nonchalant about our presence. As I peeked through the alder and leaned my rifle on the spruce log, the moose perked his ears and looked around to listen. The light breeze was in my favor and it could not smell me. The moose chewed its food, and the loud chomping waterlilies sounded like popcorn popping. As the moose submerged its head into the small river to get more food, I yelled at Kerry. The current of the small swift river gurgle and masked my yelling.

It is ironic the State of Alaska sees itself as the only one responsible for all tasks in managing all the animals that provide food security.

I grew up hunting and fishing with my family. It is easy to simplify my way of life and relate with Natives of my village, but when we lump subsistence in with other resource management concepts, I've always been partial to three objectives that tend to get mixed into other management schemes: responsibility, obligation, and trust.

I've heard arguments and issues settled with the assumption that we cannot please everyone with whatever final decision is made. My ancestors never imposed hardships on others who shared the same resource—berries, birds, fish, and small and large animals. Resources were never hoarded or recognized as property to be owned. Access was never restricted or denied or a means of negotiating an agreement. The lesson is not that what is yours is ours, but what is yours is what I respect and we share what is ours. Traditional areas were recognized and respected; imaginary lines or boundaries were never created. The concept of space was never small or enclosed. Traditional food caches were recognized as luxuries and a freedom of success in leisure activities. Over the years, when I talk with elders, I tend to get confused on issues they try to explain and how this information is related to the message being conveyed. Much of the information is abstract. I understand what they say because like minds think alike. My challenge is how to explain this to non-Natives.

Here is one example. If I have a good fishing spot with more than I need to meet my needs, I have no reason to impose or restrict anyone from using it. I recognize that others have needs, and if I have more than sufficient, there is no reason for me to restrict access. And if you have an unsuccessful opportunity, I will share my catch. This is the Native way. One general perception of visiting non-Natives is a communal relationship between the Natives. And for Natives this relationship is not only shared between people but extends to the fish, wildlife, and resources we share with Mother Nature. Many non-Natives call this harmony and respect. It sounds rubbish and spiritual, like a church.

Native and non-Native harvest ethics have created a clash of cultures. With this state of mind, fish and game harvest regulations can be traced to anecdotal evidence with the assumption that a particular regulation is necessary for conservation. Many regulations have been around for so long that they have been accepted as ethics of responsibility. Window harvesting of salmon is one example where Natives are given permission from someone of authority and told not to fish to replenish the stocks. These regulations point to scientific data as proof of potential consequences if no management guidelines are followed. When fish and animals are identified as endangered species, no harvests are acceptable. As a food security issue, suppose Natives were to argue salmon fishing—timing of harvest, preparation, and surplus—is a Native public health concern for basic sustenance.

Since 2010 ADF&G managers have started to learn about Yukon salmon and the ecological knowledge Natives tried to explain to early non-Native managers.

In an abstract sense, Natives trying to explain Native intuition is a language translation challenge. What Natives talk about is often illogical to those who have never experienced the way or reasons Natives practice the activities they do. The elders' talk did not make sense or seem relevant to the issue. The interpretation was only as good as the fluency and knowledge of the interpreter.

An example is when Uppa Kelly told the trooper that the east wind and weather would be good for salmon. This relationship of the salmon to the wind and weather is an abstract reality. For the trooper, the extension of the environment had nothing to do with salmon. The west wind is predominantly responsible for pushing in the main salmon run into the Yukon River from the Bering Sea: the west wind is an indicator of run strength and salmon abundance. But what about the east wind?

When the state BOF and BOG address regulation proposals, anyone is eligible to provide testimony and recommend alternatives to convince the board whether the proposed change is necessary. In 1980 Natives who provided testimony during Alaska board sessions often talked about abstracts as the wind and weather, but the mutual understanding could only be as good as who was speaking and translating, who was listening, and who was the final decision-maker. Many elders would start by telling stories. As a Native, I see my life as simple, but when I try to write and explain it, it is easy for me to get lost in the words. The closest analogy is the challenge poets face in writing about the simple existence of being; if they find the words that best describe it, other poets are likely to appreciate the analogy. But for people who do not care for poems, the words are all rubbish.

This relationship to the abstract and concepts of time and space is difficult to explain to others not familiar with Native culture. A difficult example is recognition of the Alaska state constitution. When early Native translators addressed BOF and BOG with elders' comments was a difficult period between cultures that are worlds apart. The reality check came with hunting and fishing closures and restrictions with possible citations, garnishment of gear, and fines to pay as lessons of obedience. The trooper telling the elders not to fish is a situation that does not need be explained. What is ironic is that there are no legal cases where Natives cite or have ever used the state constitution as legal arsenal. If anything, the constitution would not apply; there is no Native harvesting court case where the language of the state constitution could have been at risk. Unlike Katie John's case, the 2016 court case of John Sturgeon presents a paradigm about how non-Natives are very good at dissecting legal regulations to their advantage as a natural result of understanding non-Native ethics.

Since time immemorial Natives have hunted, fished, and harvested wild resources. The state constitution was signed in 1959, when Alaska was accepted as part of the union. The courts, as mandated by the same government that upholds the constitution, can only interpret their own regulations according to their own needs; they will never see this as a conflict of interest.

In the Katie John decision, the state argued that state waters belong to state management and that preferential use is unconstitutional. Eventually, the state chose to stop pursuing a preferential disclaimer because leading discussions imply that the constitution does not apply to Alaska Natives. If no action is taken, the constitution will continue to remain silent on subsistence and Alaska Native identity. This is a catch-22 situation. To circumvent any claims of preferential use, the state uses emergency orders for subsistence as a non-regulatory process with no binding language or reference to any Alaska state statutes that recognize claims of preferential use. This is a prelude to a fallacy and needs to be addressed in the Alaska Administrative Procedures Act; otherwise, Natives can claim food security concerns and harvest fish and wildlife at will. Unlike the Katie John situation, the John Sturgeon decision argued that the state constitution gives the state every right to manage all navigable rivers in Alaska, even if they are federal lands held in trust by the Department of Interior.

In June 2016 St. Mary's elder Moses Paukan Sr. wrote a letter to Governor Bill Walker and requested Yukon king salmon harvests for food security. In response, despite management closures, the ADF&G commissioner allowed harvest of Yukon kings. ADF&G Division of Subsistence collected information on king salmon caught for monitoring purposes. The Division of Subsistence is separate from the ADF&G Commercial Fisheries Division, which is responsible for management of salmon. In several villages, local hires collected genetic samples for age, sex, and length of subsistence-caught king salmon. Over the winter this information was processed.

At the annual April 2017 Yukon River Drainage Fisheries Association meeting in Fairbanks, ADF&G provided the genetic harvest data of Yukon kings. Of nine hundred samples collected, 27 percent were females. Females reaching the spawning grounds are more productive for salmon stocks of concern. In hindsight, ADF&G should allow Natives to catch as many king salmon males as needed to meet food security needs. To this day king salmon fishing continues to be micromanaged. It seems as if information of this harvest data was never released to the news media. What were the fishing gear or environmental conditions that allowed Natives to harvest king salmon males while allowing more females to reach the spawning grounds?

When my sister Agnes told the trooper that Uppa Kelly said the east wind would be good for salmon, the trooper responded that the wind and weather have nothing to do with salmon and insisted that fishing was closed. In western Alaska, the summer east wind comes from the land mass of Alaska, bringing warmer and dry weather; the east wind is like the Santa Ana winds of California but not as strong. For the month of June this is excellent weather to cut and dry salmon. No salmon will be wasted, and the Natives prepare their food security for the remainder of the year. As the season progresses into midsummer, preservation attempts will be ruined as a result of inclement weather and insect infestations.

Title V of the Alaska State Statutes addresses wildlife and fish regulations. The Alaska BOF and BOG are the final decision-makers, though anyone is eligible to submit proposals to any language of this section. Alaska is so big that the boards have sectioned Alaska into regions with proposals for different regions addressed in alternate years. Western Alaska is part of the Arctic Yukon Kuskokwim, and the proposal period for this region is usually addressed every four years.

Although the concept of sustained yield is a major provision of the Alaska State Statues, the actual use of this tool is left to the discretion of the ADF&G commissioner. To help with any final decision, the commissioner refers to the statutes as guidelines about what action should be taken, especially for management harvests that can be controversial. When the regulatory language is long and complex, the final interpretation is left to the discretion of the commissioner. To simplify this complexity, emergency orders supersede any state statute hunting or fishing regulations.

In the last decade actions from BOG have not been a concern for my part of Alaska. The wildlife issues already address the way management is applied. The wildlife biologist is an invisible person allowing Natives on the Lower Yukon lenient harvest opportunities. The wildlife manager is based out of Bethel and rarely seen on the Yukon side. Unfortunately, relations with the fish manager and Yukon River have not been cordial. This manager is based out of Anchorage or Fairbanks. Imagine someone from Kansas telling people in Oregon when, where, and how to fish. BOF continues to address challenging issues of Yukon salmon. Every AYK proposal period includes recommendations for this fishery.

In 2006, as Pilot Station tribal representative, I submitted a BOF fish regulation proposal for my portion of Alaska. This proposal was an attempt to do away with window harvesting for Yukon fish districts 1, 2, and 3 and responsibility of the commissioner. Although this was to simplify the management of current seasons with unrestricted subsistence harvests, one ADF&G historical fact included was the king salmon harvest data show healthy escapement and sustained yield during productive harvest seasons. During those times, ADF&G management actions for salmon return and size were not issues of concern. Prior to state management, there is no existing data that show unrestricted subsistence harvests led to decline or endangered salmon numbers. If anything, the state annual report to the North Pacific Management Council always claim annual statewide subsistence salmon harvests are insignificant to the total statewide harvests and all salmon stocks are healthy and sustainable. In 1980 the state started restricting net size and using harvest windows and mid-point salmon management guidelines. After these regulation guidelines became the only management tool, the fishery experienced many concerns, including smaller king salmon size, decline in fish numbers, and food insecurity.

Another unusual responsibility addressed in the Pilot Station tribal proposal was the involvement of tribal entities and tribal members who live in these communities. The proposal includes an attempt to do away with emergency orders for subsistence with the notion that emergency powers should be given to the commissioner, along with responsibility to identify and address a problem and take corrective action. According to ADF&G guidelines, emergency orders allow subsistence harvests and circumvent regulations and are not intended to recognize preferential harvests. During emergency openings, harvests for sport, commercial, and personal use are not allowed, whether one is an Alaska resident or not.

Emergency orders should not supersede the status quo. This is not power; this is lack of trust responsibility with use of emergency power to avoid civil disobedience in fear of the people—regardless of the condition of the resource. When there is no trust, emergency powers will be difficult to enforce if civil disobedience is undertaken despite the regulations. Fishery managers are only present during the fishing season and absent the rest of the year. The absentee management of subsistence does not have the trust responsibility that can be achieved with direct involvement of Natives for food security in all final management actions—not as advisers but rather as participants with stewardship obligations and full management responsibility for a trust resource.

This BOF proposal was submitted in 2006, but it did not meet language criteria for the board support selection and was not included with the packet for that year. Perhaps reference to Alaska tribes within any portion of the Alaska State Statues is not allowed.

"Repealed" is the most common regulatory language in Title V of the Alaska State Statutes.

After Kalen graduated from Pilot Station high school, he was excited to be accepted to University of Alaska–Anchorage. As a university promotion, a Fred Meyer store offered a discount midnight sale for students who show their student ID card. Shopping that midnight, the place was packed and all checkout aisles were staffed and busy. I smiled as students rushed with shopping carts full of ramen noodles, small microwaves, TVs, lamps, bean bags, bedsheets, and clothes for the new semester. Some were happy for the laptop and Xbox specials.

Although the midnight sale is normal for urban centers to entice the greatest number of shoppers willing to spend money, imagine if this event were to happen in a small village. As a result of our 2006 community development plan, one priority addressed was for a new grocery store. As a result, Pilot Station tribe invested in and opened a tribal store, and sales became a monthly event. But the tribal store went one step further.

Imagine a village with seven hundred people in one hundred households. Two small stores service the people with groceries, household supplies, and small merchandise. There is no reason for a twenty-four-hour convenience store. One fine summer day, the tribal store has a three-hour midnight sale. The next month, both stores have a midnight sale, and this becomes a monthly community event. This midnight event became popular for tribal members from neighboring villages. This is what happened in Pilot Station in middle-of-nowhere Alaska with only a certain number of people and customers crowding the store. The store sale was always on the first of the month, when the state issues new vouchers for food stamps. In June 2018 the food stamp program began to issue food vouchers well after midnight, and the midnight store sales became obsolete. There are no more midnight sales.

In addition to a tribal store, Pilot Station also has a tribal court system. Alaska has 229 tribes. Some tribal courts are active and address court cases and preside over tribal and non-tribal community members. Most cases involve the Indian Child Welfare Act, tribal child custody, parenting, and minor youth behaviors. Civil nonviolent cases involve domestic abuse, importation, and trafficking of drugs and alcohol. Penalties for serious incidents include banishment of tribal or non-tribal members from the village. Tribal courts do not address serious felony and criminal cases; these are addressed by the Alaska state troopers and state court system.

In 2010 Pilot Station had a tribal court case with the State of Alaska. The final result was a historic decision regarding the way a tribe can address the civic responsibilities of who we represent. The case highlights tribal recognition and the social obligation of every constitution as a living document. As a result of the decision, the response from the state infringed on the tribe to create a legal document for recognition of tribal citizens. On this legal document we were required to create a tribal emblem to make the procedure official for federal, state, and foreign governments. I was on the tribal council during this historic event, and I am proud about how we stood and exercised our sovereign powers.

The 2010 tribal court decision was unusual. Every existing government has constitution guidelines. Of all 573 tribes in the United States, this legal document is the first known of its kind. Internet research on similar tribal documents for reference provided no hits. We knew of no other tribe who had created such a legal document. What is this document?

18 ⋞ Misnomers of Management

"No, we are not lost. I recognize that tree," I reassured my supervisor.
"Yeah . . . right." Andy was agitated. It had been a long, hot, and humid
day. This was our first time to this area of Yakutat; the brush was thick,
and the devil's club and mosquitos had been menacing. I was enjoying
the work because the weather was overcast and not raining.

We worked for the U.S. Forest Service Forest Science Lab out of
Juneau. With my other supervisor, Paul, everyone in the lab nicknamed
us "forest pest managers." The Forest Service has many departments,
such as silviculture, sales, and management, and all staff knew who we
were when we said we were FSL. I was the forest technician used to
gather and collect data, Andy Eglitis was the entomologist, and Paul
Hennon was the pathologist. As forest pest managers we monitored the
health of forest trees and any outbreak conditions that may kill or make
trees sickly. Andy studied the bugs and insects and was a spruce beetle
and hemlock sawfly expert. Paul studied the diseases and fungi that
may cause trees to stress and become susceptible to rot or attack from
other forest pests. He was the expert studying what has been causing
the decline and slow death of the Alaska yellow cedar.

Andy and I were near Yakutat to collect observations on a previously
reported hemlock sawfly outbreak. Russell Fjord was not far away. Andy
led with the map, compass, and an old notebook with the bearings
and distance to the plots we are seeking. There was no trail. We found
our first plot and were reassured that we were not lost. As Andy was
trying to make sense of the handwritten notes, I looked around and
enjoyed not being in charge of this quest. My sense of direction was
not fixated on the map and compass. This was an old growth forest.
The trees were big and oddly forked with burls and signs of old age.

Every tree has a neat personality. The witch brooms on the birch trees looked iconic.

As we returned after a long day, I recognized a tree, and the map and odd compass reading was getting Andy frustrated with the sense that we were lost. In southeast Alaska, there are places that give odd compass readings, and these made us doubt our sense of direction. In some eerie places the compass would point to where we knew north was not supposed to be. Even though I tried to reassure Andy, Andy was not convinced and looked to see if our footprints could be found. Andy wanted to go back to the last plot and take more careful readings. This was 1990, before handheld global position systems were economical. I convinced Andy that I would be in shouting distance as I went to the truck and honked it.

After working with Andy and Paul for six seasons, Glacier Bay National Park near the community of Gustavus and Bartlett Cove became one of my favorite places. We monitored the spruce beetle outbreak. This area was covered with ice glaciers about one hundred years ago and the spruce trees are considered young. The ecological succession from a glaciated area to a forest biome is phenomenal. Visitors are amazed when we tell them that the young trees are part of a natural succession and have never been clear-cut or planted. No logging companies have been to this area, and these are natural regenerated wild trees. The amazing and neat thing about working in this young forest, similar to old-growth forests, is that there is no thick underbrush.

Unlike the old growth, the soil is thin, and the forest floor is carpeted with a soft bright colored green moss. During one work trip we helped the National Park Service with search and rescue of visitors who had wandered off the trail, got lost, and had to spend a night in the woods. When visitors walk off the trail the moss springs back to life and leaves no footprints. When the weather is overcast, the young-stand composition of these trees looks all the same in every direction. Luckily, the visitors were found before lunch.

If there is such a thing as a Bermuda Triangle of Alaska legislative politics, the Lower Yukon is the center. Like the mystery itself there is no acceptable answer to why this is. Every ten years the Alaska state redistricting board reviews legislative districts according to distribution factors of the decennial population survey. Every redistricting effort causes the committee members to scratch their heads and create an odd geographic shape for the Lower Yukon district. In every U.S. Census, the Kusilvak Census Area is the leader of low economic opportunities, low median income, high cost of living, and high unemployment: statistics no census area can be proud of. It is the poorest region of Alaska, coupled with social and health-care disparities. A misleading criterion used to create a geographic district is that communities must have similar socioeconomic characteristics. The Lower Yukon has been the responsibility of state politicians who reside in neighboring census areas with different demographic and economic characteristics. As a result, the state has successfully segregated this area.

In the last several decades the state house and senate representatives have been from Nome. Except for one year, our state representatives were based in the Upper Yukon communities. Based outside the Lower Yukon, many representatives never experience our community's hardships.

Like any politician, the only time representatives are visible in any community profile is to claim a spotlight if a large development project, energy assistance, or social service program is recognized. The only time we may see a brief glimpse is when they campaign to gather votes for office. Although their campaign signs pepper our community, the last state senator to visit Pilot Station was before the 2004 elections.

Many local Natives have no idea what our state representatives do. In the last several elections, the house and senate candidates ran unopposed. They have served so long in state politics that state issues tend to stagnate until need for help becomes critical. For us, the state legislature does not exist. Beside the state troopers who visit when something bad happens, the only other public presence is ADF&G managers, who are seen as intimidating people with the eye of the state, making sure wildlife harvests are not excessive. These are people we would rather not see, invited or not. Despite the role of politicians, it becomes ironic when they insist we must follow and respect and adhere to their rules and regulations. Considering the stagnation, it is easy to feel ire and disdain over the state's responsibility in any and all services.

Mary Sattler Peltola was a state representative who tried to help Lower Yukon residents. Based out of Bethel, Mary represented the adjacent district to the south, and it was heartwarming when she provided a weekly newspaper column about efforts, hardship, and progress in trying to help despite the fact that the Kusilvak is not her district. The Yukon Kuskokwim Delta is the home of the Yupiit, Mary Peltola's people. We never hear anything from those state representatives based out of the Nome region.

Despite the diverse Alaska Native cultures, the state legislative districts do not recognize these cultures' ethnographic regions and traditional areas of respect. Georgianna Lincoln is a well-respected Athabaskan from Rampart who once served as our district state representative and demonstrated respect for other cultures when she admitted she was not comfortable representing our region because of its demographic composition, economic characteristics, and the fact this region is Yup'ik and more than a stone's throw from her part of Alaska. Imagine someone from Kansas telling people in Oregon: *I'm your state senate representative.* And for the constituent to visit, imagine driving from Kansas to Dallas and flying through Los Angeles to get to Oregon.

In 2013, as a result of this discrepancy, Calista Corporation spearheaded a regional subcommittee of local leaders to create a regional tribal government. As a *People in Peril*, the eventual action of Native leaders of this region can decide the fate of our Native identity and whether we are ready to try and help ourselves or continue to wait and depend on others from far away.[1] One lesson tribal members need to take advantage of is that district state house and senate leaders represent a people, not a land base. We need to remind everyone that we are not only Alaska Natives . . . we are tribal members.

≥

There is special lingo fish biologists and managers speak. Although the Yukon River system is huge, using scientific methods to monitor fish passage estimates is left to a select few. Another unquestioned challenge is how agency scientists create scientific methods to monitor salmon without first consulting the people who live on the river. Unfortunately, despite what science may try to answer, what managers leave unanswered is how some fishers are better at catching fish than others. In a true scientific process, one must assume every fisher is the same for this scientific method to be quantitative, qualitative, and repeatable.

In science, for a process to be accepted as scientific, the methods and procedures need to be repeatable. The conclusion of all data and results observed is left to the person assumed to be responsible. In comparison, traditional ecological observations and conclusions are difficult for Western science to accept as reliable. For example, the neat thing that makes fishing challenging is that fishers who have developed methods to catch more fish are not willing to openly share this. Fishers like to keep trade secrets except with a relative or best friend. In this case, science attempts to infuse a random collection method and make it repeatable so others can use the same collection tools for conclusive evidence.

A major provision of the scientific method is that conclusions that are widely accepted must have supporting documentation from similar collection procedures. If this was not so, controversies would be rampant. This has been a challenging issue for the Yukon River Pilot Station Sonar Site, where scientific collection methods dictate that a scientific process must be in use. Unfortunately, when the same person collects samples, you should already expect to get similar results. Unlike bad fishers, the best fishers do not like to share secrets. For traditional Greenland Inuit seal hunters, a fisher was a bad hunter.

Although methods for catching fish vary, drift gillnet fishing is used at Pilot Station Sonar to enumerate fish species seen on sonar passage counts. This is a critical element of the whole monitoring system. Seining on the river is not an effective method. Fish-counting towers and partial weirs are effective in shallow and clear water streams. Rod and reels, fly rods, and use of lure or baits for salmon will not work on the main murky Yukon. Dip-net fishing was never used as an enumeration process for any salmon passage estimates. Whether it can be used as a fish sampling procedure depends on the ADF&G habitat biometricians who provide the statistical sampling formula.

Acronyms such as ASL and CPUE may be tongue twisters for people who have no idea what managers are talking about. In the same way, managers use numbers to assess BEG and SEG and show that escapement considerations are part of in-season monitoring tasks as principles of sustained yield. BEG and SEG, biological escapement goal and sustainable escapement goal, are guesstimate ranges as reference to assure everyone that efforts to maintain and replenish the stocks are practical. The use of these misnomers became necessary with the treaty obligation with Canada for monitoring king salmon border passage numbers. Monitoring these passage numbers assures everyone that we are indeed diligent stewards of a wild resource. Despite the range of escapement goals, the final passage numbers are available after the season is over, whether Alaska subsistence harvests have been allowed or not. This is a difficult issue managers address in season while the fish are passing Native communities and fishers who live on the river. Once salmon pass these communities, this is the end of the season, and there is no other time to harvest salmon. The salmon swim to their spawning tributaries to spawn and die.

ASL (age, sex, and length) data is collected as the main measurements that help provide a general composition profile of salmon as a school of fish. This data supports BEG and SEG. This rationalizing of data is logical of sustained yield principles, where ASL, BEG, and SEG are qualitative data supporting each other in some quantitative way within an acceptable statistical formula.

As ADF&G technicians gather test fish data, use of catch per unit effort (CPUE) as a sampling method infuriates me with the notion that the biologists are trying to simplify the rate of catching fish with the assumption that all fishers are the same. Habitat biostatisticians pondered this situation, created a statistical formula, and developed CPUE as a sampling technique. It is easy for me to look to other fishers and wonder if these statisticians have ever fished for any fish with any kind of gear. Creating fish population estimate models is a statistical challenge for reliable data gathering methods that question not the harvesting method itself but the room for error that can be achieved. Reliable CPUE data is critical depending on condition of the harvest gear, the environment, and skills of fishers.

In June 2009 I agreed to help the ADF&G Yukon River Pilot Station Sonar Site test the variance of CPUE in comparison to two different king salmon gillnet sizes. The praise and accolades I received as a skilled drift-net fisherman compared to the ADF&G fishers made me skeptical of the confidence in fishing skills that is supposedly addressed by this sampling method. Native people are good at catching fish and eating fish, statistical variance or not. The challenge is how to include the confidence skill of a good fisher in a statistical formula accepted by a scientific method. ADF&G employees who have never fished or driven an outboard motor do not show any confidence. Final management decisions to allow subsistence families a chance to harvest salmon depends on your success as a fisher. The biometricians have factored in 0.5 as a confidence interval with no moral obligations and the notion that zero is still a number.

Another tricky word often used in management is "fecundity." When managers use words alien to everyday language, the response from the public is a quiet acceptance that the managers know what they are talking about and they have a good grasp of the condition of the resource. Natives have no alternatives when managers use difficult words to recommend the proposals they support as serious alternatives to consider. Anyone can look up the word and come up with their own idea of how this applies to fish or wildlife management situations.

When managers use "fecundity" liberally as a generalized term to help answer difficult questions, they should be able to answer questions regarding every aspect of our fisheries. Questions about fishery genetics, stock timing, and analytical observations collected from ASL and CPUE data from any fishery monitoring stations, especially if used to estimate fish composition. For example, of the four thousand kings harvested in the Lower Yukon commercial fisheries, how many are male or female or bound for the Chena River or Canada where jack kings are thought to originate? These questions should be able to be answered, especially if "fecundity" is a key word of the answer. If 92 percent of female kings commercially sold in 2008 were Chena River stock, many people would not be pleased. Although this data is available at the end of the season, it is in season when run size and critical harvest decisions are pending to allow subsistence fishers food security with commercial fishers waiting on the banks.

If they use "fecundity" as a key word, managers should have a reasonable idea about the carrying capacity of the Yukon River. This information is critical. To most managers, carrying capacity is assumed to be a given number or a range of numbers. If we can assume that the Chena River can stock twenty thousand to forty thousand king salmon, the carrying capacity gives the monitoring agency an idea of the range to expect. Realistically, twenty thousand kings are phenomenal, and anything less is a reason for concern. The challenge is the carrying capacity of the ocean where all Alaska salmon live to reach adulthood.

Lower Yukon fish openings are an effort of time management. Regulations for subsistence fishing emphasize commercial fishing will not occur simultaneously. Usually, a lag between the two is necessary to prevent subsistence catches from being incorporated as commercial sales. It was a common concern that subsistence harvests should not be included for commercial fishers to sell. When the state changed to a dip-net fishery, the amount of time to harvest subsistence salmon for traditional drying and smoking became a time management issue. Although commercial fishers became proficient at targeting a specific salmon, the subsistence family network became at risk for food security.

There is a scientific method for fishers who are good at catching fish. The agencies that collect test fish data try to simplify data collection in such a way that others can verify, refute, or compare measurements of similar results. Data collected in a scientific way has to be applied in a logical procedure for anyone to repeat. When statisticians ponder a formula, they look to each other and know confidence intervals are best described as trade secrets. Unfortunately, whether these collection procedures are tested as a tried-and-true process is difficult to answer. Anytime I see other Native fishing cultures, I marvel at the innovative practices that make them special, but as a fisherman I know they have traditional trade secrets they are reluctant to share, subtle and reclusive as that may seem.

Like fishers, the technicians who collect test fish data at the Pilot Station Sonar Site attempt to support the rate of catching fish as a collective sampling method, and every technician who participates in the process contributes to this pool of data. Unlike fishers, the technicians who catch fish have no reason to question why some people are better at catching fish than others. This is a difficult statistical variance to include in a consistent sampling technique. The challenges to this sampling procedure are mechanical failures and environmental changes. ADF&G

managers who rely on CPUE data collection methods have a trump in the deck: their collection procedures will never be held accountable, especially if count estimates contradict actually population returns. For example, it is easy for managers to assume a sampling error when they have mechanical failures or environmental challenges. When the water level starts to rise due to rainfall, more wood debris floats downriver. CPUE assumes every fisher is the same; therefore, the challenge to contradict fish passage estimates depending on skills of the fishers is left without weight.

Natives tried to tell managers the traditional monitoring method was a setnet in the water twenty-four hours a day, seven days a week, until they met their subsistence needs for the season. When ADF&G restricts harvest methods with an iron fist, this takes away the traditional monitoring method. Pilot Station Sonar Site has admitted many times that yes, the water level is high and there is more wood debris hampering efforts to sample acceptable test fish and sonar operations, and we don't know what is happening on the river. This natural environmental condition should not be allowed to further restrict subsistence or justify fish companies' requests for commercial fishing at the risk of salmon escapement concerns. With high water level, the skills of ADF&G fishers are not questioned.

Unlike Native fishers, ADF&G fishers do not use scientific methods to catch more fish; they fish to get a sample of what they catch.

NOTES

1. *Anchorage Daily News*, September 11, 1988. The series A People in Peril helped document rural Alaska's economic and social problems, including alcohol and drug abuse, crime, suicide, poverty, unemployment, and cultural crisis due to desperation and despair of rural remoteness.

19 ≷ Status Quo

"Oh, I got one of those," I told Norman Xavier. He was excited after opening his mail at the post office. He looked at me, and slowly and carefully he asked, "You're over sixty?" No, I wasn't over sixty years old. He was holding an official letter from the State of Alaska and excited about this lifetime privilege of living and aging as an Alaska resident. Confused, Norman asked, "You got a permanent hunting license?"

"Yes, I always carry it," I said as I took out my picture ID card. "That's your permanent hunting license?" "And for fishing," I said. Norman looked like a methodical Native as he walked out holding his mail and wondering about my tribal ID card. Elders who turn sixty in Alaska are eligible for a permanent state hunting and fishing license.

≷

In my small village, federal and state courts are nonexistent or exist far from my mind. My concerns and issues are irrelevant in the courts. For Native Alaska, this is an acceptable existence. We also feel relatively safe because there are no lawyers living in our village. There is no local U.S. or state judicial system that is fair and impartial for subsistence regulations in which everyone participates. If every Native charged with a hunting or fishing violation pleaded not guilty, the current courts do not have the manpower, resources, or luxury of American judicial systems to argue the burden of proof. How many not guilty pleas do we need for the State of Alaska to realize that we still have a subsistence issue to address?

If you are not afraid, I will help you. Over the years I have told many Natives. Finally, in 2015, I had my chance. I was not trying to help anyone—I was there to help myself. I reminded myself that this was a situation I created and a test for me and my knowledge of the judicial system. On the teleconference court hearing, the state magistrate repeats, "Just so I get it correct, you are pleading not guilty?" Yes, it was my fault. I had irritated the Alaska state trooper and was given a citation on the Yukon River. I was not afraid. I had not done anything illegal. I had fifteen fresh salmon from the ten-hour commercial fishing period, and I told Trooper Forreste that I was taking this salmon home to feed my family and not to sell it to the fish-buying company. It did not matter whether the magistrate knew if I was a commercial fisherman or not.

Many parts of the world recognize any immediate emergency situation requires action, usually with emergency orders issued from public officials responsible for the task. In Alaska, the state has created a successful segregation with the reality that ADF&G emergency orders are not as serious as we tend believe. It has created this complacency that if a real situation requires immediate action, the emergency response may not be taken seriously or heard by those who need to hear it. It is a general state of affairs that the state is maintaining a superficial reminder that jurisdiction and political boundaries exist over all state regulations.

Contrary to the state constitution, subsistence activities cannot be effectively managed as a status quo. Unlike sport, personal, or commercial use, opening and closing the season for subsistence harvests requires an ADF&G emergency order at the discretion of the commissioner. This status quo is a confusing mind game of wildlife responsibility.

For Natives this emergency order procedure is never seen as an emergency; it is a whim of the state trying to maintain a consistent sense of dignity lost with the first emergency issued as department policy. The state is just trying to be bossy. Whether these orders have supporting scientific evidence is irrelevant to logical decision-making procedures. The state tends to believe the emergency order procedure would allow Alaska hunters and fishers to be well educated and respected; in actuality, this is a crippling process with supporting documentation that ignorance is no excuse and anyone will be penalized and treated as a criminal if this order is violated.

Take, for example, a 2008 emergency-ordered moose hunt closure. If any Alaskan was issued a citation in this closed area, there was a general assumption that they did not know of the emergency closure. Every

ADF&G regulation and USFWS federal subsistence booklet attempts to provide mirror regulations to minimize conflict and remind every hunter that they are responsible to know if current changes are issued. There is no discrepancy; the two governments act cordially and document everything with corroboration. This is a subtle way to minimize intimidation and remind everyone that *ignorance* is no excuse.

With documented regulations everywhere, ignorance is assumed to be addressed, especially for those who are actively involved in all subsistence regulations and procedures. For someone who hunts and fishes, all regulations are second nature to casting a rod, setting a net, baiting a trap, or pulling a trigger. In 2008 the Federal Subsistence Board chairman was cited for illegally harvesting a moose in a closed area.[1] The ADF&G emergency order closure had valid population concerns. Red-handed, the FSB chairman—the only Alaska Native board member responsible for all federal subsistence regulations in Alaska—donated all meat to charity and resigned in disgrace.

Regardless of the justification for season closures, every ADF&G emergency order looks so similar to the next that all Natives have grown complacent. Exclamation points or not, every emergency order is ignored unless we read the fine print and realize the reality of our current fish and wildlife situations.

If the chairman had challenged the citation, we could have learned more of our subsistence situation with the State of Alaska; meat is meat, and food on the table helps in more ways than human existence. The 2009 Yukon king salmon fishery is another example of this subsistence management dilemma. Management recognized drastic action was necessary to allow acceptable salmon escapement numbers. The Yukon River Treaty requires a certain number of salmon be allowed to pass the Canada border onto the spawning grounds. Management was faced with a dilemma between treaty requirements and Alaska salmon regulations. Much of the interpretation is based on common regulatory language understood as topics of concern.

The ADF&G commissioner is responsible for issuing emergency regulations to open or close subsistence and issue any additional changes. Standing beside the commissioner are the enforcement officers who interpret these regulations to justify citations and ensure compliance.

Every enforcement officer is familiar with current hunting and fishing regulations, season openings, bag limits, gear restrictions, and all necessary information for resident and nonresidents, but there remains a question of officers ignore civil disobedience in fear of the people. If citations are given the state courts help determine the final conclusion.

The 2009 Yukon salmon season was a funny, odd year. According to management the salmon numbers were a critical concern. Preseason indicators had predicted a dismal forecast and early in-season escapements predicted to return that year were unaccounted for. Drastic action was necessary to allow salmon to reach spawning grounds without jeopardizing the health of the fishery, so the state issue a river-wide king salmon closure. In defiance, Marshall Native subsistence fishers fished despite the closure and the State of Alaska did not take any actions. Despite the state's claim of jurisdiction, Natives tend to stick together and dare the state to take action when subsistence is restricted.

One standing qualification to be selected as a board member to any state or federal regulatory body is that the applicant must have no previous wildlife criminal violation. A clean slate is necessary to recognize theoretical skills and analytical knowledge of all hunting and fishing situations. How can policymakers expect to learn if a regulation is necessary when they have no personal experience of humility from a hunting or fishing violation and being branded as a criminal for life? We all agree illegal activities such as a market or commercial harvest in exchange for cash or taking an animal for choice parts should face prosecution, but we need to step back and reassess the monitoring of Natives who are providing food necessary for health and wellness.

According to ANILCA, the FSB chair must be filled by someone who is Alaska Native, who hunts and fishes according to subsistence, and who is respected by Natives. I applaud the chairman for subconsciously reiterating the fact that all subsistence harvesters are treated as criminals according to simple state procedures. With emergency actions the state continues to justify the status quo of hunting and fishing as a difficult definition of preferential harvests. When many Fish and Game board members have no experience of these regulation procedures, it is easy to be blinded by the glowing silhouette of these members as respectable sportsmen with their integrity intact. A tarnished reputation is not good in the limelight and a general recognition that your reputation will no longer be taken seriously or accepted by well-respected sportsmen who serve on the same board and those who testify and vigorously attend these special public functions to voice their concerns—it is ironic the disgraced FSB chairman also served as a state board of game member for more than ten years. As a result of the chairman's mishap, FSB now requires two Natives to be board members.

As a Native I trust my harvest ethics. The use of emergency orders only for subsistence is arbitrary and capricious. Following the logic behind this procedure, the commissioner is also required to issue emergency orders for all users. Alaskans relate to valid reasons about emergency orders for natural disasters necessary for the safety and well-being of every resident.

In June 2015 the state issued a ten-hour Yukon commercial dip-net fishing period. Five days a week—Monday to Friday. The commercial fish companies were happy, but the state issued no official announcement for subsistence. All subsistence salmon fishing was closed. Commercial fishing was open noon to 10 p.m., and fishers were reminded to ice and bleed their salmon, which they could *sell or keep* for personal use.

In 2013 the state allowed dip nets for the first time on the Yukon River. For decades dip nets had been accepted in other Alaska rivers. One unique statistic for Lower Yukon commercial fishery is 99 percent of fishers are Native and reside in the community where this fishery is allowed. Ray Oney is a Native, originally from Marshall, and a council member for the Yukon Kuskokwim Regional Advisory Council. He remembers dip-netting for salmon along the shale cliffs in Pilot Station many years ago as a young teen, so it is not an unusual traditional practice.

When State Trooper Forreste issued me a citation, I was dip-net fishing for salmon near home. Trooper Forreste was checking on legal gear, license requirements, and making sure personal flotation vests were used or available in the boat. Other concerns we discussed were the use of boat permits, vessel identification numbers, and boat registrations including emergency equipment such as flare guns, fog horns, and fire extinguishers. Natives in eighteen- to twenty-four-foot open skiffs call these state requirements redundant.

In 1970 an issue addressed in the Lower Yukon was allowing subsistence and commercial salmon fishing at the same time. To address this, BOF regulations created a lag time between one and the other as window management: "subsistence fishing is closed 12 hours before, during, and 12 hours after a commercial opening." With the new dipnet fishery, managers initiated salmon fish openings with no prior knowledge of why harvest windows had become a management tool. When I discussed this with Trooper Forreste, our meeting became less cordial. Trooper Forreste became irritated, looked at the salmon in my tote, looked over my boat gear, and gave me a citation. I accepted the citation and told him I was going to challenge it, and he admitted I had every right to do so. Several days later, the fish-buying boat captain told me the troopers had checked to see if I sold my salmon or if I took it home.

In June 2015 there were no legal subsistence fish openings. All state announcements opened commercial fishing ten hours a day, five days a week. My original intent when I met the troopers was to talk with them as long as I could to keep them preoccupied from visiting any other Native boats and issuing one less citation. Despite the definition of perjury, I know all Native fishers. I am familiar with most regulations, and some Native boats are not legally equipped to meet state requirements. As we talked about the concurrent commercial and subsistence fishing and the issue addressed in 1970, I asked: "How do you know subsistence fishers are not giving fish to commercial fishers to sell?"

This statement did not go over well. With the not guilty plea, the magistrate needed Trooper Forreste as presiding witness. With several attempts to contact Trooper Forreste and no response, the magistrate had no option but to dismiss the case. I did not have to pay a fine. Although Trooper Forreste looked over my boat with no obvious illegal evidence, Trooper Forreste gave me a citation regarding a U.S. Coast Guard gear requirement for operating a boat over eighteen feet on Alaska waters. I did not have a type IV throwable flotation device. Despite the flotation vests my crewmember helper and I were wearing, if I had a float seat cushion I would have been okay. I have never seen any U.S. Coast

Guard vessels in any Yukon River waters. One other citation has been issued to a Pilot Station Native for a similar minor infraction.

Although the Native FSB chairman did not challenge the state emergency regulation, in 2009 the state issued a citation to a Native subsistence fisherman in southeast Alaska for overharvesting salmon. Albert Kookesh Jr., a state legislator from Angoon, accepted and challenged the citation with an argument that subsistence regulation procedures in Alaska are redundant and arbitrary. The state supreme court agreed that subsistence harvest limits for southeast Alaska did not follow the Administrative Procedures Act dictating how state regulations are made. This is true for all of Alaska and why the commissioner should be required to issue emergency orders not only for subsistence. The charges against Albert Kookesh Jr. were dropped.

FSB was created with ANILCA and issues federal regulations for Alaska Natives and rural residents on federal lands. ANILCA and Yukon River Salmon Agreement of the Yukon River Panel address similar resource management concerns. The unique characteristic of Yukon Panel membership is that it includes Alaskan and Canadian representatives working together to address river-wide concerns. The Yukon Panel has no discretionary responsibility; it offers advice and approves federal funds for river-wide projects. As a management alternative, the Yukon Panel needs to help create a discretionary regulatory body involving Alaska tribes and Canadian First Nations to manage Yukon River resources. This regulatory body will not require the state to issue emergency orders for subsistence. Recognizing and allowing First Nations to join the Yukon River Intertribal Fish Commission is an example of this endeavor.

Through the news media it is not unusual to read and hear rumors of Yukon king harvests between Alaska and Canada. People who live on the river are familiar with Lower Yukon commercial fishing, and Canadian commercial harvests have not been significant. During seasons when fishers are adamantly restricted and significant salmon passages are reported at the Canada border with rumors of Canadian commercial fishing, Native relations to management are not cordial. Commercial fishing is one thing, but when subsistence is restricted and border estimates exceed preseason projections, there are no management guidelines for emergency disaster declaration between agencies who claim responsibility. After the season is over and border estimates have been met, management comments about surplus of Yukon kings that could have been harvested for Alaskans.

If Alaska tribes and Canadian First Nation Natives work together to sustain our salmon fisheries as our forefathers, we do not need federal or state oversight to complicate matters. The current condition and concern of Yukon salmon numbers is proof of the failure of ADF&G management efforts. More than ever, our salmon stocks have declined to drastic conditions cumulating from ADF&G telling Natives what gear to use, how to fish, where to fish, and when to fish. These are non-sustainable management tools. All Yukon salmon numbers have crashed so that no Yukon salmon fishing was allowed in 2021 and 2022. Food security was so drastic that Bristol Bay salmon was flown into every Yukon River community. We Natives need to be responsible for our destiny. There is no proof our traditional stories failed to sustain our salmon stocks.

In April 2014, during a round table discussion with First Nation Natives at the Fairbanks International Yukon River Summit, it was heartwarming to learn about similarities in cultural and traditional hardships we share when subsistence is restricted. The First Nation Natives were surprised to learn Alaska Natives have separate state and federal regulatory bodies, as if the Native has a mnemonic pseudonym image. I was asked a question only a foreigner would ask: Is this true for every U.S. citizen?

NOTES

1. *Anchorage Daily News*, February 27, 2008.

PART III

The animals were first introduced into Alaska from Siberia from 1891 to 1902 by Dr. Sheldon Jackson, the United States General Agent in Alaska. The original purpose of importation was to augment the dwindling source of native food supply consisting of game and fish, which had been seriously depleted by the whites.

— FELIX S. COHEN,
Handbook of Federal Indian Law, 1941

21 ⤝ Paimiut River

"Look! In the grass!" my brother James whispered.

"Antlers," I whispered.

It was another September moose hunt season, and we were at the Paimiut River near the village of Holy Cross. I was with my brothers Abe and James and two of Abe's boys. We stopped by the Paimiut moose hunter check station to buy current hunt licenses and visit with Randy Kacyon, the area manager for Fish and Game. This check station was jointly operated by ADF&G and USFWS. The first time I met Randy I saw a special trait I had never seen in previous managers.

Randy Kacyon was a state wildlife biologist for the region with the main office based in Bethel. In addition to working on efforts of wildlife concerns, Randy's personal endeavor and passion was working with Natives on all wildlife issues. The Yukon Kuskokwim wildlife GMU 18 is a region the size of Oregon and Washington, and Randy was the only state employee responsible for all wildlife.

Of previous wildlife biologists who worked this position, something about Randy's management contentions was different and not as intimidating. Randy was more than a public presence for the state and worked constructively to manage all hunt efforts with an understanding that Natives depend on the region's wildlife for personal sustenance. He did not create an invasive authoritative presence. Randy would explain the tasks and responsibilities of wildlife issues important for residents in simple language the Natives could understand and relate to.

A local wildlife concern is moose management. Randy started out as a wildlife technician collecting raw data, but once he became responsible, he recognized that the moose population was always stagnant. This whole region can support more moose, similar to other prime habitats of Alaska, but the numbers never seem to be there. According to population projection models, the growth rate can be exponential especially with the fact that moose females can reach maturity and breed as early as two years old. Randy recognized that it is the females that should be protected from Native poachers. Poaching was a constant issue for previous managers who tried to rule Native hunters with an iron fist. Randy learned, recognized, and spoke to Natives that female moose should be protected and allowed to breed, and the population growth could be promising.

Every season, hunters in Alaska are allowed to harvest males or moose with antlers. Female moose have no antlers. When Randy visited with Natives, he quietly emphasized, "Save the cows for the future." Save the female moose for future hunts.

Randy traveled to communities in the region, visiting elementary and high schools and educating young Natives of the activities and responsibilities of hunters in maintaining wildlife with the message that all these wild critters belong to everyone. This educational approach to teach future hunters was promising. The challenge was the older Natives, who believed the manager was an intimidating person trying to be the boss to Native way of life. As a wildlife manager recognize that animals live out in the wilderness, the rational way to teach seasoned Native hunters was out in the places where they hunt.

When Randy attended community meetings, the Natives discussed local issues created from regulations and previous managers' convictions rather than current efforts to ensure protection and conservation of wildlife. In addition to hunting, Natives also talked about fishing, social service programs, education, housing, alcohol, child custody cases, and issues Randy had no responsibility or obligation to address. Randy's Western education background is in science and wildlife. At these community meetings the Natives were trying to convey the message that all subsistence harvest decisions impact all areas of Native life. This same message was given to previous managers. Where the previous managers failed, Randy was able to connect with Native hunters and concerns of ADF&G.

Randy was instrumental in securing funds to build a log cabin with assistance from USFWS. The cabin was built in the Paimiut River and became known as the Paimiut moose hunter check station. The check station serves several functions. Although it is mainly used during the hunt season in September, USFWS employees use it for staging other fish and wildlife projects any time of the year. In September, Natives can purchase current hunt licenses for the remainder of the year, and the station served as a source for news and hunt reports of the area. Before the check station, agency staff had some idea of harvest estimates, but these numbers were questionable. The check station collected moose tooth samples for age estimates, antler size, and other data of wildlife harvested. This provided a better understanding of harvest statistics and meant that more Natives were providing real data. Usually, moose harvest tags were discarded rather than being completely filled and returned to the agency—self-addressed and stamped or not.

The other information collected from the Paimiut check station was where the Natives were from. Before, agency employees had assumed Natives only hunt in the immediate area of their own communities. What the Paimiut check station proved was that Natives from coastal communities of western Alaska and Kuskokwim villages came to hunt near the village of Holy Cross. Hunters from villages as far away as Kotlik, Newtok, and Hooper Bay traveled more than two hundred river miles to hunt. This information is documented proof that use areas were extensive. These hunters do not use any hunting guide outfits, registered or not. Natives were also harvesting animals farther upriver in the adjacent GMU, which Randy was not responsible for. This unusual fact showed an overlap of hunting areas with residents from different communities.

"Don't point at things when we are in this country," Abe reminded us—otherwise the wind and weather would change for the worse.

For four days we had been stuck at the mouth of Twelve Mile slough below the Paimiut River waiting for the stormy weather to change. With a little north wind the Yukon River was rough with waves and too dangerous to risk our little twenty-two-foot fishing boat. We stayed in our tent playing card games to pass the time. Like any game fun to play, the history of ADF&G and its role with Native wildlife resources have been precarious.

Within ADF&G, the traditional responsibilities are divided between one group that manages animals that walk and the other fish that swim. Agencies such as the Division of Commercial Fisheries and Game Division knew what they are responsible for. Some did not and eventually learned by trial and error. Every Alaskan has a voice in the system. Equal, fair, and due process is recognized. In 1989, when the state realized subsistence management efforts were unconstitutional, a nagging voice about hunting and fishing issues implied cultural issues and preferential disparities: rural verse nonrural, Native and non-Native, and those who depend on wild resources more than others. Some were aware of these issues and bias; some were not and created a self-conscious image within ADF&G.

After the 1989 state supreme court ruling, an uncomfortable situation was developing, and every ADF&G division was getting a sense of this self-conscious image. For state employees it is generally accepted that we can look to written law and interpret it and use it to settle indifferences. Additional disputes can be clarified with the help of the state attorney general. The state realized this self-image was reference to the ethics of Native Alaska and public trust resources that belong to every Alaskan.

In light of this issue, the state realized certain words can carry strong connotations and be interpreted as culturally inappropriate and sensitive. One is the definition of "game" to mean wildlife, which is difficult for many Natives to accept. In 1993 ADF&G's Game Division changed its name to Division of Wildlife Conservation. At this time, Katie John's story was pending and the previous name was appropriate for respectable sportsmen, who traditionally recognize wildlife as nothing more than a source of fun—a game to be played. These respectable hunters continue to recognize the state constitution was never meant to be culturally inappropriate and that *our* management agencies delegated wildlife authority, not intending to target preferential users. This realization compelled the name change; management for conservation sounded more acceptable and professional than managing wildlife for a special user group.

It was a quiet realization that ADF&G did not intend to recognize as special sportsmen and their activities. This was not a good time for the state; the constitution was at stake, with talks of a convention to amend ANCSA to address subsistence. The interpretation was never meant to mean this, and the name change was rational. If the state claimed subsistence was unconstitutional, the same argument would apply to personal and sport. Within this system a *board of subsistence* should also be created.

Although ADF&G self-imposed this name change, the 1989 subsistence ruling helped create the 1994 legislative Intensive Management Law to aggressively management and regulate fish and wildlife with no sympathy to any user or Native culture. As a contingency plan, the stake of any fish or wildlife would never be in jeopardy and conservation and preservation actions could be imposed to sanction harvests for all users. This plan had never been used for subsistence, but Lower Yukon Native hunters self-imposed a management action that made ADF&G skeptical of ethics of difference between non-Native and Native hunters.

In Native Alaska, the perception of a sport hunter is not a good one. Natives would rather not see any sport hunters for any wildlife that belong to all Alaskans. The first instinct about subsistence is to make it easy, cost effective, time efficient, and sufficient to feed families. Need for food to quench hunger is not a game. One peculiar hunting regulation states that all edible meat must be salvaged. As a Native I find this a redundant rule; my ancestors would squirm with envy and ask who was practicing this wanton waste behavior. The argument that wanton waste is not tolerated by the state is an irony of the Intensive Management Act. All harvestable meat must be salvaged and transported out of the field. Once transported to the home destination, use of the wild meat is left to the discretion of the user. It is not unusual to hear of spoiled wild meat and fish found discarded in garbage dumps and trash bins.

Boning out the meat in the field and discarding the bones is some hunters' practice. To do it out in the field, subsistence hunters know that this can ruin more meat—savory bone roasts are an additional delicacy. Hunger knows no laws. Boning out the meat is generally seen as a practice of hunt ethics created over time, depending on the reason of who does it. At one time every hunter was required to salvage the whole animal, including the bone. BOG legally changed this as a potential criminal charge. Regulation proposals passed by this board often intend to make it easier for sport hunters.

Before my brother James and I saw the antlers in the grass, we visited with our brother Martin and his hunting party. For the last two nights, they had listened to bull moose fighting from somewhere across the river from their camp. The Paimiut River is a prime subarctic boreal forest with spruce, birch, aspen, and thick willow and alder. Many open meadows and scattered lakes make this excellent moose habitat. Bull moose fighting can be heard from at least a mile away, and trying to triangulate the noise deep in the forest can be difficult.

As we watched the antlers, we whispered about whether to get Abe and his boys to help shoot the moose. As we were whispering, we heard this *clank . . . clank . . .* every time the antlers moved. The moose stood and gave an impressive view of its sheer size. It was a nice animal. Another bull stood on the other side and completely surprised us.

"Holy!" we gasped.

It was a giant with a large body and impressive antler racks. The field grass was five feet tall, and the two had been low to the ground, sparring with their antlers. All we saw was the antlers, and the clanking noise was the antlers hitting each other as they sparred. They looked tired. We quickly decided what to do, knowing we may not have a more open target. To increase our chances, we selected only one to target. It took seven shots to knock down the one we wanted.

When Abe, Martin, and their hunting parties saw the animal, they could not get over how big it was. Smiling, happy for the meat, James and I told them that this moose was the smaller of the two. The big one got away and we did not target it. With the adrenaline of moose sparring for the last several days, the meat of this huge prime bull was tender, fat, and delicious.

Save the cows for the future was the main emphasis Randy Kacyon discreetly told Natives. Randy was familiar with Native hunt ethics and knew poaching of female moose was common. But Randy did not emphasize *not* killing moose and especially not killing cows. From previous stories of defiance, Randy knew that trying to impose more restrictions would create reason for deterrence. In any conservation efforts, restricting hunting and fishing will provoke Natives who hunt for food.

Trying to teach Natives about not harvesting cows was difficult because of several factors, such as a spiritual belief according to some that the animals willingly give themselves to hunters, or the reasoning that killing the first animal we see would save fuel and economic costs. As a visual learning device, Randy made a drawing of concentric circles emanating with little moose silhouettes, with a female in the center. Each circle represented one year of life for the female and in subsequent years more silhouettes represented new moose. It was a family tree with the message that the growth rate could be exponential. If one female was not killed and gave birth to twins in alternate odd years, and each of those offspring gave birth, in ten years the number of offspring from this one female can be significant. According to simple population projection models, this growth rate should be accurate. As an incentive to encourage Natives to stop at the Paimiut check station, Randy gave free items useful to Natives with the message to tell other hunters of this free stuff. Natives get happy when they receive free stuff. One of these items was a ceramic coffee mug with an emblem of the moose population growth diagram.

At some point, when you say something to enough hunters, you will tell it to Natives who make a difference. Before 1990, Natives from Lower Yukon villages traveled to Paimiut River to hunt. The moose numbers in the Lower Yukon have always been stagnant, and with the price of gas needed to travel there, making one trip upriver to hunt was more cost and time effective than trying to hunt near home, where more effort is expended because the supply is less significant. The moose numbers farther upriver were more appealing. Although the moose numbers near Paimiut River have always been consistent, not every hunting trip is a guarantee. The morning coffee in the cup with the emblem stirred conversations of what moose numbers could be like. As a joint effort, Lower Yukon Natives agreed to a moratorium in 1992. Native leaders from below the community of Mountain Village agreed to no moose hunts. ADF&G and USFWS have no regulations or authority to impose wildlife moratoriums. Native hunters voluntarily agreed not to hunt.

As a result of this five-year moratorium, moose numbers have escalated to such numbers that ADF&G allow for any moose to be taken—including cows and calves, with longer hunt seasons, including winter hunts. Natives from Kuskokwim River villages saw the result of this moratorium and agreed to a similar moratorium with assistance provided by USFWS.

Randy Kacyon was the area wildlife biologist for seven years. He was also a pilot and flew a small airplane for aerial wildlife surveys. In 1996, while conducting a moose survey in the middle Yukon portion of GMU 18, Randy's plane went down. He did not survive. Small airplane fatalities are a leading cause of death in Alaska. Since 2005 the Paimiut cabin is no longer used as a moose check station. For the Lower Yukon, the moose population has escalated to such numbers that in January 2017 and 2020, BOG addressed a proposal to open snow machine winter hunts for non-residents. The state opposed this proposal.

21 ⬱ Fish and Game Hats

"How did you teach these boys to fish? These boys don't know how to fish. They fish any old way." Thecla was loudly explaining and mad at her husband, Evan Paul, for sending the three young boys to fish for salmon. Thecla looked at her son John and told him to get out of the boat and find Uncle Waskey. "There is too much fish . . ."

⬱

I was walking the spit in Homer, Alaska, fishing rod in hand and my two kids in tow. It was a nice day to try and catch salmon in the tidal pool. The spit was crowded with fishers, but I was amazed and awed at the berth I was given as I walked by. I stopped at a likely spot to cast the kiddie rods, and whispering fishers gave me more room. It was not only the tourists in plastic raincoats who smiled, nodded their heads, and silently gave me room. I know I look Native, but this self-reverence was not creating this euphoria. My sisters told me that I would look good in a uniform. A long time ago I told myself that I would never work with any resource agency that requires a uniform or in a position that requires any wildlife enforcement obligation. I was not wearing a uniform of any sort except for a hat with an ADF&G logo. I was not impersonating anyone. I was working with the ADF&G Yukon River Pilot Station Sonar Site and visiting Homer for a vacation.

I worked seven seasons at the sonar site. Every year the staff provided hats with an ADF&G emblem and sonar logo. Every season's hat was a different color. Lately I've been wondering what these hats would fetch on eBay. Imagine the elbow room if you were official-looking and fishing among the crowds on the Kenai River. But if you wore this hat for fun you would be impersonating an ADF&G sonar staff member.

Although my region of Alaska is predominantly Native, I know of only one Native state wildlife trooper who enforces wildlife regulations and none who work in ADF&G management. In the past, rumors of Natives issuing hunting or fishing violations spread fast in communities. This is not an issue taken lightly; the traditional way a Native sees another Native harvesting resources is that this is not a reason to impose hardships. I recognize you have needs, families to feed, communities to support, and I have no reason to make your life difficult. I share your way of life.

Rural Alaska has few existing roads. Flying in small airplanes is a requirement.

I am not a pilot. I have no license to fly and no interest in becoming a pilot. A pilot's license is not the same as a state driver's license; many drive vehicles because of convenience and everyone else is doing it. Driving is second nature to our notions of modern evolution and no one questions it. If anything, it is a question of when we get to that stage of life and become eligible to get a license and share the open road with likeminded people and proceed to our own destinations. Learning to fly is more complicated and challenging than learning to drive a vehicle. One of my jobs required me to fly in small airplanes.

Flying in a Cessna 207 floatplane for eight hours a day can be monotonous. When the weather is calm, the views in Alaska are mesmerizing; when it is foggy, overcast, and gloomy it is easy to be glum and accept the fact that we are just flying to do a job. Some areas of Alaska are rugged, barren, and empty, best described as a home fit only for the wild critters that live there. Ever since agencies claimed responsibility of all wild resources, one principal component is to monitor and keep count of the critters as part of the stewardship responsibilities we fulfill with Mother Nature. Through trial and error of keeping count of the critters, we have learned not only of the spatial association of these numbers as they fluctuate through time, but also the relationship of these critters with others and biomes of our ecosystem.

Population dynamics and how agencies monitor and count numbers of critters are a part of biology, the study of life. My early college sessions taught counting animals based on visual sightings and mathematical statistics to extrapolate an estimate number. Growing up with the talk of elders, I've had doubts that the state provides accurate or reliable numbers of moose, bears, or wolves as reason to restrict subsistence. Although all population estimates have a statistical variance that attempts to minimize the margin of error, one of the early counting methods was the use of flying in a straight line and counting the number of critters spotted and extrapolating the total number of animals that may inhabit the area. When I first worked at the forestry science lab in Juneau, I knew our major task was to monitor forest insect and disease outbreaks. What caused me to step back and laugh was when I was told that I was to count all the insects in southeast Alaska. I wondered if I had made a wise career choice.

Unlike the visual linear method, FSL used spatial association in a way that compliments my abstract Native way of thinking. As I used tweezers and picked, identified, and counted hemlock sawflies, brown-nosed hair loopers, and spruce budworms, trying to keep spiders from crawling away was a distracting chore. Spiders are not forest tree pests. All these pests are non-flying insects. When I traveled home to visit, it was not easy to explain what I did to my relatives, so I told them I traveled southeast Alaska in a small floatplane and looked for patches of trees that looked sick because of disease and insect outbreaks. Discoloration or lack of foliage indicates a possible outbreak. When Andy Eglitis, the entomologist, explained the insect counting method and how this practice had begun in 1940, his eyes lit up with excitement. Andy loved this job. In 1960 this counting method was refined and used as an annual monitoring system for the Tongass National Forest. FSL has data on the number and condition of the forest pests of every year since.

For ten days we flew and landed in every area of southeast Alaska, in places with names such as Naukati, Berners Bay, and Ward Cove, and collected insect samples. These same collection sites are used every year to monitor insect conditions. As insect population numbers are compared to those of every other year, a pattern can project whether a new outbreak is about to occur.

For a time before non-Natives became common visitors in rural Alaska, Natives assumed any new visitor was working for the school, the church, or Fish and Game. Anyone else of no relation had no reason to visit. The Fish and Game representative was the ominous person; Natives refer to any fish or wildlife representative as "Fish and Game." This nomenclature applies whether the representative works for the federal or state agency. Fish and wildlife troopers, USFWS, ADF&G, and organizations affiliated with these agencies are all "Fish and Game." In Pilot Station, there is no Forest Service, BLM, National Park Service, or Soil Conservation Service, but if you are a new visitor, you are most likely Fish and Game.

In March 1999 I agreed to help ADF&G Division of Wildlife Conservation with a Yukon River moose count survey. In the Lower Yukon there is no ADF&G office. State employees are seasonal visitors and depend on what critter the agency is attempting to manage. I agreed to help ADF&G with this moose count with coordinated assistance from USFWS. From Pilot Station I traveled to St. Mary's by snow machine, and with several small airplanes we flew to predesignated plots to count moose. Unlike previous moose counts based on linear flights—flying in a straight line and counting number of moose sighted—the staff used a spatial method I was familiar with from counting the number of insects in southeast Alaska. During our preflight staff meeting and site selections with this random population estimate model, I was pleased, as this spatial method was more rational and had less room for error, allowing for patience and more corrective observations than the previous fixed linear method.

To count insects, we used a ten-square-foot white sheet as an area of fixed reference. We only count the insects that land in this area. The sheet was spread on the forest floor with several forest branches overhanging, and we banged and shook the tree limbs so that all insects, spiders, and bugs would fall onto the sheet. As we identified and counted, we had a rational number of insects according to space and time. From each site, three sample counts provided current insect conditions. When there were less than a handful of insects, we counted and collected the data as is. If there were more, we collected every insect into paper lunch bags to count later at the lab. The heavily infested areas had counts of more than a thousand insects, and with average counts between three samples, we extrapolated a total number. Thus, a timeline of annual counts provides a reference on the condition of the forest pests in comparison to the island, area, or the Tongass Forest.

In comparison, to count moose with this spatial method, a grid pattern was drawn over a map and a random number of grids were selected to be counted. In theory, the ten-by-ten-foot sheet was one hundred square feet; for the moose count each area was two and a half square miles. Every critter counted in each grid area provides a statistical extrapolation. Certain areas of southeast Alaska always had some number of insects present, in the same way that moose favor certain forest areas. Winter areas near the main Yukon have the highest number of moose. As a major river system disturbance due to erosion, sandbar formation is constant and the main brush growth is willow, a winter food source for moose. The spatial method allowed moose and insect counts to be statistically extrapolated with fewer errors. The early method of linear counts often made it difficult to distinguish between male and female, whereas spatial counts allowed for leisure and ratio assurances between males, females, and calves. Along river corridors where moose spend the winter, it was not unusual to count thirty moose per square mile.

In St. Mary's, ADF&G and USFWS staff stayed at the old mission dorm and used the river as an airplane runway. All airplanes were small ski-equipped single engines, from the Cessna 185 to the Super Cub. I was a spotter and recorder, and my pilot was a young Alaska Native Yup'ik, USFWS supervisor Gene Peltola Jr. In 2020, as former director of the USFWS Office of Subsistence Management, Gene became the director of BIA for Alaska.

I was seven years old, helping my grandma Alick hand-saw firewood for her cookstove. This was several months before Donald and I snuck away to commercial fish for salmon. It was midafternoon, early June, sunny with a light breeze. Families who live along Kwicauq Slough were busy getting ready for salmon fishing season. Grandma Alick was pleased with the wood and I could go and play. I ran over to our neighbors to look for my friend John Paul.

John's parents, Evan and Thecla, were working on their fish-drying rack. Thecla told me that John was out fishing with his uncle Jimmy.

Instantly bored, I ran to Mom and my sisters as they were working on our small garden. A half hour later, I checked on the Pauls' and John was not back. Evan and Thecla talked about why the three boys were taking so long. The boys used Evan's boat and fishnet to drift for salmon. The Yukon River was calm, the sun was shining, and the boys were taking too long. Thecla was worried that something may have happened, and Evan reminded her that her brother Waskey was getting ready to fish and could check on the boys.

Dan Greene's home was on the other side of Kwicauq Slough. Dan hollered from across the river that Evan's boat was returning and it looked heavy and loaded. As the boat came up the small slough, families gathered to see how the boys had done.

"Eeggigi, chawata," I heard many people repeat.

Evan's boat was loaded with salmon. As the boat slowly docked, the boat waves rocked other boats in the calm slough, and everyone was pleased and happy. Evan smiled and beamed about their success, and Thecla was pleased her fish rack and cutting table were ready and they had fish to cut. "Eeggigi, chawata," Thecla repeated until she realized there was too much fish. Thecla had told Evan to fish and get enough salmon to cut and dry. Thecla asked her husband how much fish was there. There was too much fish. "I told you to get enough fish for us to cut," she said in Yup'ik and started to raise her voice. "These boys fish carelessly, there is too much fish!" Evan tried to reason with her that he was busy working on the fish rack and could not go and fish at the same time. Evan asked the boys why they got so much fish and how many times they set the net out to drift.

"Once. We only drift one time, but it took long time to pull in the net."

Thecla was mad at Evan and said he needed to teach these boys how to fish, in the old days fishers knew how to fish. Thecla looked to John and all the fish scales on his pants and told him to get out of the boat and find her brother. Waskey had gone to buy gas and was lucky he had no need to fish; half of this boat load was Waskey's to cut and dry.

I heard Grandma calling me to ask Thecla if she could have a fresh salmon for dinner. Evan was all smiles as Thecla yelled at the boys to unload the salmon. I asked Thecla for the one salmon; she looked to me and in a loud voice told me to take two salmon for my grandma.

This was 1970. Federal and state management oversight for Native traditional harvesting was lenient, and families met their subsistence needs. Statewide, a new salmon fishery management concept of harvest window was just beginning. For the state, this micromanagement tool actually began in the 1960s and was developed and refined through the 1980s. The 1970s was the learning phase as more public involvement influenced state management. Native traditional harvesting became an attempt to merge window harvest opportunities and favorable weather conditions for drying and smoking. In time, Native ways would falter.

Between 1990 and 2000, as salmon numbers became an issue of concern, ADF&G started to allow subsistence harvests later into the summer season. Unfortunately, late summer is not a good time for traditional preservation methods of drying and smoking. Rain showers increase in frequency and moisture content rises, allowing any salmon preservation attempts to mold and ruin. The amount of insect infestations is another culprit. As summer extends to midsummer, fly activity and larvae increase, and any host raw meat or fish is susceptible. Traditional harvesters know early June harvests minimize mold and insect infestations.

The 1970s also saw a new management concept intended to work side by side with harvest windows called mid-point salmon passage management. The mid-point estimate is used to guesstimate the mid-run of the salmon and allow commercial salmon fishing after this passage. Although these management announcements are documented with involvement of state and federal oversight, the fact that salmon did not follow projected returns proved challenging to ADF&G. In 2003 concerns about king salmon returns led to claims that Native harvesting methods had caused smaller salmon size and decline in salmon numbers—despite managers telling Natives when, how, and where to fish. In 2010 BOF passed more gear regulations, and this created tension between Native fishers and state managers. As a result, between 2010 and 2016, each summer season manager lasted only one season before quitting and leaving ADF&G for good.

Despite the ADF&G managers who have come and gone, the subsistence family network is instrumental as a traditional salmon management tool. The family niche determines the success of the season, with the mother figure as the main fish cutter and preparer. The mother knows how much salmon to prepare for the season relative to other available wild resources and family size. If there is more than enough, the mother expresses appreciation and lets everyone know that there is no need to catch one more just because we could. Unfortunately, when window harvests became the only duties of the ADF&G manager, this took away all responsibility of the mother as family manager and allowed fishers to harvest as much salmon as they can or like when permission is granted, regardless of needs for food security. In time, non-Natives told managers that the Natives were overharvesting salmon and that we need more subsistence harvest regulations to address this.

In 1968 Pilot Station elders saw an unusual ecological salmon projection. They told ADF&G managers that salmon returns were about to become an issue of concern. The managers laughed. In 1980 elders talked of favorable salmon returns, and again this raised doubt; by this time non-Natives had proposed more gear and fishing time restrictions. In response BOF restricted net size to eight and a half inches and reduced fish openings. Many of us learned that when Natives bring up an issue of concern, more state subsistence regulations are created. As a result, many became reluctant to share Native concerns.

What is this Native traditional indicator, and is there any irrefutable proof to these traditional salmon premonitions?

22   Shortsighted

"Hey, look, it's following us."

I turned and looked . . . and looked again. What was he talking about? Something was following but I didn't see anything. I turned to Henry and smiled. As he walked to inspect the smokehouse and fish-drying rack, I quickly lifted my ski goggles and looked to see what was following. It was a bright, sunny afternoon, and there was nothing but snow and ice. This was Nunivak Island: there were no trees or brush, snow and ice as far as I could see, nowhere for anything to hide. Something was following? Did Henry have a sixth sense?

It was mid-March and the winter weather had finally cleared. After five days of ground snowstorms, we finally left Mekoryuk to try and do some sort of muskox survey. Compared to many places I have worked, Nunivak Island is barren tundra with slow, small rolling hills. The island is snow covered in March, and a little wind creates ground storms with instant whiteout conditions. Everyone is used to this and uses ski goggles to keep instant blowing snow and ice particles from stinging, squinting eyes. After one day walking in the village, I gave in and bought new snow goggles from the local store. The ground storms are nothing like storms at Pilot Station.

In addition to completing an animal survey, I issued forty muskox harvest permits to Native residents of Mekoryuk. I worked for ADF&G Division of Wildlife Conservation based out of Bethel. These tier hunting permits are one method that actually works in favor of the locals. The history of muskoxen in Alaska is as interesting as the animal itself. After Secretary of Interior William Seward helped purchase Alaska from Russia, Mr. Seward reintroduced muskoxen to Alaska from Greenland and Canada. Before the turn of the century, early whaling ships and gold rush pioneers had killed and decimated the muskox from Alaska. As social creatures that help protect their young and females, muskoxen form a circle and work together to thwart any predator animal attacks, with no reason to run away. When early non-Natives arrived with their muskets and rifles, the circle defense was no match, and all animals were shot for meat and fur capes. The light, fine fur—or *qiviut*—is like no other, and the insulating qualities from the cold are phenomenal.

When the muskoxen had all been shot, this raised Native food concerns.

≥

In 2006 Pilot Station opened a tribal store with the Alaska Native Industrial Cooperative Association, known statewide as ANICA. Before this store opened, Pilot Station had one store, owned and operated by the village corporation, and tribal members were not pleased with services and cost of goods. Mail-ordering groceries and traveling to St. Mary's Alaska Commercial Company Store or Yukon Traders to shop were normal. Pilot Station tribe does not represent corporation shareholders.

After the tribal store opened, the impact to the community was immediate. Not only did the store provide alternatives, sales, and a variety of goods, the additional competition provided several economic benefits to the community. All employees and management are local, so local jobs were created, though with one exception the community had to agree to. With no community building to house this store, the tribe sacrificed the tribal bingo hall used to fundraise and help pay for local emergency assistance and food donation requests. Even though the building was over twenty years old, and constant repairs and maintenance were a weekly chore, the economic impact to the community was immediate.

In 2009 Pilot Station tribe nominated our tribal store for a Small Business Administration statewide contest as a small business promoting economic development to our village. As a local economic source, the influence and services surpassed village expectations. Unfortunately, SBA only promotes Alaska Native corporations with the rationale that tribes do not receive benefits or services from ANCSA. The contest does not apply to tribal enterprises created for small communities.

The City of Pilot Station collects a local sales tax. After the tribal store opened, the annual sales tax revenue reported to the State of Alaska is evidence that local people were spending their earned money in the community. In addition to local employment, sales tax, and weekly store sales, the impact to the existing village corporation store was significant. The tribal store grocery sales helped offset the exorbitant costs of living in rural Alaska. The impact to the Native village corporation was self-evident: several years later the corporation sold all its grocery store assets to another Alaska self-made conglomerate. The Pilot Station Native Store is now part of the Alaska Commercial Company; every Alaskan knows these stores as AC. Several years later the St. Mary's Yukon Traders closed.

The Pilot Station Tribal Store does not sell fuel. In 2022 the prices for heating fuel and gasoline are $8.90 and $8.40 a gallon, respectively. The local fuel vendor is the Native village corporation. Despite federal subsidies and dependence on a fluctuating market economy, the cost of services in rural Alaska follows an eminently escalating scale compounded with transportation costs for delivery.

Henry Ivanoff is a Native of Mekoryuk and lifelong USFWS employee as a refuge information technician. For several days in March 1999, I was alone in the USFWS bunker. The weather forecast for the next several days was not promising. Henry helped USFWS with maintaining the bunker and equipment and had done an excellent job. I had nothing else to do but wait on the storm to pass. Henry invited me to his home to eat dinner, watch March Madness basketball on TV, and visit. The bunker had no telephone or TV. There were several interesting old *Alaska Sportsman* magazines to read.

As Henry and I were completing a muskox ground survey on the east side of the island, we came across a young pair of male muskoxen. At a safe distance we stopped to observe. These are not pets and we had no intention of getting any closer. Henry knew that the main herd was on the west side of the island, but because of weather conditions we were limited to this part of the island. Although there were no trees, we could see distances, especially on cool crisp afternoons. It was sunny on this side of the island, and we saw the luminous heavy clouds of the weather front to the west. After leaving the muskoxen, we traveled another twelve miles and stopped to inspect a smokehouse and fish-drying rack.

After Henry inspected the smokehouse, I looked back the way we came and with courage meekly asked Henry about what was following. Everywhere I looked I saw nothing but snow and ice. Henry looked the direction we had come from and told me to follow the trail of our snow machine tracks. He asked if I saw the muskoxen coming this way. I did a double take. I could not get over it. I felt like an embarrassed idiot: these animals are completely black with a backdrop of a bright white snow-covered blanket. There was no easier contrast to see, and I am not colorblind. When we stopped Henry turned and took one look and recognized the animals for what they were. I had looked and looked and did not see them because they were more than four miles away and tiny little specks! I was looking for something closer and less than a mile away.

My visual perception acuity is not nurtured for this barren environment. Because I grew up in woody brush and forest, my visual acuity is focused on objects closer than a mile. Places thick with brush and trees, where sight is not my only sense but where my hearing and smell play an important role in my sixth sense of the environment.

In mid-1990, during one successful moose hunt in the Paimiut River, my brothers and I came across Native hunters from the coastal community of Scammon Bay. They were beached in one fork of the river. We recognized the hunters so we stopped to see if they were okay. One was a young elder who had traveled for the first time this far into interior Alaska. The young elder was more comfortable hunting seals and traveling on broken sea ice and boating in the stormy waters of the Bering Sea. They saw our meat load and asked how they could be as successful. My brother told them that it would be easier if they walked into the trees and brush and looked for open meadows where moose are likely to be spotted. We watched with amusement when his eyes roved the trees and grew with realization that they would have to get out of the boat and venture into thick trees and brush where everything is unknown. After this conversation, a young hunter came out of the woods and made our day. Speaking loudly and excitedly in their coastal Yup'ik dialect, strapping on his Gore-Tex chest waders, the young hunter talked about how he had gone into the woods and taken care of business and was not afraid and brave for doing all this. We burst out laughing and when he realized there was another boat of strangers, his face turned red with embarrassment. We questioned how and why he did not hear our boat motor as we stopped.

It is not unusual for Native hunters from coastal communities, where trees and brush are scarce, to be apprehensive of hunting in areas thick with underbrush. It is not unusual to see these hunters sleep in blue tarps inside the relative safety of their boats. When we are not familiar with each other's hunt areas, these lessons can be formidable. In 1989, while visiting Kotlik, I was invited to go jackrabbit hunting. This area was new to me and one hunter told me that I should not drive fast just anywhere. Even if there was a snow machine trial, don't follow it driving fast; it is not like hunting at home. In Kotlik, hunters travel through thick willows often make odd ninety-degree turns to avoid ten-foot cutbanks of small rivers and sloughs.

Although we were not able to complete a thorough muskox ground survey, Henry reassured me that the local Natives were not concerned about muskox numbers. Nunivak Island is an island, and the Arctic fox is the largest predatory animal with the exception of an occasional lost, wandering polar bear. Mainland wolves or bears have no chance of making it onto the island. If there was any concern about the muskoxen, the Natives from Mekoryuk would be the first to notice and inform the agencies. Mekoryuk is the only community on this island.

As part of working with the ADF&G Division of Wildlife Conservation, I also had the privilege to work at the Paimiut moose hunter check station in the same cabin Randy Kacyon built. I completed similar tasks Randy had started, from selling and issuing state hunting licenses and moose harvest tags to visiting with hunters. I knew many of the hunters, and many were surprised to see me working there. A Native working for Fish and Game is a major broken public relation image of cultural significance. Natives have never trusted Fish and Game, and many questioned me. My parents asked me the same question: Why are you working for *them*?

One early morning at the Paimiut cabin, I was enjoying my coffee and the cool fall colors and the misty shine of the sunrise when I heard a boat coming from around the bend. It was my Uncle John Thompson Sr. and several of his boys from St. Mary's. They were happy and surprised to see me as my cabinmate came out and greeted the hunters and offered fresh campfire coffee. My cabinmate was an elder non-Native who was visiting from the Lower 48 and volunteering with USFWS with a chance to work and experience the rural remote Alaska wilderness. For the elder, this was an Alaska vacation, and he was about the same age as Uncle John. The hunters started talking to the elder, and the elder pointed and told them to talk to me. John Jr. said that they were there to talk to Fish and Game, and I told them that I was Fish and Game. They were surprised and could not get over it, despite the Fish and Game hat I was wearing. I reassured them we were the only ones there and I could answer any questions. The elder amused the Natives when he announced that he was my camp cook.

I offered Uncle John food, coffee, and anything they might need. They started talking about last night and stopping at this cabin before midnight. The wind was howling and the spruce and birch trees swayed and creaked all night, but we woke to a calm morning. They talked about beaching their boat, shining a spotlight over the dark cabin, and hollering trying to get anyone's attention. This cabin is in the middle of wilderness, and any Native should be able to hear any commotion. I am a light sleeper and did not hear them at all. Embarrassed, as my cabinmate went to check on his cooking, I told them about my cabinmate's sleep apnea and his sawing logs that shake the cabin. To sleep, I put on my high-tech earphones and turned up the volume on my Walkman cassette music as loud as I could. I keep up with technology. My cousins looked to me and marveled that I had my own cook, and I told them that they should try his sourdough pancakes.

I reassured my cousins as I measured their moose antler size and collected a tooth sample and moose harvest tag. I sold licenses and monitored and recorded what was caught, but I was not a trooper and did not issue hunt citations, and I had no reason to report Natives. As

I reassured every hunter that I knew what home was like, every Native offered me fresh moose meat. Uncle John was pleased that his moose was the largest antler size measured. Several months later, the tooth sample aged his moose as the oldest for the season at twelve years old.

The Paimiut cabin is an hour boat ride below the village of Holy Cross and two hours above Russian Mission. Uncle John stopped to see if we could call and reassure my auntie in St. Mary's that they were safe. I told him that we had an emergency satellite phone and short-wave radio if we needed to request an emergency response. We also had a VHF radio, which had the same limited range as Uncle John's boat radio. With the weather clearing, they felt confident they could make it to Russian Mission and call home.

Henry Ivanoff helped build the Paimiut River log cabin as a refuge information technician or RIT for USFWS. Visiting in Mekoryuk, Henry laughed when he told me the place he felt safest was not in the cabin but on the cabin working on the roof, even though he was afraid of heights. For Henry, the thick trees and brush kept the bears hidden, and Natives who grew up on treeless tundra do not like surprises. Standing on the roof was refreshing, allowing him to see distances. The RIT program is a local observer program monitoring and reporting any wildlife, fishery, or refuge concerns. The RITS visit local schools and community organizations and provide information or collect concerns any Natives may have. The most influential program the RITS address is goose conservation and the Yukon Kuskokwim Goose Management Plan.

Although I have met many RITS and Native USFWS employees, Natives actually working for the state ADF&G are fewer in comparison. I have never worked for USFWS. One of the first Native RITS was Mr. Chuck Hunt from Kotlik, who helped initiate the statewide program as a Native liaison. One afternoon at the Paimiut cabin, I was surprised to see Chuck stop by to drop off his moose harvest tag, and he was not happy. Chuck and Donald Mike had boated all day from Kotlik and planned to spend a week camping and enjoying the outdoors. Just as they reached a favorite campsite, two good size bull moose stood side by side. Instead of camping on vacation as planned, they had to head home before the meat could ruin. Both Natives worked for USFWS and had taken time off from work, but in two days they were done and not pleased. Going out hunting is not the same as camping or going for a ride.

At the end of my work season, a small floatplane came to pick me up and fly me home. With the moose season winding, down the number of visiting hunters has reduced significantly; my elder cabinmate was flown home earlier that week. On the flight home, sitting in the copilot seat, I was mesmerized by the views. The pilot is a non-Native, and as we reached a safe altitude we saw flocks of geese, swans, and birds everywhere. The Yukon Delta National Wildlife Refuge is a major bird breeding site. At a higher elevation, we flew behind two large birds of prey soaring. In the small plane we felt the thermal lifts of the wind. Before I could say anything, the pilot was coasting behind the two birds, when all of a sudden one of the huge birds made a turn reacting to wind turbulence and hit the propeller and splattered all over the windshield! Surprised, I shielded my arms and knee over my face and cussed at the pilot. The engine sputtered but did not die. The bird disappeared and was all gone.

We were still flying. We landed on the river and checked the prop and engine radiator. The pilot washed blood, feathers, and gore from the windshield and was lucky the windshield was not cracked. Standing on my side of the pontoon floats, I looked for any damage and found a single claw. Cussing I threw it to the pilot . . . and he was happy for a souvenir. Ospreys are amazing birds. This one had over a seven-foot wingspan. What is it like to think like a gussak?

23 ⋜ Genetic Tributaries

"This is killing the animals! This is causing the animals to suffer," the three students yell. My classmates and I looked to each other and instantly knew we did not want to be associated with this group, so we slumped into our seats and I shielded my eyes with the bill of my cap. The conference members were startled and looked to the commotion. The protesters were sitting in front of us and one was waving a Conibear trap over their heads.

Why were these students protesting? This was a co-management wildlife conference, where everyone was supposed to cooperate with shared responsibility. Every government entity was there, the conference table at center stage had several Native representatives, the state management was supposedly there, and the federal presence was already seated. Everyone was there to discuss the preservation and conservation concerns of the large wildlife addressed at this conference.

The Native representatives claimed Native activities and monitoring efforts had identified the resource as sustainable with sufficient traditional population estimates, not a complete conservation concern, and that further management actions were not necessary. Other non-Native user groups were not convinced because recent state-conducted population estimates indicated a reason for concern and that large number of animals were unaccounted for. Rumors of wanton waste and massive die-offs due to natural phenomena with Mother Nature plagued the news media. The federal presence was there to help coordinate the meeting because of some fiduciary mission. The university coordinating the event found several campus security guards to help escort the three misfit protesters and their Conibear trap out of the conference stadium.

This was not a national televised event, and no video cameras or radio stations were present, so I don't know what the protesters were hoping to achieve. With sighs of relief, coordinators for the event introduced the participants and addressed the issues before further harvest restrictions or hunt regulations were set. The Eskimo and other Native leaders on the table sat serious and would not accede to whatever sanctions without resistance; their lives were at stake again with more impending regulations. The non-Natives represented the government and seemed nervous and apprehensive. These Natives were not Yup'ik Eskimos or any Alaska Natives. I look to the agenda; this was exciting for me, and I wondered how this kind of meeting could be set in Alaska with the Natives, state, and federal government on the same table.

In 1985 the fur trade industry and means of catching fur critters on traps was a circumpolar issue. The agony and suffering of fur animals are compelling, and efforts to boycott fur garments as fashion trends was receiving national and worldwide attention. As a result, the fur market experienced hard repercussions, and this recession impacted Native communities who depended on fur trapping as a local source of income. Unfortunately, this market has never recovered. The harvest of baby seals with their unique fur properties and texture had started this retribution effort to save all fur animals. Despite that, fur is an Alaska Native commodity, and efforts to boycott fur garments within the fashion industry have forever changed Alaska Native lives. Although empathy for fur animals began a worldwide trend, this co-management conference was not there to address this. This conference is not in the United States, it is in Canada, and the Natives present are the Nunamiut Inuits, Dene Athabaskans, and Métis—Natives who depend on harvests of the Beverly and Qamanirjuaq (Kaminuriak) caribou.

The co-management conference was on the McGill University campus in Montreal, Quebec. I was a young student, and talks of co-management schemes interested me because at home in Pilot Station, there had been reports of creation of a Yukon Delta Goose Management Plan. Although the goose management plan did not have much clout because the State of Alaska has no management authority over migratory birds, it was still a player with conservation concerns and harvests applying to Alaska residents. USFWS coordinated the goose management plan because it included several western states essential as seasonal flyway migration routes. Therefore, a migratory bird agreement needed state sanction approval and participation regarding conservation and preservation efforts of a harvestable resource.

Forty years later, in November 2015, UAF hosted the only Alaska co-management conference coordinated by the campus tribal management services. Claims of extinguishment of aboriginal rights are a reason triparty conference meetings between federal, state, and Native Alaskans are not necessary. Recent creation and actions of the Kuskokwim River Intertribal Fish Commission helped initiate the co-management conference, recognizing Native participants and shared responsibility with an emphasis on conservation of king salmon. The Kuskokwim Commission was created following similar guidelines as the Columbia River Intertribal Fish Commission. Development of the Yukon River Intertribal Fish Commission was also initiated for my part of Alaska. These fish commissions only focus on salmon. Pilot Station tribe has not joined the Yukon River commission and therefore has no obligation to help with shared responsibility of any fisheries. In June 2016 a Yukon Intertribal representative called Pilot Station and asked for a tribal resolution for Pilot Station to join as a member of this cooperative management scheme. In response, Pilot Station told the representative that we would rather work cooperatively or directly with the State of Alaska. An intertribal commission puts tribal powers at risk. What tribal powers?

Whenever there is discussion of Yukon River salmon, it may seem easy to question everything about anything and accept the answers at face value. For those of us who live on the river, are we asking questions that need to be asked?

In 1994 the first Yukon salmon genetic samples were collected at the Pilot Station Sonar Site. Samples of chum salmon heart, liver, and muscle tissue were collected to get a better grasp of stock and timing difference between summer and fall chum salmon. Several years later king salmon samples were collected. Another several years later, it was disheartening to learn that samples of the king salmon had not been analyzed because of state department funding shortfalls. Finally, in 2009, the king salmon genetic samples were analyzed, but the conclusions created conflicting points of view that would ultimately create more state subsistence gear regulations.

At the annual AFN convention or any large Native gathering, it is easy to observe, differentiate, and speculate where any unknown Native came from in the state. For people, the most prominent distinguishing trait of identity is our facial features. This is a genetic feature, and for humans, it is most distinguishable between cultures that are worlds apart where shades of color are a dominant trait. Although some facial features may be deceptive, the way a person talks is another distinguishable trait. At face value, the way non-Natives speak and look may all seem the same as the next non-Native, in the same way we Natives may all look the same to others. When Natives talk to other Natives of different cultures, it is easy to differentiate facial features, dialect, accents, and certain phrases that can be comical to hear for the first time, like hearing a Canadian speak the first time. To Canadians, we will always sound comical. Genetic features such as similarities in facial structures also help identify family relations.

The agencies that manage Yukon River fisheries often estimate at least 50 percent of Yukon king salmon spawn in Canadian rivers. Most seasons, this is the assumption. If our managers could take a look at a salmon caught in the lower river and immediately identify which river tributary the salmon originated in, or speculate which tributary this salmon was swimming to, this would be an excellent management application skill. It would immediately support the managers with reasonable efforts to understand a small aspect of the physiology and ecology of salmon than just claiming responsibility of our fisheries as mandated. Especially if managers can look at a salmon and immediately identify if it is bound to spawn in Alaska or Canadian waters. Unfortunately, the managers who take a look at salmon just see a fish. Other than recognizing what species of salmon—king, chum, or pink—there are no easy physical traits to identify which river the salmon originated in or where it is swimming to. This is true for king salmon. I am curious to know where this salmon is going if I caught it near the mouth of the Yukon River. Yukon kings are deceptive; managers shy away if we ask if a large king is male or female from its general physical features.

In the summer season the Yukon River Drainage Fisheries Association has a weekly teleconference meeting for communities along the Yukon River. If I lived in a community farther up the Yukon, I would be curious to ask management, "In last week's Y1 and Y2 commercial opening, what percentage of kings sold to the fish buyers was Canadian or bound for the Chena or Andreafsky River?" Would 90, 20, and 10 percent, respectively, be acceptable?

If management had been around for a time and could look to historical data to answer this question and could explain and justify current regulations with sound scientific information in a reasonable way that common people could understand, I could accept the comfort in knowing the majority of harvests are not from river tributaries near where I live. This data should be available in season so that Natives who live on the river have a chance to harvest salmon for food security without scrutiny toward commercial harvests. If we know the number of salmon harvests in the Lower Yukon is consistent between stocks of every tributary, everyone would feel comfortable that no particular stock was targeted, and BEG and SEG goals within all tributaries would have certainty of salmon escapement for spawning.

If questions like this can be answered, I accept the manager's current regulation schemes, especially in regard to window harvest subsistence fishing and timing sequence of commercial fishing. But if there is no answer, I am likely to weigh the concerns, recommendations, and management options from people who live permanently on the river. This lifelong collection of observations has often been traditionally ignored by management because of lack of substantial scientific significance. We Native people take pride in our collection of customary traditional practice and information about traditional ecological knowledge, but this information cannot be used for current management when managers regard traditional information as trivial.

Use of genetic information during the season can help accurately verify salmon bycatch in the Bering Sea pollock fisheries where salmon live to maturity. With this technology, we can learn to appreciate how real science is used to estimate stock numbers and help manage our fisheries with food security as hindsight.

Traditional Natives caught salmon randomly for subsistence. When we need the fish and are prepared to handle bulk numbers of salmon, when the weather is favorable, when fish drying racks are cleaned and ready . . . when we know this—we will go and fish. This is the principal doctrine of traditional sustained yield, that Natives will fish when ready to safely prepare and preserve bulk salmon, recognizing food security as a goal and that no food will be wasted. This is not the same as the manager giving permission for everyone to fish at the same time. This traditional harvest practice contradicts current regulations riddled with non-Native harvest ethics. There was no practice of window harvesting when my ancestors fished. Ecologically, my ancestors looked to the weather and determined whether it was a good day for salmon to smoke and dry; if not we waited until favorable conditions. Window management targets a certain pulse of salmon, allowing Natives to fish or close the fishery to protect the stock. Traditional methods used random harvests, consistent through the season, allowing for greater salmon diversity and gender escapement. Once the family harvested their needs, they were done for the season.

Like my ancestors I am against non-Native harvest regulations because of what I have experienced. Managers have no idea of what happens when they claim full responsibility and follow regulations telling Natives when to fish. Harvest window dictate how and when I have to fish. If the fishery is to be closed for the next three days, I have no choice but to fish tonight, regardless of the weather.

Before my sister Melgie passed, the state announced a subsistence emergency opening for Natives to legally fish for salmon, closing the next morning. Early to mid-June are favorable weather conditions for drying and smoking salmon. Any later into the season, and rain and insects will cause mold and infestations to ruin salmon. The day was Thursday, June 10. Subsistence fishing was open and would close Friday morning at 8 a.m. till 8 p.m. Sunday. This is window management, with a set amount of time to fish. I had no other choice besides poaching. If I fished against the regulations and got caught by the wildlife troopers, there would be serious penalties like garnishment of boat, motor, and gear if I was unable to pay penalty fines.

Subsistence fishing would be closed for three days. I needed at least one fish tote of salmon to start processing on my fish-drying rack. My family was ready. Before I left, Melgie found out fishing would be closed after she got off work on Friday, and she had been planning to fish on Saturday. Melgie worked with the summer school students and Friday was payday, and her family had no money to buy gas for the boat. Sunday night was too far into the future and the weather did not look promising for the next week. So I agreed I would get her a fish tote of salmon. This is what subsistence means: helping each other. Late Thursday night into Friday morning, I got two fish totes of salmon well before the 8 a.m. closure. At least 120 salmon can fit into a fish tote.

My family processed one tote of salmon because this was what could fit on our fish rack and was more than sufficient for our needs for the winter. Friday was hot and sunny, excellent weather for drying, but the other fish tote was left in the boat, ruined. In hot humid weather it does not take long for fish to ruin. Melgie was not ready, busy at work. Seething with anger I cursed the state manager and *their* regulatory rules as I threw the ruined salmon into the river and washed out my tote. We have no available ice machines or dog team kennels in any Lower Yukon community. And here our tribal organization wants to work with the state, and not as a member of the intertribal fish commission. Perhaps Natives should gather together on our side of the river and tell the state to go manage the salmon on the Mississippi River. Window harvesting gives me no respect for managers.

Other Natives have similar stories. It is hard to speculate how much salmon is wasted. It is a difficult Native custom to admit wasting of fish or wildlife. It is discouraging to see managers blind to the Native world and Native economics. I have contempt for managers who use harvest windows because they encourage wasting of salmon. King salmon have had to be thrown out because the weather was not favorable and ruined the drying process. This is counterintuitive to intensive management plans and efforts to conserve stocks of concern. ADF&G representatives falter when they try to explain what sustained yield means and giving Natives permission to fish at the same time to allow for some food security needs.

In all these years of fish meetings with state and federal managers, Native fishers never questioned the Whitehorse Rapids Fish Hatchery program of enhancing Yukon king salmon stocks with hatchery fish. In the past, about 150,000 hatchery-raised king salmon fry were released, and management has no idea of how much of an enhancement or impact these salmon have had on Yukon salmon numbers. This is a non-Native effort to manage Mother Nature. We can only look to our current numbers to determine whether these stocking efforts have worked or whether the released salmon is an overstocking oversight. Before these salmon fry were released, permission from Alaska Natives was never asked.

The Nunamiut Inuits were significant participants at the caribou co-management conference at McGill University. With Dene and Métis, these Canadian Natives were concerned about claims that the caribou numbers were in a perceived state of decline. Non-Native hunter reports and Canadian wildlife surveys indicated that populations were not as abundant as before. Stories of caribou succumbing to a flash flood and poaching of animals had everyone's attention. Efforts to restrict seasons and harvests were proposed. In response, the Natives argued that the caribou numbers were there but that they had migrated through different routes and wintering grounds, corroborated by a traditional ecological network with other Natives who live and observe these animals for food security. Maps and traditional migration routes and wintering grounds were identified, and cooperative efforts were addressed.

After the co-management conference, visiting two of my professors amid a livid crowd of Montreal Canadians and Boston Bruins fans, I cannot marvel the fact that this sport is a national event. Despite all the ice and snow in Native Alaska, hockey is not practical as a sport. The main Alaska Native sport is basketball—indoors, out of the cold, with no major gear investments. George Wenzel and Steve Cox were my instructors at the Center for Northern Studies; one is an anthropologist and the other is an archaeologist. Both had completed work and research on the Eskimo and we got into a discussion of the traditional Native word *muit*. At first, they had me confused about what they were trying to explain as they argued about what this word meant in the complicated language of Western academia. When professors talk like this, they have a secret language that tends to confuse people in general. Common phrases and linguistic associations help explain how Natives share the same attributes of the Northern Hemisphere as a part of our shared cultural lineage.

The Yup'ik name for Pilot Station is Tuutalgaq. When this name is used with *muit*, it becomes *Tuutalgaqmuit*, which means "people of Pilot Station." In Inuit, *Nunamiut* translates as "Eskimos" or "people of the land." Within Eskimo language, *muit* is universal and understood with similar meaning between Eskimo cultures. Between Athabascan and Navajo Indians, fluent language speakers also recognize similar words and linguistic associations that provide cultural significance of meaning. Because of these similarities between cultures that seem to be worlds apart, people of like minds think alike.

In Yukon River communities, I know of many Native dignitaries concerned about our issues and not enough entrepreneurs. Especially when fishery issues are passionately discussed and the eventual penalty only includes more restrictions. In early 1990, who would have imagined that masses of plastic pint-size drinking water could be marketed and sold as it is now. This same scenario should apply for Yukon River water. Suppose you were from the community of Fort Yukon or Eagle: step out your front door, dip a sterile bottle into the Yukon River, and try and sell it. Who would buy it?

I would. I am a commercial fisherman. This sample of dirty water would make me successful at catching salmon. If you were from the Lower Yukon community of Kotlik or Nunam Iqua and try to sell the river water collected from there, I would have no reason to buy it. The span of the Yukon River is more than two thousand miles. For salmon, there is a molecular difference between Lower and Upper Yukon River water.

24   John Paul Edwards (1971–2001)

"Looks like arms and legs," Peter whispered, and Tony nodded his head.

As we boated, we watched the monitor and tried to gauge our bearings every time we saw this shape on the screen. The light green hues indicate that it was not a hard object. We went a little farther downriver and slowly turned around for another look-see. To compensate for the current, Tony sped up his outboard motor until the picture on the screen cleared to a visual profile. This equipment is tricky. It took us some practice to gauge our boat speed to get a picture of what we saw on the screen. Every time we went upriver the river current gave an illusion that we were going too fast. We looked to the beach to visualize landmarks, clumps of trees, the distance out, the current ripples, and looked to the other side of the bank toward Pilot Station. We neared the spot where my brother Donald and I had run over someone's set-net when we were young. We saw the object again and Peter threw out a rock with string tied to several empty quart-size oil containers as a buoy. This was our marker.

We headed toward home watching the screen. Closer to the other bank, the river current picked up and we started losing the picture. I increased the gain and the power to clear some of the clutter. The river current was too strong and there was no bottom picture. The computer screen was a mass of red and difficult to read. We tried in grayscale and got the same results. The river current was too strong and fast for our ping rate.

After thirteen hours, we quietly conceded that it was time to go home. We found a likely spot and marked it. It was four in the morning and everything was quiet. We told search and rescue of where to concentrate search efforts. The picture on the screen looked like a body flailing on the bottom of the river. We went home thinking about the picture. It was etched in my mind and I had a hard time falling asleep. I felt restless.

Later that morning, search and rescue pulled out a log from near our marker. After ten days of looking, this was frustrating news.

John Paul Edwards, where are you?

≥

It is common to see young Native boys walking with guns. Everyone knows they are hunting. In the winter it is rabbits and ptarmigan, in the spring ducks and geese, and in the fall it is spruce hens. Many boys hunt with friends in their age group. In addition to improving marksmanship skills, many are fostering hunting partnerships. Kids who are most familiar with hunting and guns teach those who are not. In our villages, kids teaching kids gun handling is our only hunter safety program. Although ADF&G has a hunter's education and gun safety program, these services are not available in rural Alaska. Funds used for this program are subsidized from hunting license fees. For many of these boys, gun handling and learning to hunt are safety issues they take at their own risk. In addition to gun safety, one of the most important skills these boys learn is in making decisions. Learning from Mother Nature is unlike any school classroom. In a classroom, a wrong answer may give you a chance to do it over again. Learning from Mother Nature is not a lesson for novices; one mistake may be your last.

≥

May 22, 2001. Bruce and I were returning from geese hunting. The weather was quickly warming and conditions on the Yukon River did not look safe. There were darker colors on the river. Traveling at thirty miles per hour, we tried not to overheat our engines. At this time of year young hunters learn from seasoned hunters about traveling on the river. Learning about traveling in conditions like this is risky and especially dangerous for hunters who travel alone. As we reached the sandbar, we killed our engines and we agreed that we were done using our snow machines for the season. The ice on the Yukon River was not safe. Spring ice breakup was almost here.

May 24, 2001. After winterizing and putting away my snow machine, I listened to chatter on the VHF radio about hunters who needed help to pull out a snow machine stuck on the ice. The hunters were part of a search-and-rescue crew looking for John Paul Edwards, who had not been seen since yesterday morning.

Earl Samuelson landed his airplane at Pilot Station and picked up my brother Abe as a spotter to help look in the most familiar geese hunting sites and routes of travel. Until Earl Samuelson retired, he was the most recognized pilot in the Yukon Kuskokwim Delta. He was commemorated for his skills as a search-and-rescue pilot for the Alaska Department of Public Safety. That evening, Matty and I took our ATVs and drove to Qaskicaq, the tallest tundra hill near home. With binoculars we looked for any smoke or signal fires and listened to our portable VHF radio. Around midnight, the snow machine search parties and Earl Samuelson returned ... nothing.

On the morning of May 23, several of John Paul Edward's friends told him they were going geese hunting and asked if he wanted to come. For some reason, John was indecisive and not sure what to do. A few minutes after his friends left, John decided to go. He quickly prepped his snow machine and gathered his hunting supplies. When he left the village, this was the last anyone saw John or his snow machine.

Weather conditions had been warming, and the ice and snow were melting fast. In conditions like this, it is easy for fresh snow machine trails to look old after less than an hour in the sun. Snow machines are the only means of traveling in this part of Alaska. There are no roads for cars and trucks between villages. Every household owns at least one snow machine and trails on the river crisscross everywhere at this time of the year. Travelers familiar with freezing conditions of any river know certain areas usually do not freeze because of strong river currents or some other natural feature. If they do freeze over, these areas are the first to open or melt and avoid during spring snow machine travel. Experienced hunters know of these areas.

Of all spring ice conditions, needle ice is most dangerous and deceptive to read during certain light conditions or glare from the sun. For newly formed needle ice before spring breakup, the color is not a good indicator of its stability. It can fool the most experienced travelers. The hunters who needed the extra rope to pull out a snow machine had stopped to cool off their engines when one of their snow machines quickly sunk on top of needle ice. They were lucky one end of a ski was caught stuck on the edge of solid ice, and with the extra rope they were able to pull and recover the snow machine. These hunters are experienced in traveling conditions at this time of season. Snow machines have fallen through ice on more than one occasion.

May 25, 2001. The condition of the river ice was worse. Max Nicolai, a village public safety officer from the Kuskokwim River village of Kwethluk, was flown in to help coordinate the search. A search-and-rescue meeting recommended all snow machines be put away after yesterday's mishap. We did not want to look for anyone else. That afternoon, six of us gathered supplies and three canoes to ground search at more bird hunting sites, while volunteers dragged hooks and sinkers in broken patches of ice close to home.

Going upriver, we walked and dragged the canoes and paddled in deeper water between leads of ice. After sixteen hours and no evidence, we headed home or risked getting caught on the wrong side of the river during ice breakup. As we returned to the north side of the Yukon, the same side Pilot Station is on, our route was blocked by large sheets of ice. This part of the river is the base of the shale rock cliffs, and the ice had climbed thirty feet, creating unstable footing. Breakup was hours away. We stashed our canoes on high ground and walked an old path the three miles over the cliffs, where a cross is placed in remembrance of John Paul Edwards.

The Yukon River is murky and brown from all the mud, sand, and silt. The river water is not clear. The Yukon provides the best-tasting wild salmon in all of Alaska. Counting fish and extrapolating population estimates is the task of ADF&G Commercial Fisheries Division at the Pilot Station Sonar Site. The high-tech equipment used at the sonar site is complicated and not easily understood. Small portable fish finders and depth meters are commonly used by Native fishers. Almost every commercial fishing boat has portable sonar equipment.

Before the season startup, I called my supervisor and asked if they could bring out the side-scanner. It is portable sonar equipment rarely used but can provides an excellent picture of what is on the bottom of the river. In the past, we used this equipment to locate snags or tree stumps that some of our fishnets had gotten caught on. This can be frustrating; the sonar site has lost whole gillnet lead-lines to logs stuck on the bottom of the river, only to recover them later in the season when the logs are finally freed.

After use of the side-scanner was approved, local Natives Tony Hoover, Peter Joseph, and Nolan Joseph volunteered to help. We used Tony's boat with the transducer rigged to the side of the boat. Unlike a fish finder or sonar that echolocates fish and gives the depth of the river, the side-scanner paints a profile of objects on the river bottom or suspended in the water column. The trick to get a picture on the screen is that the scanner transducer or the boat has to be moving. This is similar to how a paper printer or copier works: When a copier works perfectly, it can duplicate what is on one paper onto another. If there is a paper jam, the duplication is a mess of lines and impossible to read. A sonar side-scanner, instead of using beams of light like a copier, uses pings of sound.

To test the equipment, Pilot Station Search and Rescue dropped an old snow machine body into a clear water lake inside First Slough, where the water was calm and the empty hull was not likely to drift away. Peter, Tony, and I had no idea of where it was. Our task was to find it, get familiar with the equipment and gauge, and try different boating speeds to differentiate what we could see on the computer screen. After searching for a half hour, we had a likely spot but it was questionable. The fact we overlooked was that hard surface on the bottom returns as a shade of red on the monitor. Softer objects like mud and silt return a picture in soft hues of green. The bottom of the lake in First Slough has rocks and gravel, so we were getting some hard signals that were difficult to interpret and made us unsure of the equipment. Although the equipment could allow us to view the picture in grayscale, the color and infrared pictures provide an easier differentiation between hard and soft objects. We thought we had found the snow machine hull; it almost looked like the right shape and size, but we were unsure.

We tried the Yukon River and boated upstream. The sand and silt bottom gave us some idea of what to look for. Our confidence boosted when an object on the bottom of the river appeared on the screen and amazed us. At low water level, this object would be visible, but at twelve feet of water, we could see on the screen the clear outline of an old empty oil drum standing upright and stuck halfway in the mud. The hard surface of the drum stuck in the soft mud painted this picture that would have been otherwise impossible to see. Later we were amazed to see truck-size boulders we had never known to exist in the deepest part of the river.

In 2003 Yukon River salmon were an issue of concern, and the fishery was declared an economic disaster. Disaster food relief was provided by the Food Bank of Alaska and several Anchorage-based organizations. In addition to canned vegetables, peanut butter, and dry goods such as rice, one item was a cardboard box of frozen Prince William Sound pink salmon. Each box included about ten whole salmon. Days later, there were many discarded fish boxes at the local community landfill with pink salmon still inside. Pink salmon is a major commercial fishery in the Prince William Sound and Cook Inlet. Despite food relief intentions, why these Natives just threw away pink salmon is not difficult to answer.

When many needs in the home are not met, there is less effort within the community to volunteer and support efforts for family health initiatives, fundraising activities, or education reform endeavors. There are no philanthropists in Native villages. Providing a free meal is more likely to encourage participants to attend a community meeting than providing the service to benefit the community. The reason that some service would be good for the community is not appealing enough to encourage participation. When food or other economic needs are in short supply, the needs in the home are recognized as a priority above all else. If the community can help with immediate assistance, Natives recognize that there is something special about living in small villages where everyone knows everyone.

In the United States, when economic conditions fluctuate between the extremes, living conditions in rural Alaska are taken for granted, with the assumption that such small economic niches are more likely to be protected than areas hardest hit by job loss and economic hardship. Although economic indicators and data from rural Alaska are not reliable sources for forecasting conditions of the economy months in advance, rural communities experience latent repercussions several months after economic crises, and recovery may take twice as long, if recovery ever occurs. One economic reality that is linked to this relationship is the cost of fuel. Regardless of fluctuating markets that determine the cost of fuel in mainstream America, the cost of fuel and energy in Native Alaska is always escalating.

During the 2003 Yukon River fishery disaster, Pilot Station tribe distributed the emergency food donation to every household. Although many used the rice, flour, and peanut butter as everyday staples, use of the Prince William Sound pink salmon depended on which household needed it. Yukon pink salmon is not unusual in Pilot Station and many have never been concerned for this fish. The Yukon pink is an odd fish. Some years Yukon pinks do not return and some years they return in such abundance that it is considered a nuisance to commercial and subsistence fishers. It is an odd fish, and managers have no idea what to do with it.

The Prince William Sound pinks were bright colored, small, and looked like trout. But the Yukon pinks in Pilot Station have already matured to their spawning physical features. This is a unique characteristic of all Pacific salmon. When salmon reach freshwater tributaries, the sleek streamline body starts to deform and change shape, their silver shine change to pastel colors, and huge teeth grow and protrude in every direction. They shapeshift into Franken-fish. Minerals and sulfites provided from ocean saltwater are not available in freshwater and this transformation occurs quickly in Yukon pinks. At this stage, the pinks are called humpbacks, and males are more pronounced and deformed in shape. Some Natives prefer the taste of Yukon pinks in this physical state. The humps are not made of meat but more gelatinous with fatty tissue, and the taste is unique. There is no market value for Yukon pinks. With their many teeth these salmon are easily caught in abundance in gillnets, and fishers cuss and throw this salmon back into the river. The Pilot Station Kwicauq Slough is alive when pinks return, and children play and gather to watch the salmon.

The Prince William Sound pink salmon fishery is a major industry with a developed hatchery stock program to help escapement. Through trial and error, the State of Alaska is learning the impacts of hatchery stock salmon and economic importance of all other salmon fisheries. Smallest of all salmon, the pink salmon's abundance has significant impacts on all five salmon stock and other wild resources that depend on feeder stock within every tropic level of the North Pacific and Bering Sea ecology. Millions of juvenile pink salmon are released, and the need for wild feeder stock to sustain these numbers is critical. ADF&G has no idea of the impact these "wild" salmon have to the marine ecosystem.

Lower Yukon residents do not prefer pink salmon. The traditional salmon preferred is the chum salmon. Unlike the rich content of kings, the chum salmon has a unique Yukon River flavor. It is most abundant and harvested in bulk, prepared in bulk, and stored in bulk. It is the main salmon dried and smoked as dry fish and a daily household staple. As dry fish, it is enjoyed any time of the day and easy to pack and carry in the lunchbox. It is comfort food. The Prince William Sound pink salmon discarded at the landfill have a taste unlike the rich flavors of Yukon salmon. The odd years when Yukon pinks do not return, there is no local concern or management effort to determine why this is so. In 2018 the State of Alaska declared the Prince William Sound pink salmon commercial fishery an economic disaster. What happened to all pink salmon expected to return that year is a mystery. The impact of this fishery is an indicator of things yet to come for all other Alaska salmon fisheries that depend on the marine ecosystem for feeder stock sources.

In 2020, 2021, and 2022, the Yukon River salmon season was a disaster. No commercial or subsistence fishing was allowed for the whole season. ADF&G has no idea of what happened to all Yukon salmon that were expected to return.

An aggressive instinct to hunt and provide families with food is in the nature of being an Alaska Native. For hunters and their catches, there is nothing more gratifying than to feed and share with family and community. Many experienced hunters have tamed this aggression, honed their skills, and recognize that making decisions is a risk for living the life we live. John Paul Edwards's family was given a critical reminder of the risks we take. Although the search-and-rescue crews looked in the most likely spots where John could have gone, there has been no evidence found of his passing. No one knows where he is. The side-scanner only gave us an idea of where he was not to be found.

Like stories of natural and spiritual phenomena of small villages, we heard later that winter of rumors from snow machine travelers from communities of the Lower Yukon meeting a bundled lone snow machine traveler telling them that he was the son of Duia and Pat Edwards of Pilot Station. John Paul Edwards was named after my young childhood friend John Paul. In 1971 John Paul was accidently shot during a ptarmigan and rabbit hunt with his young relatives.

Caution is not only important for safety. In Mother Nature, risks do not only affect the young and inexperienced; they also affect the elder and experienced travelers. We often hear of close lessons, but we do hear about lessons that are tragic after the fact. Several years before we lost John Paul Edwards, a local Native elder and experienced outdoorsman succumbed to the elements. In early winter 1999, Anthony Tony, locally known as 197, was found succumbed to hypothermia after his snow machine got bogged in slushy snow on a small stream used as a trail crossing. Mr. Tony was on his way to his hunting and trapping cabin where he collected a lifetime of stories. His moniker 197 was his call sign for the early CB and VHF radios used to keep in touch with family and communities. In winter of 2007 the village of Barrow also lost an elder hunter in a similar tragic situation.

25 ≋ River Ecology

"I shouldn't have cinched that knot!" Carl yelled to me. We were in the Yukon River and we watched the outboard motor sputter as the prop spun slowly to a stop. We floated downriver. The life vests kept us bobbing and the internal float pontoons kept the boat afloat, but still the twenty-foot boat looked awkward floating upside-down.

It was Father's Day, middle of June. The Yukon River was calm, the sun was shining, and there was no wind and clouds. It was a beautiful day and I looked forward to our family gathering plans to barbecue moose ribs after I got off work. Because it was a special day, I had agreed to work at the sonar site for half a day. After my afternoon shift, I helped my supervisor quickly move one of our markers on the other side of the river. This task does not take more than ten minutes, an easy quick chore we have done many times.

The Yukon River was picturesque. It was not meant to be an easy day. I grew up on this river and should have seen the warnings, but my supervisor was insistent and captained the boat. I was preoccupied with thoughts of barbecued moose ribs, a family gathering, and enjoying the view of Pilot Station from this side of the river. I love it. I did not realize my supervisor had taken the Yukon River for granted and tried to fool with Mother Nature. I felt responsible for this mishap.

In stunned surprise, I grabbed the steering wheel and gunned the throttle-shift full power forward. With the engine roaring, trying to get power to pull the thing out of the mud, it was no help—too late. I looked to the beach, the river current, and turned around to see my supervisor mid-air, jumping into the Yukon and abandoning me to the situation at hand. His outstretched arms and flailing legs are a vivid picture permanently etched in my mind. The motor was screaming, there was no safety splash guard, and water was gushing in over the rear transom. Roaring at full throttle, the one-hundred-horsepower outboard quickly sunk, and there was no tilt leverage and torque power for what I was trying to attempt. In seconds the bow of the boat was pointing into the air. The motor was helpless. The boat overturned and toppled swiftly with the pull of the river current. With seconds to pull the throttle into neutral I grabbed the port side of the boat rail and hung on as it toppled. In the water I kicked off the boat as we watched the propeller spin. The boat was overturned and we were in the cold Yukon. The motor gurgled, puttered, coughed, and died.

Awed with surprise, I laughed at what had just happened. As if humiliating us, the thing stuck in the mud pulled free and the boat floated downriver. Mother Nature smiled. The marker we had intended to move was a red buoy on a twenty-pound anchor to keep it in place. The buoy is a marker for reference. It was one hundred meters from the beach and our initial plan had been to move it closer to the beach because of the high water level.

On calm days it is easy to take the Yukon River for granted as something that can be mastered by novice people who do not live on the river. This was the same spot where my wife, Janice, and I had seen a whirlwind eddy pull in logs and floating ice bergs during spring breakup, long before Fish and Game ever set up their sonar site. When I first saw this eddy, it was not the motion that caught our attention, despite the sound of our boat motor, it was the roaring sound and cackling of ice being crushed. The logs and ice are swallowed whole and spit out among us, popping up from the river. The Yukon River has no sympathy. The river current flipped the Fish and Game boat as if it were a toy. Natives from Pilot Station heard what had happened and laughed at Fish and Game. It was excellent Father's Day weather.

"Information from this site was instrumental in setting our gillnet size restrictions by the board of fish in January." I commented this in the testimony of Gene Sandone at the 2010 Arctic Yukon Kuskokwim Regional Advisory Council fall meeting in Bethel. I was not pleased with what Gene had brought to the attention of the council members. Gene was a longtime retired ADF&G Yukon River employee working as a lobbyist and consultant for the Yukon Delta Fisheries Development Association, the CDQ program created for the Bering Sea. I was a council member for the AYK Regional Advisory Council, and we had an opportunity to question anyone providing comments. People who provide comments to the regional advisory councils have no obligation to do so.

At the January 2010 BOF meeting in Fairbanks, Lower Yukon residents opposed a proposal to reduce the king salmon gillnet size from eight and a half inches to anything smaller. People most familiar with Alaska fisheries were concerned about the king salmon size getting smaller. The concern is statewide in every salmon fishery, and to date a single cause has not been determined. There are many theories but no actual burning proof. There was a similar situation in the late 1970s, and many pointed to the gillnet size used by Lower Yukon Native fishers as the cause.

In 2009 the argument was the same: gillnet size is causing the kings to become small. The ADF&G Pilot Station Sonar and Emmonak setnet site helped provide river-wide salmon passage estimates. In 1997 ADF&G received federal funds to start another sonar project near the community of Eagle, providing enumeration numbers for Canadian stock salmon. A traditional fishwheel was used to collect salmon information. In January 2010 comments on a BOF proposal to reduce gillnet size include incriminating evidence of the three-year salmon data collected from the fishwheel as influential hard data that the king salmon were getting smaller. With no evidence to counter this argument many upriver residents were pleased with the BOF net size reduction.

At the fall AYK regional council meeting Gene Sandone provided an update of the 2010 Eagle fishwheel king salmon data. Gene was pleased to comment that the fishwheel had been moved farther out to the deeper river channel and was catching bigger kings, as if to say that this was proof the net size reduction is working and that we were getting larger king salmon, despite the fact that there had been no gillnet fishing for several years. Regardless of how deep the fishwheel was, bigger king salmon swim farther out in deeper water where the river current is strong and swift.

Although BOF made this gillnet size requirement, there is one salmon bycatch issue Pilot Station tribe continues to ask ADF&G management.

Many Alaska fishers are familiar with bycatch of king salmon by the Bering Sea trawl fisheries. As traditional fishers, my family harvests thirty Yukon kings and eighty chum salmon to dry as smoke salmon every year. This is something we learned from our parents as a traditional safe preservation method to make it last for at least a year. This is our food security. Since 1982 we have accepted the eight-and-a-half-inch state regulation as the legal net size to harvest all our kings and about half of our chum salmon needs, which is more than sufficient. The king and summer chum salmon arrive at Pilot Station about the same time. When we meet our king salmon needs, we are done, but when more chum salmon is needed, a smaller six-inch gillnet size is used to target chum salmon.

The Pilot Station Sonar test fish crew provides twice daily salmon fish deliveries to the community dock for residents to select fresh salmon, whitefish, sheefish, burbot, cisco, or pike. The test fish crew helps the community with fresh salmon when subsistence fishing is closed. Many residents have become dependent on these deliveries, including local teachers and their families. Every delivery is on a first come, first served basis. Usually, families who have access to fish boats and gear allow elders and families without fishing gear a first opportunity to select salmon out of courtesy. When there is no more salmon to deliver, many have to wait for delivery the next day or for permission from ADF&G to fish.

Catch per unit effort is not a kind phrase to Native fishers. When fishers use the eight-and-a-half-inch net, the number of chum salmon caught is enough to help traditional needs. But as the net size gets smaller to seven and a half inches, more variety salmon size is caught, including more chum salmon. I know I need thirty kings, so I expend as much time to catch this number, but the more I try to get kings, the more chums I get. Instead of 80 chums, I get more than 120. Subsistence fishing and commercial fishing are not allowed at the same time, so I cannot sell any excess. I give away as much as I can, but every subsistence family is fishing because ADF&G gave Natives permission to fish. Everyone has a similar excess situation, and the community is saturated with salmon; this is window fishing.

Pilot Station tribe tried to educate managers about this excess chum harvest and provide a recommendation about what Natives should do with the excess fish. One non-Native recommended throwing out the dead salmon, but this wanton waste contradicts ADF&G principles of sustained yield as management guidelines. Natives throwing away salmon and being charged with wanton waste is double jeopardy. ADF&G has given no recommendations for this excess harvest. When the community is saturated with fish and not every salmon is taken from the daily ADF&G fish tote, the test fish crew tosses this salmon into the river and records it as a loss. When permission is granted for Natives to fish with the seven-and-a-half-inch net size, subsistence fishers will keep kings and toss excess chum salmon into the ADF&G fish tote for them to toss into the river. We can only look at our current chum salmon returns and ask ADF&G what are they hoping to achieve.

The reason Lower Yukon Natives do not use fishwheels is that we do not need that much fish. We have no reason for maximum harvest limits; we have no dog kennels to feed. Families will harvest what they need, pending permission from ADF&G.

In fall 2010, after I reported an update of the AYK regional council meeting to my community, Pilot Station tribe sent a letter to Governor Sean Parnell requesting that the state either rescind the BOF net size reduction or provide a state recommendation on the incidental catch of summer chum salmon. In response Governor Parnell sent a letter explaining that the actions and decisions of BOF are based on the best scientific information available with the rationale that larger fish at the spawning ground provide greater productivity. This rationale has no scientific data to verify it, only anecdotal information. It is like saying the tallest people make the healthiest families. With no recommendation for the incidental harvest, Governor Parnell concluded that further investigation and a dedicated staff working together to gain a greater understanding of Yukon salmon would take time. The next five ADF&G managers lasted only a season before quitting and leaving ADF&G for good.

Although the state responded about gillnet size and incidental catch response with silence, we asked managers another question about the scientific language used by the staff and the layman's language understood by BOF. In Western science, genetics is universal accepted in everything scientific and is the basis of understanding life from biology, chemistry, physics, and so on. In fact, every high school student biology book has reference to Charles Darwin, the theory of survival of the fittest, and story of genetic drift. In any given population, a normal bell curve describes the phenotypical physical characteristics of individuals within the population. Height is one physical example: in our human population we have tall and short people, but most everyone is an average height. But our population is changing from short people to more tall people; scientists are familiar with this concept as genetic drift. The bell curve of population height is moving toward taller people. If managers keep using the argument that larger net size used by Native fishers is causing king salmon to become smaller, we should see this same scenario in similar salmon species harvested by the same Natives on the same river using the same methods. Everything in science needs sound reasoning to explain how it is compatible with human understanding of the laws of nature.

Pilot Station tribe asked the ADF&G manager whether the fall chum salmon were also getting smaller as a result of gillnet size. The king salmon size has been scrutinized by agency staff, saying that here is the proof, so it is a done deal. Following scientific theory, we should see similar results in like situations. One of the neat things about science is the results allow anyone to discuss the conclusions, and any number of conclusions can be drawn as long as the theory is sound.

Pilot Station Sonar Site has collected data on all salmon species since 1985; the fall salmon size contradicts this net size reasoning. If anything, fall salmon have been fished by Native fishers with longer commercial fish periods and consistent harvests with the same six-inch gillnet size. The fall salmon have been fished without prejudice. Since 2016 Native fishers have commented about the size and abundance of bigger fall salmon. All these fall salmon were larger; ADF&G has no explanation for this salmon observation. Perhaps time is necessary for these observations to become factual. Many Natives accept the claim that nature will do whatever it does when it wants.

In 1970 Pilot Station Natives experienced this similar phenotypic characteristic in the fall salmon size. Natives told ADF&G managers that larger king salmon were returning as a result of the salmon food situation in the Bering Sea. When fall salmon return bigger, the kings following in several years also return bigger. The lifespan of fall salmon is shorter than kings.' In 1980 Native fishers voluntarily agreed to reduce their net size to eight and a half inches to quell any intents of management to shut the fishery. In response, the 1982 BOF made this gillnet size a state regulation. ADF&G recorded consistent and phenomenal salmon harvests in the 1980s and allowed subsistence families to fish leniently. Native families met their king salmon food security and accepted the use of the eight-and-a-half-inch gillnet.

In June 2016 Lieutenant Governor Byron Mallot visited St. Mary's tribal members and overrode the ADF&G manager to allow subsistence king salmon harvests. In one drift, one lone St. Mary's fisher caught more than one hundred king salmon with the seven-and-a-half-inch gillnet during a time when all Natives were fishing at the same time. Even if Yukon king salmon numbers continue to be a stock of concern, excessive harvests make it difficult to determine whether escapement window management goals are working or if net size reductions guarantee larger king salmon size returns.

It is easy to take the Yukon River for granted during calm conditions. During stormy weather the Yukon can be menacing and may be better avoided. In 2003 two new teachers moved to Pilot Station, and they considered themselves an avid outdoor couple. They had an eighteen-foot aluminum boat with a seventy-horsepower outboard motor. One of the teachers' parents came to visit Alaska for the first time and the four went for a Yukon boat ride. The sun was shining, but the wind was blowing and the river rough with waves.

Upriver from Pilot Station, the river current and a perfect southwest wind create an aberration of waves that can fool novice boaters. During this condition, Natives will drive as close and slow near the shale cliff to avoid pounding of the waves and ride every crest with caution. The teachers and parents were riding this part of the river, and they were lucky a Native was watching and saw the boat topple and capsize. None of the four were wearing personal flotation vests. The Native quickly rescued the four as they were trying to hang on to the upside-down boat. River drowning is a major Alaska cause of death.

The waves on the Yukon are nothing like ocean waves where swells seem constant and usually move from one direction to another. It is common to perceive ocean waves as following a pattern or a vicissitude of rise and fall. In the Yukon, there is no such wave pattern. It is very much like whitewater, and the height can vary between four and seven feet. It is unexpected and a sober realization that more caution is necessary than previously thought. After the Native rescued the four from impending doom, he later admitted that he was very scared for his own safety and he was wearing his own flotation vest. This was the roughest river condition my cousin Ignatius Alick had ever boated, and only because it was an emergency response.

If there is one rule of thumb regarding boating conditions on the Yukon, it is this: if Natives are not going to risk it because of inclement weather, rough waters, or any Native reason, then it is safe to assume that most everyone should not risk it either.

26 ⪻ Civil Obedience

"Have you ever thought about joining the military?" the staff sergeant asked me as we were having dinner at the Black Rapids barracks. As part of a UAF outdoor survival class, we were in the middle of the Alaska Range mountains for winter survival training. Despite this training, I never joined any of the armed services.

Before anyone can join any U.S. Armed Forces, they must clearly understand the question of *conscientious objections*. Without a doubt, the answer to this way of thinking gives us safety in numbers. Mom told stories of blackout conditions during World War II, in which everyone was told to close curtains to keep homes in darkness. During the war period, creation of the Alaska Territorial Guard for homeland protection against enemy invasion gave a sense that Native Alaskans were participants in a massive war effort, but many had no idea of what it was all about.

There are oral stories of Natives buried near Pilot Station who were killed from bow and arrow wars with Yup'ik Natives from Chevak. Elders from Chevak have similar oral stories. No one knows why these wars were fought or whether any victory privileges were lost or won. Some rumors say shamans were involved.

In affluent societies the winning nation in wars and epic battles also captured the privilege to claim all resources—to own the people, timber to build homes, fish to feed families, soil to grow crops, and wildlife to claim and hunt at will. It is hard to imagine this scenario occurring in Native Alaska or communities within the Arctic Circle. Natives who inhabited these cold and bleak areas had no reason to covet what their neighbors had. No reason to start feuds or warfare to capture neighboring hunting or fishing areas where everyone shared similar hardships.

In the Northern Hemisphere and high altitudes such as the Rocky Mountains, there is one tree unique to the cold temperate environment. In the foothills and boreal forest of Pilot Station this tree is called the tamarack, also known as larch or lodge pole pine. It does not grow very big; it is skinny and scrawny and Natives have no traditional use for it other than as occasional firewood. Its green leaves are needles like those of spruce and pine, with a similar woody stem bark composition. Unlike spruce or pine needles, stiff and sharp pointed, Tamarack needles are fine and soft like those of fir, cedar, and hemlock. During summer, it is like a conifer and picturesque like a postcard Christmas tree. During fall it sheds its needles like aspen, birch, and alder and stays dormant during winter. Except for needles falling, this tree is similar to fir, but fir trees are not native to Alaska.

In southeast Alaska with the Forest Science Lab, I helped my supervisor, Paul Hennon, on an Alaska yellow cedar project. Paul is a forest pathologist and studies the forest diseases and microbiological pests that cause trees to be sickly and susceptible to insect attacks. It is ironic that these two pests will work together to wreak havoc on a single tree: one will weaken the immune system and the other will attack and feed on the host while it is trying to recover. Sounds like the federal and state relations over the Native. Nonetheless, Paul and Andy Eglitis, the forest entomologist who studies forest insects, work very well together to monitor forest pests of the Tongass National Forest.

Conifer trees are an important forest economic product. Every tree is susceptible to forest insect and disease attacks that cause the tree to rot and decay from within. Forest pests include insects such as spruce bark beetle and hemlock sawfly and diseases such as rusts, mistletoe, and conks. Serious outbreaks can affect large forest areas, leading to a quicker rate of decay and susceptibility to environmental influences such as groves of trees falling from strong winds and altered soil and stream stability. Mud slides and stream erosion all depend on a healthy forest ecosystem. It is all a natural progression of forest dynamics. In a forest ecosystem, change is a natural event. Some trees have developed more resistance than others and some have adapted evolutionary changes to survive a changing global environment. The fossil record shows how natural evolution is not considerate of those who do not adapt and at risk of existence. Is the tamarack one of these species at risk, or is it evolving to a changing environment?

In several Alaska yellow cedar study plots, FSL monitored the rate of decay and the rate at which the tree slowly dies. Every living tree is kept alive by the nutrients, water, and minerals from the soil and environment. Underneath every tree bark is the veins of the tree, the sap of life, and this provides the mechanism to transport food and sustenance of life to the leaves and overall growth. Every tree grows from the very tip of the stems to the girth of the column and leaves. In turn, the leaves provide energy from sunlight to make life possible with kinetic and chemical reactions at the cellular level, invisible to the naked eye. FSL intentionally killed cedar trees in several plots to study the rate of decay in comparison to other conifer and deciduous trees, trees that have leaves in all seasons and trees whose leaves fall before winter. When a tree's bark is damaged, the natural healing reaction is seepage of pitch to help cover the wound and allow sap to continue to provide sustenance around the wound. FSL girdled the bark off around the selected trees to cause the slow death. Sometimes, people who tie a clothesline around a tree and leave it for several years will slowly kill the tree.

Trees without vibrant defense mechanisms like natural vaccines did not stand as long as those without. Deciduous trees such as alder and willow did not last as long as birch. Conifer trees such as spruce and hemlock did not last as long as cedar. What was amazing about the Alaska yellow cedar is that they were girdled in 1950, and forty years later, remnants of these trees were still standing. Rugged looking and void of branches, trees as large as forty inches in diameter had outlasted smaller cedar. Remnants of the spruce and hemlock logs had fallen, decayed, and been absorbed by the earth as soil nutrients. For birch trees, the amount of tannin is the main defense against aging and insect and microorganism attacks. The cedar defense mechanism is similar and it is a longer-lasting tree. The natural preservatives of cedar give it longevity and make it a desired building material with structural strength and construction engineering features. In comparison, the tamarack does not have much of any engineering structural integrity or desired preservative characteristics, yet it continues to exist in a cold barren environment where conditions can be harsh and unforgiving. The tamarack is found in areas of southeast Alaska but not in abundance.

There is something about the Alaska yellow cedar that had Paul Hennon preoccupied with his profession since he was a young college student. For all insect infestations, the telltale sign of boring holes, insect trails, and sawdust are a quick indicator of the cause. Discolored and premature falling of leaves, including insect teeth marks on the leaves, provide a hint of what may be causing a tree to stress and decay. For most forest pest outbreaks, it is easy to assume the cause by tree species with symptoms of the outbreak. Spruce trees may be attacked by spruce beetles, hemlock trees by the hemlock sawfly, and alder leaves by the alder rust disease. Every tree has a host number of insects or diseases as potential threats.

If it were not for the longevity preservation characteristic of Alaska yellow cedar, the slow die-off might not have been noticeable. In southeast Alaska, huge swaths of cedar were slowly dying, and Paul Hennon started a lifetime career studying the cause. Cedar trees with dying white needles are visible in many areas, including areas on Admiralty and Chichagof Island and the base of Mt. Edgecumbe. For Natives in southeast Alaska, this tree is valuable for cedar bark canoes, totem poles, and building material. The engineering qualities, pliability, and strength are phenomenal. In a remote area on Prince of Wales Island, we found an old cedar dugout meant to be a canoe, but the log had cracked and ruined the effort. This remnant was two miles from the ocean and was built where the tree was cut.

In several areas, I helped Paul dissect cedar trees, cutting the column of the tree for obvious injuries, collecting needle and branch samples, digging and dissecting the roots and collecting primary, secondary, and tertiary root samples to try and determine cause of death. We collected micro and mycelium samples to determine whether the tree might be a host to a parasite feeding, as well as soil and associated vegetation samples. With support, assistance, and encouragement from other FSL forest pathologists, Paul tackled this as a forensic science expert.

A similar tree project was started to get an idea of what might be causing the cedar decline and to study the growth and health of tree species that may have succumbed to a similar die-off. In fact, one tree was thought to be extinct. For a long time, this tree was known only as a fossil tree, found in fossil rocks from when the dinosaurs roamed. What is unique is that this tree is similar to the tamarack and redwoods. It is known as the dawn redwood.

≥

At the outskirts of Petersburg is a state forest nursery. Dawn redwood seeds were planted and grown there as a pilot project. Dawn redwood and Alaska yellow cedar seedlings were transplanted to several mixed biomes to compare growth rates and monitor whether they can survive the southeast maritime forest. The dawn redwood leaves are soft and similar to cedar, except cedar is a conifer and the dawn redwood is deciduous and similar to tamarack. As a fossil tree, this tree had grown worldwide, and large fossil forest remnants are found in the Canadian high Arctic, at Elsmere Island, as well as Nunivak and St. Lawrence Island in Alaska. The first time I heard the intriguing story about the dawn redwood was at this nursery.

Charles Darwin was an explorer of the natural world, collecting, identifying, and naming species in nature and others lost and found in the fossil world. Fossils of dawn redwood have been found with those of dinosaurs and other extinct species. For a time, the dawn redwood was believed to be extinct. During the Korean War, a U.S. soldier was crawling wounded on the forest floor when he picked up branches and leaves of this unusual tree and tried to recall what it was. When this soldier realized that this was a live sample of a fossil tree, it gave him every reason to make it out alive. Hobbling with a branch and leaf sample inside his blood-soaked shirt, the soldier lived to show other botanists and academics what he had found. After the war was over, it took several years of searching for where the soldier had been wounded and found the tree sample. It turns out that this tree was growing only in a valley forest in this one remote province of China and nowhere else. This was the first story I heard of this tree, and after my own research, I found out my co-worker had embellished the story of how it was found to present the significance and handle each seedling with reverence and care.

In a similar project with the Fairbanks State Division of Forestry, I helped plant Kantishna River white spruce seedlings in several boreal forests near Fairbanks. The desired traits of Kantishna River white spruce include uniform stand composition of strait taper trees and consistent seasonal growth rate. When we collected Kantishna River spruce seeds for planting, the three of us started by collecting individual spruce cones on the forest floor. After some time doing this backbreaking chore, we found it easier to raid squirrel caches and collect bushels at a time. At an airplane hangar, we spread out the cones to dry and open. With a hand-crank drum tumbler made of chicken wire, we tumbled the cones to collect the seeds. The seeds of this vibrant native species were planted in recently clear-cut forest. Unfortunately, it was discouraging several years later when a natural forest fire ravaged the seedlings. Forest fires are a natural ecological event.

Loss of forests as a result of insect infestations is unavoidable. In Alaska, spruce beetle infestation in areas such as Glacier Bay National Park and the Kenai Peninsula have destroyed acres of spruce forests. Ecological events such as forest fires and insect outbreaks are elements of nature and it is not unusual for the two to work in tandem. Dead-standing spruce-beetle-damaged trees are susceptible to large forest fires, and trees damaged by forest fires are potential hosts for insect and forest disease outbreaks. The Alaska yellow cedar's decline may be a result of a changing global environment, and it is unfortunate for these trees to succumb. Nonetheless, efforts to monitor and determine the cause of the decline must not be set aside without first learning and examining all evidence with skills of a forensic scientist. Stories of dawn redwood and tamarack in remote harsh environments provide significant evidence of global climate change and forest succession. As a result, it is difficult to accept climate change as a result of manmade development of industry. All data of climate change as a result of humans is anecdotal or insignificant compared to evidence of catastrophic events such as a major meteor strike.

Use of global thermonuclear weapons for terraforming land masses has been rumored in Alaska. One story was of Cape Thompson and Project Chariot, where use of a nuclear device was proposed to create a deep-sea port. Elders heard about Hiroshima, Japan, as a significant

World War II event and were familiar with stories of nuclear weapons. Weapons of mass destruction tend to heighten worldwide issues and discussion of fear. One environmental concern in 1960 was the theory of nuclear weapons creating nuclear winter and global temperature cooling. For common Natives, it was a god-fearing tabernacle story of a colder climate. Nonetheless, this nationwide story initiated public opposition to nuclear devices. In 1980 stories of global warming brought similar public support for banning CFCs and mass smoke and carbon pollution affecting the earth's ionosphere and ozone. It is an accepted theory that the mass extinction of dinosaurs was a result of a global ecological event caused by a meteor strike. The dawn redwood witnessed this time period. That this tree exists in a small forest valley is a favorite story among botanists. The slow demise of the Alaska yellow cedar is evidence of a non-catastrophic event.

In Pilot Station, the tamarack is not a dominant tree and will not be found in a forest stand with other tamaracks. It is widely scattered among the tundra foothills where spruce and birch forests are dominant. Pilot Station is the westernmost extent of the range of this tree; it is not unusual to find one tamarack every square mile or so.

In Alaska there is another plant succession taking over and replacing tundra. Many Natives have old family photos with backgrounds of tundra, brush, and trees as reference to this natural succession of a changing climate. In Kashunuk Slough, between Pilot Station and Chevak, are the old village sites of Chakaktolik and Owl Village. This area of Alaska has no significant manmade impacts. These old villages are favorite campsites for spring geese hunting and summer berry picking. In the sixties, boating along Kashunuk Slough, we used to see tundra hillsides and berry patches accessible from the beach. Now, there are many areas where willow, alder, and legume grasses have overgrown and replaced tundra.

The tundra is a natural biome of a cold barren desolate land with extreme weather conditions, cool temperatures, and permafrost. Brush and grass growth is best associated as a warmer temperate world. This is all evidence of a natural succession of climate. Every time I travel and check on abundance of berries, there is one legume plant that is evidence of a warmer temperate biome. It is a plant indicator of environmental change and loss of tundra plants, moss, and berries. Although willow and alder brush are abundant along corridors near rivers, streams, and waterways, this growth of brush is the edge where brush meets tundra, where tundra meets soil. This keystone plant is the foxtail grass. This grass is not a major plant that grows after a disturbance; this plant will slowly creep, grow, and help take over tundra. The unusual feature of foxtail grass is a brushy tip with soft prickly barbs where the seeds of the plant are housed. The seeds are not like pollen or winged like spruce cones. The foxtail grows on corridors commonly used by animals. As the plant matures, the foxtail barbs attach to fur and clothing, and this is how the seeds are dispersed.

As the foxtail grows, soil is developed with less humus than tundra, with a natural change in rate of decay. As this succession transforms tundra to organic soil matter, plants that favor soil grow with taproots downward and outward. Tundra is a mass collection of moss, lichen, and roots that mesh together as a living, breathing organism. Tundra contains more humus than organic and started to grow when the ground layer was permanently frozen. In turn the tundra helps create and maintain permafrost. The foxtail is a pioneer plant of a developing soil.

As soil develops, nutrients and organic layers provide sustenance for brush and legume plants. With this trend, the tundra characteristic of a cool temperate world creeps farther from traditional berry-picking sites near the top of the riverbank. When we traveled to pick berries, my parents often talked of these changes and areas where they used to pick berries when they were young, and how much farther we now have to travel to find salmonberry-picking sites.

Imagine stories of urban sprawl and changes to our natural world. Try as we might, we cannot hold this back.

27 ⪜ Sense of Time

"The people who need to hear this are here," the elder told the event coordinator as we waited for more people to come into our community city hall. We were twenty minutes behind schedule. There were more elders present. The high school students were nervous because they knew the elders and they were here to talk about the school Natural Helpers program.

⪜

A Wrinkle in Time is a favorite book I read while commercial fishing. When I started fishing with Uncle William, he smiled every time I went to the bow of his boat and took out a paperback book. I started out as a deckhand when I was ten years old. Uncle William had an eighteen-foot wooden boat with a twenty-five-horse outboard. Twenty-four-hour commercial fishing was normal. After the first two or three commercial openings, the excitement of driftnet fishing turned monotonous—unless we were catching lots of fish, which was fun and exciting. When the weather was calm and dry, reading a paperback made time entertaining. During fishing season there was no such thing as summer school and teachers to assign homework. As an elementary school teacher in Pilot Station, my sister Louise had a large collection of paperback books for anyone to borrow. I was reading for fun. The idea of a tesseract fascinated me.

It is often taken for granted that any Alaska commercial fisher can make money from catching and selling fish. Pilot Station has fifty-four commercial fishers who can legally catch and sell Lower Yukon salmon. Before dip-net commercial fishing, the average income was seven thousand dollars for the season. With the annual Alaska Permanent Fund dividend, this is the yearly income for many fishers. With fishing expenses such as boat, motor, fuel, gear, and supplies compared to the cost of living in the Kusilvak area, this income is dismal compared to any full-time job. Many fishing families are recipients of welfare and social service programs.

Fifty-four commercial fishers is a deceptive number. Deckhand helpers and families look forward to season openings and a chance to earn money to pay past-due and immediate bills or to get electricity hooked up again. Some fish to restock freezers with salmon.

There is something about fishing that makes some fishers better than others. People who do not participate do not know that some commercial fishers catch more fish and get paid a little more than others. Seven thousand dollars is an average; some make more and many make less. Everything is based on how much fish one catches, especially in a river system where every fisher is required to use similar gear and to fish at the same time.

The change from a gillnet fishery to a dip-net fishery is a recent gear restriction. At one time the maximum net depth for eight-and-a-half-inch net was 60 mesh deep. In 1980 concerns from non-locals that this deep mesh was catching too much big fish made Native fishers agree to reduce net depth to 45 mesh. At this time, commercial fishing periods of thirty-six- to seventy-two-hour openings were not unusual. BOF made the 45 mesh a regulation requirement, and ADF&G started to issue shorter commercial fishing times with the intent that shorter periods would allow more salmon escapement. As a result, Native fishers adapted and became proficient at catching fish. But what was unusual was that more commercial fishers were catching as much fish despite the difference in gear requirement and time allotment. In 2019 most gillnet openings in Pilot Station were restricted to three hours or less, and many fishers were catching as much salmon despite the time limit.

Fishers are happy when catching fish. In 2012, when ADF&G recommended use of dip nets for commercial fishing, Natives' opposition and reluctance to change gear went ignored. The managers are not there to please anyone. The dip-net fishing has become a niche fishery method and changed the way fishers perceive fishing times and success. Time management and location of the main pulse of salmon became harvest guidelines for Natives who live on the river. Natives call ADF&G daily to find out what time fishing is allowed. The last commercial Yukon salmon fishing season was in 2019, and commercial dip-net opening was allowed ten hours a day, five days a week. One question ADF&G frowns on is "What time do salmon enter the river?" Elders familiar with Mother Nature know this time of day and have passed this knowledge to successful commercial fishers.

≷

The Yukon River Drainage Fisheries Association is a river-wide organization addressing salmon concerns. It is not unusual for recommendations to reduce fishing efforts to help conserve Canadian salmon escapement. Although many assume the first pulse of king salmon enter the river as mainly Canadian stock and mostly small males, efforts to restrict fishing to allow this escapement are counterintuitive to conservation. Every year, an effort to conserve the first pulse is a priority. If they are mostly small and males, why members recommend conserving the first pulse and encourage harvests later in the season when the salmon are mostly female and larger contradicts principles of sustained yield. Allowing female salmon to reach spawning grounds is more productive. The rationale to protect the first pulse because they are king salmon is arbitrary.

In July 2009 the state issued an emergency order requiring fishers to release incidental-caught king salmon during chum commercial fishing—an example of classic actions the state has administered over the years. Although the state says that actions to conserve king salmon are necessary to allow commercial fishing, this creates and encourages wanton waste of king salmon as the only alternative. None of these managers have ever fished following regulation guidelines, and this management approach for conservation is impractical to sustained yield principles. In 2009 Yukon king salmon numbers were a critical concern, and sonar numbers were dismal. Marshall Natives had already harvested kings, and the state emergency regulation required commercial fishers to release all kings. As a Native, it is hard to release a limp lifeless salmon caught in a fishnet.

The ethics of catching fish is different between subsistence and sport fishers. A sport fisher may release a fish and fulfill a thrill of catching, but when the state pounds a fist and requires the Native to do the same, this requirement is against Native ethics. Native ethics is to respect all wild resources as a traditional management doctrine. During these trying times with the state and regulations that always change, elders went through a difficult period adjusting to regulations and the values that continue to redefine culture and respect.

The Yukon River is immense. It is a huge river. I don't know how many times I can say this and still fathom the truth of its size. Although the recent salmon declines have raised many concerns, subsistence fishers are still catching fish, commercial fishers are still catching fish when they can, and sport and personal-use fishers are somewhat content. This historical data of Natives' catching fish since statehood is hard proof of a sustainable fishery. The Yukon salmon is not listed as an endangered species.

The basic function of a gillnet is to hang loose in the water and let fish swim into it. In shallow water, eight feet or less, a long-depth net has different dimensions than a shorter net. Depending on the rate of the current, a longer-depth net is slack in shallow water and creates a different curtain as the river deepens. Whether that is good or bad depends on the fisher. It is common for people who have never fished to assume every fisher practices the same methods and is just as successful as the next. This perception changes when Kenai River fishers fish shoulder to shoulder. Although a fishwheel may not seem as effective as a gillnet, it does matter where in the river the contraption should be placed to be most effective.

In the Upper Yukon River, the ADF&G Eagle Sonar Site use a fishwheel to collect salmon data to help monitor the condition of the fishery. Although the fishwheel is a traditional Native innovative harvesting technique that sustained the people and communities for generations, the fact that this method is acceptable as a sampling collection method is ironic. Fishwheels do not extend all the way across the river, and a partial weir helps channel the fish traffic from near shore, but the fish that swim in the deepest river are not sampled.

While working at the Pilot Station Sonar Site, I witnessed one of the largest kings caught for sampling not in the eight-and-a-half-inch mesh but in the two-and-a-half-inch. This small net size is meant to sample cisco and little whitefish. The largest king was caught on the little protruding cartilage of the upper lip. Larger fish are likely to be caught on smaller nets than smaller fish are to be caught on larger mesh. It is easy for small fish to swim through bigger nets. Commercial fishers makes money pound per pound, where size is not a factor. Granted, a large fish weighs more than a small fish, but small fish are appealing if non-fishers argue that larger fish are not as plentiful as before. A dollar per pound is the same value to the big and little king salmon; size is not a factor.

Pilot Station Sonar Site uses six gillnet mesh sizes to collect fish samples. During heavy salmon runs, smaller net sizes are fished for a shorter length of time relative to larger nets because smaller nets catch more fish regardless of fish size. One requirement for collecting CPUE data is timing of the drift. During heavy salmon runs, a five-and-a-half-inch mesh catches more fish than a seven-and-a-half-inch net for the same amount of fishing time. Logically, the five-and-a-half-inch mesh catches more variety of fish as chums, kings, and sheefish. If smaller net mesh allows commercial fishers to harvest a broader range of sizes and more salmon pound per pound, fishers are happy.

After a good fishing, fishers will wash the slime and fish scales from their boat. Something a little clean is more appealing. The practice of washing fishnets differs between fishers, and whether they use a household detergent or not varies. It is common to use Pine-Sol to wash nets, but local fish buyers have discouraged fishers from using this as a detergent.

All Alaska salmon are anadromous, meaning the salmon spawn and breed in fresh water and live their adult life in saltwater, in the Bering Sea and Pacific Ocean. For managers and ecologists, this is described as a complex life cycle. As mature adults, the salmon return from the ocean to the very same tributaries in which they were born to spawn a new cycle of life.

Many fishers recognize the practice of using bait as a lure for catching fish. It is common with rod and reels and a hook, line, and sinker. Some fishers prefer fake lures over bait. Fake lures are not as messy. And some fishers like to use bright shiny flashers to get the fish's attention that food is right here. Every fisher is different. Unfortunately, using bait or flashers is a tactic that will never work for salmon in a dark, silty river system. Unlike Atlantic salmon that can spawn several life cycles, once Pacific salmon enter a freshwater system, they tend to stop feeding and eventually they die. It is a natural, important cycle of life for the way salmon have evolved. As part of growing up on the river, the main purpose I remember for fishers washing their nets was to keep the smell of fish from being overpowering.

Every fisher is different. A clean net and boat are more appealing than smelling like fish all the time. I remember Uppa Walter Kelly practiced things differently with his net. As I fished with Uncle William, I noticed Dad practiced the same things as Uppa Kelly. Dad picked a certain plant from a certain river tributary and rubbed, soaked, and scented his nets with this smell, not necessarily to mask the fish smell, but as an attractant to lure and catch more fish with this pungent flowery smell. It worked. This smelly plant attracted salmon to the net.

In addition to practicing subsistence fishing, I am a commercial fisherman. As a subsistence fisherman, I have a vested interest as part of my culture. As a commercial fisherman, I have a monetary interest. The future of this fishery will always be a concern for me, my family, and every fisher in my community.

As one of the largest deltas in the world, the Yukon River has a large drainage basin. For people who have never seen it, know that the Yukon is dirty with silt and sand. It is impossible for salmon to see more than a few feet. With water from all tributaries, tons of gallons of water flow hourly and daily. In theory, the salmon use their sense of smell to guide them back to the same rivers in which they were born to breed again. In the Lower Yukon, the water from every tributary is mixed; therefore, the concentration of water from any single tributary is diluted and not as concentrated as river tributaries closer to the source.

In Pilot Station, the most diluted concentration is Canadian water. The plant Dad collected and the fragrant smell he soaked into his net made a source of smell for salmon to help guide them back to their spawning site. With this same thought, here is another scenario. Suppose you became an entrepreneur and sold a bottle of Yukon River water. In an earlier chapter, I said I would buy a bottle of Yukon water from farther upriver, as at Fort Yukon or Eagle. Not to drink or quench thirst, but to catch more fish. If I soaked my net with this river water, the salmon swimming in Pilot Station would smell this strong concentration, get excited, and know where they are going. The fish that spawn farther upriver have a long journey to get to the other side of Alaska. The best-kept fishing secret is to keep others second-guessing. This is what fishing is all about.

What time do fish enter the Yukon River? Since the dip net is now primary gear for chum salmon commercial fishing, Natives have adapted, and those most successful incorporate traditional ecological observations. One benefit of observing Mother Nature is that patterns and sequences of ecology become clear. Fish are not like people who go and travel anywhere and everywhere; fish, like all wildlife, are creatures of habit. All salmon stick together as a school of fish and travel together to their spawning ground. Regardless of the time of day, ADF&G allows fishers to fish, and as long as they are fishing within this school, catching fish is guaranteed.

When ADF&G first announced dip-net commercial fishing, many Natives were fishing at the sonar site because we know this area always has salmon. We were mad at Fish and Game for restricting gillnets. As protest, more than twenty fishing boats crowded the ADF&G test fish boat and rendered the sample collection method questionable. ADF&G managers implored the Natives to allow the test fish crew to accurately collect fish samples. As a result, the next commercial fish announcement included language excluding the sonar test fish site, with a three-hundred-foot buffer zone. Anyone fishing within this zone was warned of possible citations and garnishment of fishing gear and possible closure of the fishery. ADF&G was adamant and would not change this new fishing method.

Realizing this, fishers talked and elders reminded Natives about traditional ecological knowledge and times when Natives caught fish efficiently before the influence of ADF&G management.

Unlike creatures of habit who go to work every morning at 9 a.m., wild animals take advantage of natural ecological events to minimize hardships and expend as little energy as possible. With this strategy, salmon enter the Yukon River as a school of fish during high tide times. Unlike chronological order and time sequencing, ADF&G is adamant about collecting fish samples at a certain time of day. Regardless of where the main salmon pulse is, Pilot Station sonar will sample test fish at 9 a.m. and 5 p.m., similar to every river-monitoring site.

High and low tide occurs every day, twice a day, every morning and every evening. As high tide enters the river, salmon will expend as little energy as possible and swim with the current with the least drag resistance. The main school of salmon will enter the river with the incoming tide and favorable tailwind conditions to minimize energy expenditures. Natives know the west wind and incoming high tide are favorable for large pulse of salmon to enter the river. The most successful fisher will follow and fish over this pulse.

How fast do salmon swim up the river?

28 ⤜ Lessons of Humility

"No, come up here and dance," John Pingayak told the audience member. John used his hands to shoo away the two university security guards standing side by side to block the young Native and his erratic behavior.

Traditional Eskimo dancing events are excellent entertainment. At the 1983 annual UAF Festival of Native Arts, John Pingayak and the Chevak Traditional Yup'ik dancers were a crowd favorite. In one skit, the troupe had a member in the audience who started pointing and yelling at the singers and dancers and behaving erratically. As part of the repertoire, the dancers danced and singers sang and the Native audience member started to raise his voice, yell more loudly, stagger, and become belligerent. Becoming brave . . . being a drunk Native. The sound of the drums triggered the Native to his part. The drunk started to dance any old way. Audience members start to cringe, shyly look away. A disgrace, this is embarrassing. Volunteers started to intervene. The man was getting too loud for the audience to enjoy. Minutes later, two campus security guards tried to usher the drunk Native out. It was all convincing until John Pingayak told security that everything was okay and motioned the Native to the stage. The drunk Native danced and sang and security continued to keep a watchful eye.

In every culture, alcohol abuse by a few members of the culture creates a broader negative image. As in the Prohibition era, alcohol prohibitions in rural Alaska create bootleggers who sneak in bottles of hard liquor and sell them at ten times the Anchorage and Fairbanks market value. Some Natives pay the bootleggers exorbitant prices. Local homebrew alcohol is common, but this alcohol is not distilled in any way. Addressing alcohol abuse is a more daunting task than creating fish and wildlife regulations. Mix the two together and the concoction created is a volatile, sensitive Native issue. The drunk Native played a skit with the Chevak dance group, and John Pingayak was familiar with the impact of alcohol in rural Alaska.

John was also familiar with our story of teasing cousins.

≥

Over dinner at the cook tent, Carleen and I tried to keep a straight face as Alex apologized to our supervisor about missing work. It was my entire fault. Carleen and I started to giggle and laugh. We couldn't hold it in anymore.

In Alaska Native cultures, teasing cousins or teasing other Natives is a social custom that recognizes the friendship, even though laughing at our differences is something outside cultures may not see as appropriate or socially acceptable to their way of life. It is all fun in nature when Natives make fun of other Natives as teasing cousins. Teasing cousins know each other. Someone non-Native teasing a Native may be offensive or racial.

People tend to think alike when they have grown up in similar situations, unique from other places. When a culture is large and diverse, sensitivity issues are not as serious as in small cultures enclosed and protected within their own realm. Mainstream culture has been desensitized to sensitive issues, and making light of these situations is fun and exciting entertainment—a reason for viewers to stay up and never miss an episode of late-night talk shows. When the masses gather every issue is game; any person and every culture is an open target for entertainment. The more successful a person, the more exposed they are in news media, the more likely comedians are to make jokes of their behavior or existence. We've grown to see it as acceptable that laughter and making fun of people is good medicine for the soul.

Carleen and I tried to keep a straight face as Alex apologized; we had teased him good. Alcohol and Natives are not good companions. In every culture this is true. We had picked up Alex at the boat dock and returned to the Yukon sonar site; today was his day off for the work week, and yesterday evening he had been invited to a party. It is not hard to hear village rumors of who is partying where and with whom. Before we picked up Alex, I told Carleen not to say anything and just to play along; I had heard Alex was partying and we were going to play a trick.

Carleen and Alex are people like me. I relate to them and can tease them about our differences. They are both Yup'ik. It is not offensive for us to tease each other about alcohol. Recognizing someone we know as hungover and buzzed from the night before is fair game, but playing the same trick on a stranger would be offensive and rude and may include overtones of racism or general dislike of that person.

≈

"Alex, where have you been? I've been covering your work shift today. How come you missed work?" I asked.

"I didn't miss work. Today's my day off."

"No. I covered your work shifts today. Yesterday was your day off."

"What! No. Today's Saturday. Today's my day off."

"No. Today's Sunday. We've been calling for you. They said you were drunk. You've been drunk for two days."

≈

We worked for the ADF&G Yukon River Pilot Station Sonar Site. Working for the state includes excellent pay and benefits unlike any mediocre job. During the off-season, the unemployment benefits were incomparable and exceeded the minimum hourly wage of the federal income guidelines. For me it was beneficial to be unemployed during the winter, receiving a comfortable biweekly unemployment check that was comparable to my wife's paycheck from working long hours at our only local elementary school.

In a 1997 ADF&G BOG meeting in which all governor-appointed and legislature-approved board members were collecting public information about hunt issues sensitive to Natives, board member Ron Somerville implied that Native participants who were providing sensitive testimony might rather be drinking than attending the meeting. Ron Somerville asked the Alaska Natives if they didn't like beer. Many Natives were offended. Regardless of ethnicity, I know I can offend many white people if I stereotype all gussak as the same.

It is generally accepted that making fun of people is not acceptable when issues of alcohol are involved. Recognizing taboo as taboo and avoiding ridiculing certain issues are community lessons nurtured where issues and constraints are similar. I relate to hardships many Natives endure as everyday issues. When anyone is selected to serve with public authority, insensitively addressing such issues challenges anyone to provide public testimony. As a result, it is easy to assume all ADF&G board members think the same as Ron Somerville. If state officials had thought or said they were different, an immediate reprimand would have been convincing. Somerville did apologize for his remark, but it is unfortunate that board members stereotype all Natives as similar to each other.

Native elders had a challenge with this mentality. When Ron Somerville moved to Alaska, it was not unusual for Native representatives to attend Fish and Game meetings where agency staff served alcohol. Perhaps if this was still allowed, Natives would be happy to attend and provide testimony on every fish and game issue.

The intimidating remark by Ron Somerville and presence of those who think alike makes it challenging. Include the wildlife troopers who enforce these regulations, it is easy to see the relationship of fear and trepidation Natives associate with the State of Alaska. If there is one thing we share, we often look to history and see similarities in many of our current situations. If you want a quote of inspiration relevant to any situation, it is easy to find one in the deep archive catalogs of the Library of Congress. *Oderint dum metuant.* I believe it was a favorite Latin phrase of Roman emperor Caligula. *Let them hate, so long as they fear.*

In June 2009 Lieutenant Governor Sean Parnell signed an emergency order prohibiting the sale or possession of Yukon king salmon during commercial salmon fishing. The concerns for king salmon were at their peak, and conservation efforts had not worked despite the efforts of those who claimed to be managers. The treaty obligation with Canada on the number of kings to cross the border was projected to fall short, allowing no subsistence king salmon harvest.

Before this emergency order, incidental-caught king salmon were allowed to be kept as subsistence during commercial summer chum fishing. Fishers know how much salmon is needed until the next season, and if their own personal needs are met, they will share with others who have no chance to harvest salmon. This is a standard, common Native practice. The commercial harvests allow for some to meet their food security needs, and usually managers and commercial processors knew this but overlooked it, because any time serious prosecution is undertaken, Natives tend to stick together and create civil disobedience that managers cannot directly address. Wildlife troopers cannot take action based on hearsay. The subsistence fishing event in Marshall supports this claim. Even though the state had created maximum sustained yield conservation measures supported by the Intensive Management Act of 1994, the recognition that there are no other options for Native food security will always be an issue to address.

As soon as this emergency order was issued, ADF&G announced a commercial fish opening, and all king salmon caught had to be released. For people who do not live on the river, actions like this create a conscientious duty of stewardship; conservation efforts have been taken and guilt has been absolved. This action allows fishers to catch salmon to sell as an economic opportunity and requires that wild critters of concern must be released to help replenish the stock. Canadians tied with the Yukon River Salmon Treaty and Yukon River Panel were pleased that the state had taken restrictions to meet obligations of the agreement. If any fisher was caught with a king salmon, sanctions would be harsh and the whole fishing fleet could be closed. The commercial fish-buying companies reminded fishers of this and that the state was taking this action to help, otherwise no commercial fishing would be allowed. As soon as I read the emergency order, I was furious. As a commercial fisherman I called the manager who was based out of Emmonak for the summer to reconsider whether fishers could keep king salmon for subsistence.

Without options, I told the manager that I was not going to release kings. I was going to deliver king salmon to the ADF&G Pilot Station Sonar Site. For Native fishers CPUE is not a kind word; commercial gillnets do not discriminate what is caught, regardless of net size. The first reaction of any critter caught in a trap is to fight and get free. This is the same for fish caught in gillnet, and the more the fish fights, the more entangled it gets. It is common to catch fish with gillnet scars from previous entanglements. The name of this net has a meaning. The fish are caught on the gills, the only breathing apparatus that provides oxygen to the lungs. If the gills are damaged, survival is at risk, and succumbing to these injuries is eminent.

Catch per unit effort is a statistical sampling method ADF&G uses to help monitor passage estimates. At Pilot Station Sonar, all five wild Yukon salmon are caught and monitored. The test fish method is the same as the drift gillnet fishery used by Native fishers. CPUE is real-time data that incorporates the net size, the amount of time the net is in the water, and the number, size, sex and species of fish caught. As part of this procedure fish scales are collected to get the relative age of the salmon. All things being equal, it is a liberal sampling procedure and accepted as an agency-wide method. Used with sonar counts that cannot differentiate fish species on a computer screen where each blip is a fish, the test fish data is used to extrapolate the number of blips to assume the kind of fish.

If 20 percent of test fish catches are kings, then it is assumed that 20 percent of the sonar blips are kings that day. But unlike ADF&G CPUE, where the average length of gillnet time in the water is six minutes, the commercial fisher's gillnet time varies between forty minutes to two hours. Commercial fishers are there to catch fish, and the more fish caught, the more economic return for this effort. These fishers have a vested business interest, like a for-profit corporation. It is not a catch-share or quota program, and no commercial catches are shared among the fleet. Each fisher is there for themselves and their families.

Unlike when Donald and I fished for two hours as juveniles, commercial fishing is not the same as it once was. I am a commercial fisherman, and my average length of gillnet time in the water is fifty minutes. The longer the net is in the water, the more fish I can catch. Fifty minutes compared to six minutes is a significant difference. As I slowly pull in my net the fish have lost all hope and are limp with exhaustion from fighting to get free. After being entangled for fifty minutes many show no sign of life, and they go into the fish tote, ready to be sold. Some feebly struggle. I am a fisherman.

And the king salmon, I am mandated to release this fish. I was furious at the manager when I tried to explain that I was going to bring my king salmon to the sonar site for ADF&G to release as they wished. In response, the manager informed the Alaska state troopers and there was rumor among the fleet about protesting fishers. The troopers patrolled Pilot Station and issued several citations for minor infractions. The king salmon I planned to give to the sonar site were immediately taken by my nephew's family. They had no king salmon because of the closures, and none of them owned a commercial fishing permit to legally participate in this fishery. Like Natives, they were taking a boat ride and stopped by my boat as I was pulling in my last drift, and they were happy to sneak the king salmon home. Several weeks before, despite the closures, I had caught all the king salmon for my family and received a hundred-dollar payment from the Pilot Station Sonar Site. My subsistence king salmon needs were met, but many families were not as fortunate. There are no Native words to describe CPUE.

During traditional potlatches, we have Native guests who know what it is like to live on our river. During these ceremonial events, we honor and share wild foods and stories that keep cultures vibrant with the drum and dancing as homage to our ancestors. We tell stories about Mother Nature and keep intimate our harvests by sharing the catch of our traditions. The state regulations have impeded this part of our lives. When the state restricts king salmon harvests, we cannot openly share this salmon without admitting guilt of what we have done. We feel guilty as if we have committed a crime if we keep king salmon against our own cultural practice and do not share this heritage. The state sanctions make us ashamed; they create doubt about our traditions and endorse non-Native harvest ethics of assimilation and create tensions among our own.

Beginning in 2013, dip-net fishing allows immediate release of healthy king salmon with no gillnet scars or stress from prolonged net entanglement. Fishers know when a king salmon is caught because it is a strong fighter and will shake and rattle the dip net. The dip-net fishery allows managers to offer lenient commercial openings. As a Native, it is hard to release a limp lifeless gillnet-caught salmon that has no chance for survival. The dip-net fishery has relieved this guilt. I do not have a drinking problem; guilt-sanctioned regulations or not, I am not ashamed to share Yukon kings as a practice of my ancestors.

No Native should be ashamed to share traditions because of regulations imposed by another ... Native or not. Perhaps it is time to talk about working together to answer questions so that together we can help manage resources and look at cooperative management schemes to relieve guilt associations about cultural and ethnic disparity.

There is a promising future for all wild resources we share in common.

29 ⋐ A Whale, a Whale

"Look! A bear!"

Someone yelled as we were resting on the Bartlett Cove beach in Glacier Bay National Park. It was 79 degrees Fahrenheit, calm and sunny. After sweating and working for the Forest Science Lab in the damp brush, our workday for Uncle Sam was over. We sat up and looked at the black bear as happy tourists stood at attention. The bear was busy digging roots of cow parsnips, which were ready and delicious at that time of year. With one eye on the bear, someone else yelled.

"Look! A whale!"

Out on the cove, a humpback whale broke the calm surface and gave a view of what pristine Alaska must mean to tourists. For us, sighting these natural wonders was just another day of working out in the field. For the tourists, it was a spectacle; many would go home and tell stories about this and encourage others to visit and see the beauty Alaska has to offer.

Elders told stories about one of these mammal sightings in Pilot Station. They foretold hard times to come, food shortages, bad luck, and said that people need to get ready.

⋝

"Don't shoot! Don't shoot the seal." The elder held her arms up and motioned for the high school students to lower their rifles.

In October 2015 I chaperoned several Pilot Station school students on a seal and whale hunting trip to the Lower Yukon near the coastal community of Kotlik. The school district encouraged traditional and cultural education activities such as winter ice fishing and moose and seal hunts. From home we boated six hours to the middle mouth of the

Yukon River. As we reached our camp site, the students were thrilled to be chasing and hunting seals for the first time in their lives.

Although ten students had signed up for this cultural event, the snowfall on the morning of our departure caused several students to change their minds and cancel. We had four boats, eight students, and five adults. Boating in an open skiff at this time of year is not for the foolhardy. A strong traditional mindset is necessary to face the snow, cold, and wind. To encourage several students who were undecided to brave this trip, I told them about the stories they would return with, tales no one could ever take away.

The Native elder women did not want our students to shoot at seals with rifles. Hunting seals with rifles is not the same as hunting moose or geese. Shooting and killing a seal will cause it to sink, drown, and be a complete loss. The elder had seen upriver hunters who had never hunted seal before shoot at seals, only to lose and waste. Many students did not know this. We had serval spears and harpoons to help teach how to hunt and retrieve seals caught in fresh water. We were seal hunting with traditional spear designs and method perfected by our ancestors.

One spear is used with the atlatl or the throwing stick. The spear is four feet long, lightweight, and less than an inch in diameter. It is the same design as a bow arrow with a three-feather tail for aerodynamic stability and accuracy. Throwing the spear by itself with a hand and arm motion is a physical challenge with little trajectory force and no accuracy. Using a throwing stick makes the spear a deadly weapon with a phenomenal increase in force and distance. The throwing stick is two feet long and operates with similar physics as a catapult. The tool has a handle on one end and a small groove on which to rest the spear, and the throwing motion of the arm provides a phenomenal trajectory force that can send the spear flying as far as fifty feet with ease. The spear tip is a detachable arrow tied to a fifteen-foot string coiled along the column. As the arrow penetrates the seal skin, the tip detaches and unravels the string, and the wooden stick floats, allowing hunters to see where the seal dives, swims, and surfaces. The hunters watch the spear and shoot and kill the seal with a rifle, then retrieve it with the string.

With this traditional method, young hunters have caught seals with spear and atlatl made to fit their small stature. The larger harpoons, similar in design, are used to retrieve large seals and beluga whales. Although we had looked for whales along the coast, we had not spotted any of the telltale water spouts that can be seen for miles. Everyone was pleased when we returned home with three seals to share with community elders.

≈

My camera, oh shoot, the fish. I had a choice as I turned to get my camera to take a snapshot of the huge black bear. Two steps toward my camera and I instantly decided to save the fish meant for dinner. The salmon was not a Yukon salmon, it was a Bartlett River salmon, and I had not had any fresh salmon in a long time. I turned to the salmon lying between me and the bear, and like an idiot I raised my arms and started jumping and making noise. FSL had invited a forest scientist to observe the impact of the spruce beetle infestation in Glacier Bay National Park, and after a long day's work, we hiked to fish for coho salmon with rod and reels. I scared the bear away, and we headed back to the tent campground to cook our dinner. The presence of salmon in this part of Alaska was unusual.

After dinner, resting on the Bartlett Cove beach, it was hard to imagine this area covered with giant sheets of ice as observed by naturalist John Muir. The current lush growth of plants and trees has grown over where the glacier once existed. Recession of glaciers is a natural procession of nature. Man did not come to this area to plant trees. In all its beauty, there are things in nature that are undesirable or hideous creations, not as aesthetically pleasing. One of these in southeast Alaska is a plant called the devil's club.

The devil's club is a common plant that grows in temperate to maritime rainforests of Alaska. It grows everywhere in southeast and south central Alaska. Seen from a safe distance, it is picturesque with huge leaves, especially when the sun and shade give it a dimensional beauty. Don't let that fool you. If you have never seen this plant before, it is as hideous as it sounds. It is a plant to stay away from and best to avoid. In the dark forests it creates thick underbrush. On the woody stalks, huge, menacing, spiny thorns make it very uncomfortable if one is poked. When a stalk springs back, as many as ten thorns can dislodge and prick into the skin.

Across the bay from Bartlett Cove where the spruce trees are older and natural succession had time to grow, we walked into the forest and into a huge grove of devil's club. I stood on a fallen log to find easier passage, and fifteen feet above the ground I looked and saw devil's club everywhere. Unlike typical devil's club, four to eight feet tall, these plants were giants. We could only see five to ten feet in front of us. Sometimes unsure of our hand compass reading, we stood on a fallen spruce log to get a better sense of our bearings. It is hard to imagine what getting lost in this area is like. There are no foot trails, roads, or paths. A soft spongy moss covers the trees and the forest floor. We walked on this and no footprints marked our passing. When the glaciers were here, there were no plants or trees and no streams for salmon. Nature always finds a way.

The glaciers in Glacier Bay National Park have been retreating since the last ice age. As the glaciers retreated, plants and trees grew and streams and rivers were formed. As life began to inhabit this area, salmon eventually start to spawn in the streams and encourage the cycle of life. Coho and chum salmon spawn in Bartlett River and many salmon die and replenish the river with nutrients and salmon eggs, and a new generation of salmon is born. In this area of Alaska there is another unusual salmon similar to Atlantic salmon. Locals call it the steelhead salmon. Unlike Pacific salmon that die after spawning, Atlantic and steelhead salmon return to the same river tributary to spawn several life cycles. The steelhead is more like a large trout. The steelhead salmon does not spawn in the Yukon River, and some consider it a genetically altered salmon created by Mother Nature.

In 1970 the State of Alaska issued limited-entry permits for commercial fishers in many fisheries statewide. This generation of fishers has aged, and many of the permits have passed on to heirs. In 2013, when the state started the use of dip-net gear for commercial fishing, many elder fishers opposed it because it was a young man's method. Dip-net fishing is labor intensive and time consuming. The gear has to be monitored all the time, and every time a fish is caught, the dip net is pulled and fish taken out. The first season, many fishers complained of blistered hands, sore backs, and constant sore muscles. Aspirin and soothing ointments become part of the lunchbox remedies.

It is a young man's fishery. All king salmon are released and all chum salmon kept and sold. With the success of this salmon selectivity, ADF&G allows fish openings five days a week, ten hours a day. The first season provided a learning lesson about how to fish with this gear and how to catch fish; many observations were collected and discussed about what was working and who was catching and why. Many learned new tricks to catching fish, and one of these tricks is a compliment from ADF&G.

ADF&G is responsible for management of the fisheries for sustained yield, and the dip-net fishery compliments this management concept. ADF&G monitors salmon passage and provides daily reports for every fishery statewide as an open fiduciary responsibility to transparency. The fisheries in Alaska belong to everyone. The daily passage estimates became a fishers' tool. Every day ADF&G provides estimates at Emmonak, and this information prepares the Pilot Station Sonar Site for any large school or pulse of salmon. Dip-net commercial fishing is allowed in districts Y1 and Y2. The border of Y1 extends from the coast to an area just below Mountain Village, and the upper Y2 border extends to an area just above Marshall. These borders are ninety miles apart. A pulse of salmon travels twenty to twenty-six miles a day. As the pulse moves upriver, young fishers travel with this pulse and catch as many fish as possible before the opening closes for that day.

One entertaining story Mom told was of a whale sighting. Mom laughed every time, but she would say that it was not a laughing matter when we suffer hard times, being able to laugh at our differences is special. Grieving historical trauma taught elders that one of the comforts of healing is to talk with someone. Pilot Station is one hundred river miles from the mouth of the river; there is no estuary, tidal, or saltwater influence. Sighting of sea mammals such as whales and seals is not uncommon. On a late summer eve, there was a large commotion as people were yelling and running to see the excitement. "A whale! A whale!" everyone was yelling. In the excitement, they started to laugh as this naked man came running from the steam house qasgiq with heat and steam emanating from his body. The man was a fisher, and sighting of whales in Pilot Station is a bad omen. Whales and seals feed on fish. Beluga whales feed on salmon. Sightings of these animals miles from the ocean is an indicator of fish conditions in the Bering Sea.

In 2004 several beluga whales were reported on the Yukon River, and one was later found dead in the Nenana River. The Nenana River is one thousand river miles from the Bering Sea, and traveling this silt-concentrated freshwater will cause whales to slowly suffocate without air exchange. The size of silt particles is not the same as sand. Silt is smaller and finer grained. Imagine what it is like for this tiny particle to get lodged in the lungs. The whales were traveling the river following the salmon. For elders, this meant that the salmon numbers out in the Bering Sea were critical and that salmon returns in the next several years were not promising.

Pilot Station elders had seen the same premonition in 1965, and when they tried to tell the managers through the language translators, the managers laughed. In this time period traditional ecological knowledge was seen as archaic. It was widely accepted that the Natives had no science, no technology, and no sense of management. This was a difficult time period for everything Native.

In 2015 Pilot Station tribe explained to the ADF&G manager this traditional observation and that traditional forecast of king salmon returns in the next several years was promising. Although sightings of seals and whales are an indicator of dire situations, consecutive years with no sightings is a good indicator of good salmon numbers. When we have no whale or seal sightings in Pilot Station, salmon numbers in the Bering Sea are sufficient, and we can expect good returns the next year.

Another observation Pilot Station tribe reminded ADF&G was the statewide conventional assumption that salmon numbers in the U.S. West Coast and Alaska tend to switch as a result of cycles. When the West Coast has poor salmon numbers, Alaska numbers tend to be higher, and vice versa—when Alaska has low numbers, the West Coast tends to have higher returns. Communication between fishers and families along the Yukon River is another monitoring system. Seal and whale sightings are not unusual in Pilot Station, and when we do not see these critters, Natives living in the Lower Yukon will reassure everyone that they are not worried about these mammals. No sightings in Pilot Station means good salmon returns, and not because there are fewer seals and whales.

The ADF&G Pilot Station Sonar Site has monitored salmon since 1982. When it is operational, they fish every day, twice a day, and record and measure all fish caught. They talk about bear sightings and any encounters in camp and note this information in their daily logs. All these years of collecting data and they do not keep track of whale or seal sightings. Seal sightings are a precursor to whale sightings and future condition of salmon. Although seals mainly feed on fish such as whitefish and cisco, whales feed on salmon. There is an adverse relationship of whale sightings to small critters that live in the ocean. In 2018 the Pilot Station Sonar test fish crew caught a small beluga whale, and Natives were happy as mangtak was distributed. Whales in Pilot Station are a bad omen for salmon returns for the next several years.

Commercial fishery of cisco, whitefish, lamprey eels, and pink salmon in the Lower Yukon have never provided significant transfer payments to commercial fishers. Kwik'Pak Fisheries has convinced ADF&G to allow commercial harvests of some of these critters. In 2014 Kwik'Pak reported a commercial lamprey eel harvest of more than forty thousand pounds, as well as significant commercial harvests of Yukon River pink salmon, whitefish, and cisco. Although ADF&G does not monitor or have data available on the impact of these commercial harvests, in any ecosystem predator-prey relationship, offspring of any brood stock help juvenile fish to sustain the ecosystem as feeder stock. The cumulative effect of impacting any species has potential repercussions to every tropic level within the system. Every fish provides little fish that big fish eat in the survival of the fittest. If there are multiple impacts to more than one feeder stock source, there will not be enough feeder stock to sustain all fish and bird species in the Bering Sea. The cumulative impact will be most significant to those on the highest level of the food chain. It is easy for ADF&G leaders to say that they have a difficult management task, but they have no idea of exclusive and excessive harvests of all feeder stock sources.

Since 2016 Natives have reported no harvests of lamprey eels in all Yukon River communities. ADF&G attributes these absences to warming climate conditions. Similarly, in the winter of 2018, the number of whitefish caught in subsistence fishnets under the ice has reduced significantly. The absence of lamprey eels and Yukon River whitefish is a traditional indicator of poor king salmon returns several years from now.

In summer 2019 dead seal carcasses were found in the Bering Sea, and dead gray whales were found on the West Coast. Abundant seabird carcasses were also found out in the ocean. Many indicate these animals died of starvation. Beluga whale sightings were also reported above Pilot Station chasing salmon. The 2020, 2021, and 2022 poor Yukon salmon returns of all salmon species were a river-wide concern.

Another traditional observation that is adverse to promising returns of salmon is the abundance of other fish species that provide feeder stock to many sea creatures. Statewide, ADF&G does not monitor or recognize feeder stock sources and overharvest concerns for wild salmon, unlike farm-raised salmon that are manually given food to eat. The lamprey eel and whitefish commercial fishing that occur on the Lower Yukon has tremendous impact on all animals at the top of these food chains. In spring 2021 and 2022 subsistence harvests of Bering Sea herring eggs were more than sufficient for many Native families. There had been no Bering Sea commercial herring fishery for several decades. In November 2022, after six years of no returns, lamprey eels were caught in Pilot Station. The recent abundant herring eggs and lamprey eels are promising as future feeder stock sources and returns of Yukon salmon numbers several years from now. As a cycle of life, the future of salmon returns is promising.

We need to treat the Bering Sea and the Yukon River as a living, breathing organism.

PART IV

Native American tribes are political entities with extensive powers of self-government. The political status of tribes actually precedes the formation of the Constitution and the United States.... Four kinds of sovereign governments are recognized in U.S. law: the federal government, state government, foreign governments, and tribal governments.

Tribal governments have self-governance powers that include: the right to form their own government; the power to make and enforce both civil and criminal laws; the power to tax; the power to establish membership; the right to license, zone and regulate activities; the power to engage in commercial activity; and the power to exclude persons (Indian and non-Indian) from tribal territories.

— NATIVE AMERICAN MANAGEMENT SERVICES

30 ⋨ Bad to the Bone

"Hey, look, berry-pickers!" I yelled over the roar of the motor and nodded to the hillside.

Along the tundra hillside we saw three berry-pickers. Gus nodded his head and smiled. We were on our way to fish for grayling in the national wild and scenic Andreafsky River.

As we turned a riverbend and lost sight of the berry-pickers, we surprised a good-size black bear eating a salmon carcass. Startled, it looked like it wanted to run into the trees but hesitated and did not want to leave its fish behind. Still puttering upriver, we watched the bear as if we had caught it in the act and it did not know what to do.

The Andreafsky flows into the Yukon River and the village of St. Mary's. Many travel the Andreafsky for berry picking, camping, fishing, and hunting. We turned another bend and saw the berry-pickers and we knew we are not alone in this scenic wilderness. Maybe those berry-pickers were people we knew from St. Mary's; the big one reminded me of one of my cousins, and I smiled. Curious, we got closer; something did not look right. They were too big.

Brown bears!

Gus and I grabbed high-powered rifles. The next bend of the river would bring us closer. There was too much trees, willows, and brush. It was a huge mother with two good-size cubs. The splattering of gravel off the propeller got the mother's attention. A hundred yards away she was immense, towering over the brush, watching us. The cubs munched on juicy blueberries. With a grunt from the mother, the huge cubs looked at us and ran lazily into the thick brush. Mother followed and was gone before we can get a shot.

At camp, Gus stayed up all night fishing. Late summertime in Alaska, daylight all night is common. Every camping trip that Gus goes on, if there is fish for fishing, he would rather fish and tells everyone that he can sleep all he wants at home. At 4 a.m., Gus peeked into the tent and woke us about a young black bear near camp. Every half hour he gave an update. Finally at 6 a.m. he warned that the bear was coming closer and asked if he could shoot it. I told him to go ahead, I don't care. I lay my head down and waited for the shot.

~

Alaska Natives are at an identity crossroads between recognition as true Alaska Natives or as tribal members. In my village, elders did not see themselves as tribal members living on an Indian reservation. For many this is not a good analogy; many grew up with stories and movies of segregation with unpleasant treatment and historical trauma from non-Natives. They could never see themselves like Indians living on reservations. Many are truthful and honest when they say: *I am not a tribal member.* The self-image is stereotyped, like that of an unkempt Native or an incoherent drunk Native, as socially unacceptable. This perception was created from early Western cinema in which cowboy actor John Wayne and his sidekick cowboys were the good guys and the Indians or tribal members were seen as bad people. More and more, Hollywood has changed this perception and recognizes in film that many cultures have their own stories to tell.

A Native hunter's natural instinct around a bear is to shoot first and ask questions later. Ethics about shooting bears are not complicated when the bear is in the sights of a rifle. A dead bear is not a threat to anyone or to all the critters this bear terrorizes. Natives will not go out to hunt black or brown bears. Many will go for moose, caribou, or geese. The real Natives will go out for a ride, and if they see bear it is an instant target to be shot. Seeing a bear does not have the same aesthetic or intrinsic sentiment that many non-Natives associate with nature. Natives see a bear as a nuisance and threat rather than as a source for food. Times have changed. For Natives who do not hunt and have grown accustomed to this sedentary and digital lifestyle, a bear is something to be feared as a creature that lives in the deep woods and to cringe and shutter about with stories of hunters crawling into bear dens during middle of winter.

In western Alaska there are black and brown, or grizzly bears. The Western Alaska Brown Bear Management Plan applies, but Natives are not familiar with this management plan. Bears in general are considered a nuisance, and brown bears are a dangerous nuisance. Between the two, brown bears are immediate targets to be shot because of their carnivorous and often predatory nature, and black bears may or may not be shot, depending on ethics of the hunter. If two Natives sit and talk bear ethics, they would rather shoot the bear than make it complicated. Every bear sighting is different. If Natives were geese hunting with shotguns and had left their rifles at home, that bear will live to see another day unless it becomes a life-threatening situation. Or if the fish and wildlife trooper airplane is flying, it is best to play it safe and let the bear go its way.

The U.S. Indian Wars were not a good time for promises of tribal sovereignty with the U.S. government. As a federal program, BIA has never had reason to be seen as mavericks or a department agency that is "bad to the bone." A 2007 Native hip-hop song many Natives relate to sings about that fear of BIA, though the government is not taken as serious as it once was: "I'm not afraid of aliens." This general perception of being afraid of government agents has changed significantly, especially since BIA is seen helping Natives to settle differences and address issues constructively, working together. This is a good start.

Before he lost his reelection, Senator Ted Stevens addressed the Native gathering at the annual AFN convention of corporation shareholders with the claim that Alaska Native tribes exist but that they could never be sovereign because they did not own the land. Senator Stevens reassure shareholders that they did not need to be afraid of tribes and that tribes would never take away what the corporations already have. The Native corporation investment in their stocks was sound, more than solvent, and still protected by ANCSA. Stevens reminded the corporation shareholders to respect the tribes and claims of Alaska tribal sovereignty would never be a threat. Ownership of land is settled, and due process is no longer necessary in any legal land claim disputes. Stevens tried to explain the role of tribes and the fiduciary responsibility of the federal government and made it confusing as Natives looked to each other as shareholders and tribal members. Was he telling the Natives that the corporations are sovereign because they own the land? Standing beside Native shareholders and tribal members were the Natives born after 1971.

For those Alaska Natives who have never received Native corporation shares, ANCSA was a one-time deal, and anyone born after 1971 is not an automatic shareholder. This act was never intended for this generation of Natives. What the regional and village corporation board decide for this young generation is not an issue taken lightly.

My Alaska corporation is bound by the same laws every corporation in America is required to follow. Although there are special provisions that make my corporation special, it can never do anything that I as an individual tell it to do. Like every corporation, it can lobby on issues as long as these issues are not controversial. It has an image to keep up, and this image is not benefited if any issue becomes liable to stocks and investment potential. As a prominent reminder of success, a dividend payment reassures my confidence. If non-shareholder members are a concern, the board can let the shareholders decide. This was ultimately what Calista Corporation addressed in 2013, when it started incorporating descendants born after 1971 with a different class of stock separate from the main provisions of ANCSA. In hindsight, the act of the Calista board members was a result of a kindling sense of leadership radiating the elder qualities of our culture. We are in a sense one people, and to succeed, we must help each other and leave no one behind.

The extinguishment of aboriginal rights has had a major impact on the way Natives view wildlife and changed many traditional customs of sharing harvests within the community. Federal and state management came to rural Natives, imposed, and told them what to do and warned of penalties if they did not comply, whether they were shareholders or not. Ted Stevens was a congressional representative for more than forty years. For this generation of public servants, animosity against tribal existence was a challenge. Ted Stevens was instrumental in the passing of ANCSA and believed that Alaska tribes do not exist.

It is difficult to fathom if ANCSA intended to decimate the Native perception of being aboriginal. Either way, it worked. The idea to incorporate Native identity into that of modern corporation shareholders was an attempt to fast-track assimilation. As this existence developed, Natives born after 1971 grew to realize that they are different from elder Natives with no other reason than that they were born in a different time. They were special with a sense of cultural pride radiating from elders and customs, but this rift of existence as shareholders and tribal members is a question that could not be clearly answered. The confusion centered on the fact that not all Alaskans are eligible to be tribal members. Talks about tribal existence created identity confusion where every Native was an Alaska resident, some were corporation shareholders . . . and every Native with ancestral ties to an Alaska Native culture is eligible to be a tribal member. Young leaders grew up learning about hunting and fishing issues, aboriginal rights, and ANCSA, and see the rich cultural traditions and customs still practiced and quietly question, why are we are different? Many would question why they are eligible to be tribal members but not eligible as Native corporation shareholders.

Natives born after 1971 matured with many unanswered questions about the role of tribes. Every true Alaska Native is eligible to be a tribal member, but not every tribal member is a corporation shareholder. This is not a situation the Natives created. It is a leading perception that Alaska tribes are sovereign but not sovereign because they do not own land. A reminder that tribes cannot do certain things that other sovereign governments can do within the body of law; this is what sovereignty entitles. In simple words, this sovereignty is a practice of power from one government that other governments accept and respect. For many the concept is mind-blowingly abstract. I have a hard time understanding this, but I know the federal Indian Wars were the result of sovereignty.

To put it simply, sovereignty is an *exercise* of power. How policymakers create and recognize federal and state laws is relevant to tribes. The theme of who enforces these regulations or who has an obligation to enforce regulations as collateral responsibility is relevant to each government, where I promise to be a responsible citizen of one government or the other if we work together to address these goals.

Every village is special to the people who live there. Roadless rural communities like Pilot Station and Fort Yukon, where tribal members live safe from non-tribal members who may be seen as a threat. Small-town Hollywood sheriffs played by Brian Dennehy and Sylvester Stallone would relate to this. In small villages, locals who are hired to police and enforce laws have quit instead of dealing with a situation seen as a potential threat. Honor, dignity, and any sense of public service for the good of the people are silly assumptions. For village police, a paycheck to buy gas for a hunting trip is not worth any claims of dereliction of duties. Almost everyone employed in Pilot Station, as part of their job experience, claims to have worked at the local police station as a city police officer or jail clerk. There are no local tribal police due to lack of tribal funds—the same reason there are no local state or federal troopers.

In 1990 a non-Native living in Pilot Station was seen as a growing threat. Fear of this person was real, and local police found reasons to be at the other end of town and work till the end of the week for a final paycheck—before quitting. Although this non-tribal person lived in the village for more than ten years, for some reason this person's behavior changed and became belligerent and menacing. The federal and state governments do not live in the community, and the city government feared this person and had no jurisdiction regarding federal and state laws. Jurisdiction of sovereign power can be confusing when the constitution is used to argue what is right and wrong.

For the village corporation, this non-tribal member was a liability. Besides, the non-tribal member is not a shareholder. As long as the shares and stocks were not an issue, the village corporation could do nothing. Regardless, the corporations were liable if they claimed they had the right to refuse services to anyone for any reason. A restraining order issued from courts that are not in the village would make everyone an instant target of resentment. Any confrontations would be complicated, coupled with the fact that there was no one to enforce a restraining order issued from the other side of Alaska. Because of their pay scale and lack of employment benefits, we do not have brave Native police. This became an ugly situation.

Without options to preserve the safety of the community, Pilot Station tribal government asserted its sovereign responsibility and banned the non-tribal member from the community. In response, the State of Alaska respected the tribal government's assertion of power, and Alaska state troopers escorted the non-tribal member away from the village, never to return. Several years later, the rest of Alaska took notice when the *Anchorage Daily* newspaper printed a full-page article of this person's belligerent behavior and the sovereign responsibility Pilot Station tribal government successfully asserted.[1]

Pilot Station is my tribe and I know my tribe does not own land to assert sovereign powers. If this is something we can create and ultimately recognize case by case and situation by situation, I want more of this to help my tribal members. Many people often assume landownership and Indian Country status is proof of sovereignty.

As Americans we all sense that Americans own America, Alaskans own Alaska, and Alaska Native tribes own the communities where they reside. We don't need a paper document to verify this proof. This sense of ownership embodied in where you live is a tickling sense that is always there when we leave and return. It is reassuring and comforting. When I travel to other communities, I respect the people and local customs; otherwise, situations can be uncomfortable.

When I was going to school in Vermont and saw Alaska from far away, I learned sovereignty is something simple and subtle and is always there. Sovereignty is *respect*. There is no American authority that can intervene and remind the Native community of who they are and what they can or cannot do. Federal and state managers do not see this as a conflict; ignorant of the Native world, they do not see Native hunting and fishing as social activities.

NOTES

1. *Anchorage Daily News*, August 1, 1993.

31 Alaska Sovereignty and Land

"My check was only $16. I hear some people got over $100—that is not fair," a tribal member commented to our council.

"We are not a corporation. We don't have any stocks and we do not have corporation shares. It is a rebate program, it is our tribal store, and the more money you spend, the more you will be paid back," I explained this to tribal members attending our annual community meeting. Someone else raised a hand and commented that we should provide dividends and make it fair for everyone, just like our Native corporation.

"Rebate money is tax-free patronage. You do not need to report it to IRS. If you spend your Alaska PFD at our tribal store, the more money you will be paid back." All corporation and Alaska Permanent Fund Dividends are reported to IRS as income.

It is accepted that the Alaska Native regional and village corporations own the land. The role of these Native corporations and the existence of Alaska tribes and tribal members is a challenge. Although every Native is eligible to enroll as a tribal member, Natives born after 1971 is a challenge for corporation identity. For Calista Corporation, as the new Natives matured and participated in regional issues, Calista started a decade of discussion and educating shareholders on options available for this new generation. Calista ultimately allowed shareholders to vote whether to make these new Natives eligible to enroll with a new class of stock. With unanimous support, in January 2017 Calista enrolled eligible descendants as new-generation shareholders with stocks that can never be inherited to their descendants, unlike original shares created from ANCSA. In 2018 these new enrollees received their first dividend payments.

Many regional corporations have done well with their investment and corporate portfolios. The village corporations, on the other hand, have their own challenges. Information from the regional corporations is available on their websites, with the exception of executive, capital, and investment information that provides a corporate edge. The village corporations are more reclusive with information. Although I am a shareholder of Pilot Station Native Corporation and receive an annual dividend from local investments, how this corporation relates to tribal members and the new generation of Natives is not an issue of concern. As a corporation, it is a capital investment machine to make money. Any other services depend on the corporate leadership structure and sentiments of board members, not the shareholders, community, or tribal members.

The ethnic identity of Calista shareholders is Yup'ik. Each village corporation's shareholders have similar ethnic ties to the regional corporation. Provisions of ANCSA require corporations to support each other to potentially operate in perpetuity with the Native identity and ancestral lineage as core values of the corporation. The actions taken by the regional or village corporation to include the new generation are not an ANCSA requirement. The ethnic identity of Native American Indians and Alaska Natives is often recognized as one under federal law. There have been some precarious situations about whether Native American Indians who move to Alaska are eligible to enroll as Alaska tribal members.

In March 2014 Calista Corporation started to address an identity issue not as shareholders or Natives, but as tribal members addressing the role of federally recognized tribes. Calista created a regional steering committee, and I became a committee member and attended several meetings about creating a regional tribal government. The March 2014 meeting was in Bethel. As part of a caucus, every member convened within their own regional unit following the same regional representation of the corporation structure. My unit includes Pilot Station, St. Mary's, Marshall, Ohogamiut, and Russian Mission. Some units from the Kuskokwim had as many as ten representatives, and each unit was to vote and select a subcommittee member for the steering committee. One Kuskokwim River unit voted several times for their representative after each candidate voiced their opinion and why they should be selected. Throughout this process, I watched and listened as each caucus voted, and without saying a word I was unanimously voted as a representative because I was the only tribal member attending from my portion of the Yukon River.

As Pilot Station tribal council leader, our tribe has always had an identity issue addressing sovereignty. When Calista sent notice it was creating a regional tribal entity, the main concern our council addressed was of a regional corporation taking over the role of tribes and operating as a pseudo-tribal government corporation, including possible loss of federal funds and loss of tribal powers with a corporate entity telling non-shareholder tribal members what to do. Every Native is eligible to be a tribal member, but not every Native is eligible to be a shareholder. Like every tribe, Pilot Station does not receive funding or operation support from any Native corporation.

Pilot Station did not want to lose tribal funds from the U.S. federal taxpayers network. Every tribal operating budget comes from Tribal Priority Allocations/Aid to Tribal Governments through BIA. The budget of all tribes in Alaska is at the generous hands of the federal government, and we did not want the regional corporation to take this away. The State of Alaska does not provide any tribal funds. When ANCSA created the corporation with the notion that an Indian reservation system is counterintuitive to state and federal jurisdiction, the question of Native sovereignty was left unanswered—until the state attorney general admitted in 2017 that tribal sovereignty was a sought-after claim in a state where 229 tribes exist. The only reason Calista had interest in a regional tribal government was regarding development of the Donlin Gold mine project on the Kuskokwim River. There is no regional tribal organization. There are many nongovernment and nonprofit organizations and corporations that serve Alaska Natives. Unlike borough governments, a tribal government is not required to follow state rule.

The main interest for Calista is payment in lieu of taxes that can be collected as part of the Donlin Gold mine project with the funds used regionally to help tribal members through a regional tribal government. Although municipal and borough governments collect taxes, the question of tribes collecting taxes has never been addressed. In 2015 the Pilot Station Traditional Council levied a tribal fish tax to the fish-buying companies for our portion of the Yukon River. No taxes have been collected yet.

In the last twenty years the Pilot Station annual tribal fund from BIA was $104,000. The tribal office is a former BIA elementary classroom built in 1976 with no water or sewer system. This funding is used to pay for office expenses such as electricity, phone, copy machine, office supplies, and salaries of our bookkeeper, secretary, and tribal administrator. At least 25 percent of this allocation is used for annual heating fuel costs. For any business in rural Alaska, operation costs are a reality check. Pilot Station pays three different out-of-town phone companies to maintain and operate the one office phone for telecommunications: AT&T for long distance calls, GCI for faxes, and United Utilities Inc. for local calls. In the last twenty years, none of our tribal employees have ever received a pay raise. There are no employee benefits or retirement plan. Many full-time employees qualify for Medicaid and Medicare benefits, Denali KidCare, heating assistance, and food stamps serviced by the State of Alaska. Working for a tribal government is not appealing.

As a tribal entity, Pilot Station provides emergency donation assistance to help with emergency food and funerary costs. In the last several years donation funds have been closed, and all we can do is refer tribal members to the state welfare food stamp program and Temporary Assistance for Needy Families operated through AVCP. Pilot Station tribe has a gaming operation with a gaming permit issued by the State of Alaska. Bingo and pull-tab proceeds help cover donation requests and salaries for bingo workers. With current economic conditions, gaming funds have been insufficient for any assistance. What is ironic is that every tribe pays a gaming tax to the State of Alaska intended to help families in need. Pilot Station tribe has reminded many state employees: people who need the help most will not ask for it.

As a society, we traditionally look at creation of projects to create job opportunities and infuse cash into the economy. Someone gets a job, gets paid, and turns around and spends the earned money for groceries, fuel, restaurants, clothing, and other needs where retail and service are part of a community. In a capitalist world the economics of supply and demand require funds necessary for an exchange of commodities. In a government world this supply-and-demand relationship is best described as a trust or a trilateral trust relationship between a government entity, a resource association, and people in the midst. Pilot Station tribe does not own land. In the last several years the land-into-trust program for Alaska Native corporations has become accepted as a program where the corporation land transferred to the tribe can be protected and exempt from federal and state taxes. The land-into-trust program is a similar situation as tribal gaming and bingo taxes collected by the State of Alaska. If one is exempt, the other should also be exempt as a tribal trust program.

To be honest, as council leader, the most challenging issue we address is tribal child custody cases. Many are difficult to listen to. Alaska tribes should tell stories of child custody cases to BOG and BOF and the impact of their decisions on Alaska Natives.

At the 2016 annual AFN conference in Fairbanks, the Tanana Chiefs Council hosted a tribal meeting to discuss options of creating a statewide tribal government. Like many tribes, Pilot Station is unable to pay the annual dues to be a member of AFN or send a tribal delegate to attend the largest gathering of Natives. Claims that AFN represents tribal members have no merit. There is an irony regarding the U.S. Code of Federal Regulations for tribes to receive their share of federal funds. It is not unusual for tribal budgets to include AFN membership fees. To receive these federal funds every tribe signs an agreement that no funds will be used for lobbying or lobbying groups. AFN is an influential conglomerate of corporations lobbying for statewide Native support.

"Helpers of Today, Leaders of Tomorrow" was the slogan for the Lower Yukon School District Natural Helpers. In Alaska, there is no statewide non-curricular, non-sporting, and non-governing school youth program. Every school program promotes education resources for a learning atmosphere to every student. Local schools in rural Alaska have no other option except homeschool or boarding schools such as Mt. Edgecumbe. The Bethel Regional High School has a youth group, Teens Acting against Violence, that promotes community wellness and youth empowerment. The Tanana City School has a similar youth program, and this group works with the nationwide 4H program in rural communities that originally depended on agriculture and services of the USDA Cooperative Extension Service. The Tanana 4H program also addresses local disparities such as challenges for community and youth.

In 2009 Lower Yukon Natural Helper students created school posters informing all students of the Natural Helpers program and identified student leaders in each school. Student leaders from Russian Mission School made a school poster and coined the slogan "Helpers of Today, Leaders of Tomorrow."

As an incentive to participate, student leaders were eligible for a group trip outside of Alaska. The Natural Helper program is not a student council or youth government program; the main incentive for Natural Helpers is peer support and leadership. The Lower Yukon School Natural Helpers, Teens Acting against Violence, and the Tanana 4H provided presentations at the 2011 AFN Elders and Youth Conference. Each program educates the elders and youth of issues and risk behaviors related to growing up in small villages.

One place I was fortunate to chaperone sixteen student leaders was the island of Oahu, Hawaii. Although Native Hawaiians and Native Alaskans seem to be worlds apart, the main theme that created the Lower Yukon Natural Helpers was a concern in Hawaii.

For Native students, this trip to Hawaii was a lifetime experience and perhaps the only trip many would ever take outside of Alaska. The swimming, snorkeling, surfing, sunning, and sandy beaches were a daily vacation in paradise. The visit and live performance of the Polynesian Cultural Center was immaculate. The thrill of traveling to an iconic vacation spot was incomparable to actually being there. With donations from Donlin Gold and Yukon Delta Fisheries Development Association, student leaders from Hooper Bay, Scammon Bay, Nunam Iqua, Kotlik, Alakanuk, Emmonak, Mountain Village, Pilot Station, Marshall, and Russian Mission visited Hawaii for ten days. Every day was a learning experience with a chance for Natural Helpers to talk about the program and tell stories to Hawaiian students. Students learned from each other about similar issues and youth risk behaviors. The main theme shared by both cultures is the high rates of youth suicide.

"You guys live in a beautiful place, why would you want to kill yourself?" many Natives asked Hawaiian students, and the Hawaiians asked the same question to our young Alaskans. The stigma and cause of suicide comes in many forms, and this issue is a challenge for anyone to address. Perhaps it is true that beauty is in the eyes of the beholder. As students talked about the issue, the peer support network promotes youth leadership, empowerment, and an open assessment program. It also offers a health and wellness peer support network. As adults we tend to offer advice or alternatives, and some will say that suicide is not an issue to talk about. The peer support network allows students to talk, offer advice, and refer statewide assistance programs available for health and wellness.

One example is the nationwide suicide hotline. Do you know the number for this hotline?

32 ⬈ Cooperative Management / Co-management

"I would like to thank ADF&G Pilot Station Sonar for allowing me to fish with my king salmon net and harvest my king salmon needs," I commented with my opening statement. I had a three-minute time limit. What could I tell BOF of the traditional knowledge I was trying to convey without offending anyone?

⬈

Hooper Bay, March 2007. I was one of eleven council members with the AYK Regional Advisory Council discussing wildlife and fishery issues for our portion of Alaska. The wildlife issues are not a concern. Our main concern is additional Kuskokwim and Yukon River fishing regulations on closures and gear restrictions that are creating community and family hardships.

Several years later, in January 2010, BOF passed Yukon River gear restrictions despite opposition from the testimony of Hooper Bay resident and AYK regional chairman Lester Wilde. No regional advisory council has management authority; they only provide recommendations. The BOF meeting was in Fairbanks, and many Lower Yukon residents attended with funding and transportation provided by the CDQ Yukon Delta Fisheries Development Association.

BOF members have a strong conviction that these regulations are necessary and that catering to the wishes of any preferential user would jeopardize the future of any resource. When I provided testimony on behalf of Pilot Station, the BOF chairman was not pleased when I mentioned that I was also a member of the AYK Regional Advisory Council.

These state regulations applied to my part of Alaska and tribal members I represent. My challenge was trying to explain how respectable sportsmen who submitted these regulation proposals were concerned about the size of Yukon kings and that catching small salmon was not as enjoyable or aesthetically pleasing.

ADF&G staff had provided the data on small salmon size to convince the board that these regulations were necessary. After this BOF action, Pilot Station tribe sent letters to ADF&G managers asking for evidence of genetic drift as a result of gear use with the rationale that we should see this same discrepancy in other salmon species harvested on the same Yukon by the same Natives with the same gear. No response has been given yet—scientific or otherwise. Western science is adamant that if what is true and happening to this species is a result of a particular action or change in environment, then the same should happen to similar species as a result of similar actions in the same environment. This is a major virtue of Western science; ADF&G biologists are familiar with this genetic drift concept.

I served four years with the AYK Regional Advisory Council, where every member is recommended by OSM and appointed by the secretary of interior. My term was up in April 2011, and I was encouraged to reapply. Recalling the treatment and scowling remarks from the BOF chairman, I did not apply for AYK council membership. Instead, I applied on behalf of the Pilot Station Traditional Council. Several months later OSM sent our tribe a letter that, according to ANILCA, organizations cannot apply for membership because ANILCA does not apply or cater to tribes or tribal members.

Before applying, Pilot Station tribe agreed that if our tribe was selected, council leaders would appoint our most qualified tribal member to attend fish and wildlife meetings and address concerns and monthly reports in all our community gatherings. This sounded rational and was included on the application. As it is now, regional advisory members are not required to attend community meetings, give reports or updates, or gather or provide community or tribal recommendations. According to ANILCA, the only qualification for advisory council membership is knowledge of hunting and fishing use by Alaska Natives and rural Alaskans. The application for Pilot Station was not eligible, and another applicant was selected.

With concerns about our salmon, Pilot Station wrote letters to Governor Sean Parnell and the Federal Subsistence Board and consulted with ADF&G staff on fishery issues. In response Governor Parnell appointed ADF&G Yukon River Supervisor John Linderman to respond with a letter citing and explaining the Alaska State Statues, the rationale for these management requirements, and the regulatory process. With recognition of unmet salmon needs and food security concerns, John agreed to meet with Pilot Station tribal members. John Linderman, sonar staff, a USFWS manager, and ADF&G Commissioner Cora Campbell met with tribal members. The summary conclusion of that meeting from the State of Alaska was: *It is difficult . . .*

FSB chairman Tim Towarak sent a cordial letter explaining subsistence provisions of ANILCA, tribal consultation, and tribal government-to-government relations FSB has to follow.

Regardless, subsistence salmon harvest restrictions continued through the season. The Yukon salmon fishery is a difficult management issue. Pilot Station tribe printed an information pamphlet educating everyone about the salmon situation and tribal issues. With volunteers Pilot Station created a Yukon salmon documentary. In April 2014 this video was the only Alaska documentary shown at the International Yukon River Salmon Summit meeting in Fairbanks. Canadian representatives showed five documentaries. After the annual 2014 community meeting the video was posted on YouTube.

In summer 2014 Pilot Station sent a letter to ADF&G manager Eric Newland. The issues addressed were the same but a tribal recommendation for action was new and compelling, compared to what management had grown accustomed to. We were entering quiet waters with a recommendation that could not be fathomed. Kuskokwim River tribal members were becoming organized and vocal with efforts of an Intertribal Fish Commission and more of their issues were addressed with USFWS, OSM, and Department of Interior. Talks of a similar Yukon River Intertribal Fish Commission were addressed for our portion of Alaska. Immediately after the 2014 salmon season, ADF&G manager Eric

Newland quit and left the department for good. Several months later ADF&G manager Stephanie Schmidt was hired.

In April 2015 Pilot Station tribe sent a similar letter to Schmidt including a traditional projection of more king salmon returns and a request for unrestricted subsistence harvests. Pilot Station also offered tribal assistance to Schmidt. Instead of complete silence, Schmidt set up a community meeting and visit along with sonar staff, USFWS manager, and a USFWS trooper—they find it comforting to travel in numbers when visiting Native communities. Although this meeting seemed more productive and educational, salmon fishing continued to mirror dismal subsistence restrictions of previous years, despite the higher number of kings. In 2015 Pilot Station tribal members had more fishing restrictions and less king salmon harvest.

Tribal food security for the winter was at risk. In June 2015 Pilot Station faxed a letter to Schmidt requesting to declare the Yukon king salmon fishery an economic disaster. Schmidt immediately called the tribal office and reminded us that we need to request disaster declaration from the state governor or Alaska's U.S. congressional representative. We reminded Schmidt why we want to work with the state. No disaster declaration request was issued.

April 10, 2015. Before sending the letter to Schmidt, Pilot Station tribe had testified at an OSM public hearing in St. Mary's to exclude Pilot Station as a community eligible for federally qualified users to harvest king salmon. In 2014 the newly organized Kuskokwim fish commission used provisions of ANILCA to allow king salmon harvests for eligible federally qualified users. With recognition of this provision, several Yukon River tribes submitted similar special action requests to allow Yukon federally qualified users to harvest king salmon. Pilot Station tribe testified to OSM that Pilot Station does not have any federal presence and that we would rather work directly with the State of Alaska. As a result, FSB deferred action on the Yukon special action request and did not allow king salmon harvests for federally qualified users. Pilot Station tribe told Schmidt that we commended this decision, and as a tribal government, our traditional wildlife management doctrines are similar to the guidelines used by the State of Alaska.

The Katie John story and John Sturgeon court case each claim that the federal and state have jurisdiction of Alaska's navigable waterways as public lands, including rivers and streams, protected on federal reserves and national parks. These two cases address use and access, the similar reasons the intertribal fish commissions were created—unlike use and access, the obligation of those responsible for management authority of a trust resource needs to be clarified.

The Kuskokwim River Intertribal Fish Commission was created with similar principles and management doctrines as the Columbia River Intertribal Fish Commission for tribal members living in Oregon and Washington. For the Kuskokwim, local tribal representatives and usfws Yukon Delta Wildlife Refuge management signed a memorandum of agreement with approval from the U.S. Department of Interior. The State of Alaska was not involved. To demonstrate the power of this agreement, the fish commission with usfws authority usurped management authority from ADF&G and allowed subsistence king salmon harvests for eligible federally qualified users. After the majority of salmon reach their spawning grounds, the commission returns management authority back to ADF&G. The Kuskokwim and Columbia fish commissions are co-management examples between two governing entities: tribal and federal. No state government is involved, regardless of resident and non-resident regulatory provisions of jurisdiction. *Federally qualified users* have no management responsibility, only claims to harvest salmon for use and access.

Following similar guideline efforts, the Yukon River Intertribal Fish Commission was spearheaded by Tanana Chiefs Conference and Association of Village Council Presidents, the nonprofit, nongovernment organizations representing tribal members in their respective regions. The Yukon River is huge, and for an intertribal commission to exist, all involved tribes must coordinate and collaborate on all fishery issues. In May 2016 a representative from the Yukon River Intertribal Fish Commission called and reminded Pilot Station of the need for a tribal resolution to be eligible for membership. About thirty tribes had submitted resolutions the year before. A copy of the fish commission constitution was available for review. Once a tribe submits a resolution, the tribe becomes a constituent and has a shared responsibility to harvest salmon according to bylaws of the commission.

Shared responsibility is the main theme for members of the commission, and the more tribes that join, the more tribal powers of support. The Alaska portion has sixty tribes that harvest Yukon salmon. Pilot Station told the commission representative that we were concerned our tribe would lose sovereign powers because the commission constitution language and tribal representative puts tribal powers at risk. Shared responsibility sounded promising, but *jurisdiction* was one misconception that needed to be clarified and addressed. This was where tribal powers could be in jeopardy.

The U.S. government has three powers of sovereignty: an executive branch where the hierarchy of the government is recognized, a legislative branch where the rules of the government are made, and a judicial branch to assure enforcement of the rules for citizens or non-citizens represented by the government within claims of territorial jurisdiction. Landownership is the main clause to support this jurisdiction claim and the reason why many assume Alaska tribes are not sovereign.

The Kuskokwim co-management agreement is with a branch of the U.S. government. Any agreement between tribes and the federal government is guaranteed just like the early treaties that once promised working together.

Alaskans have a fair understanding that the federal government has broad discretionary powers. Pilot Station tribe agrees that a co-management agreement of shared responsibility with the State of Alaska is more rational, with authority where jurisdiction is prudent. Usurping power from one government to serve the needs represented by another is not an act of civility or respect of sovereign powers. The State of Alaska has since statehood been involved with fish and wildlife management. As it is now, provisions of state sovereignty include state regulations with state troopers and state courts to enforce regulations to citizens recognized as Alaska residents and non-residents.

If a state-tribal co-management agreement is created, tribal sovereignty is the base of all tribal laws, tribal police and tribal courts will provide enforcement, and jurisdiction will apply to *tribal and non-tribal members*. For this co-management agreement to be rational, the State of Alaska must be willing to give tribal jurisdiction to tribal and *non-tribal* members for personal, subsistence, and commercial activities. Rationally, no federal provisions will apply and make this complicated or cumbersome. It is hard to tell if the state was offended when the Kuskokwim Commission exercised usurping power and took away all management authority. The federal government will be offended if it is excluded and a tribal co-management agreement is signed with the state. Are there any federal laws that will prevent this?

The Kuskokwim fish commission agreement with usfws derives sovereign and legislative powers from federal and tribal laws, enforcement from tribal courts with tribal police and usfws troopers with federal courts, and jurisdiction among citizens recognized as *federally and non-federally qualified users* according to a tier system created by anilca. Non-federally qualified users are not eligible to harvest salmon. Because this is an agreement with the federal government, provisional powers of broad jurisdiction are derived from anilca guidelines. Federal jurisdiction overrides state regulations. Any tribal agreement with the federal government will challenge the state to step back and watch.

All harvest provisions of this co-management agreement apply on federal lands and waters, and harvests are only allowed for federally qualified users. According to the Katie John decision, federal oversight applies to state waters for Native subsistence harvests. Because this overrides state regulations, the users are not resident or non-resident—instead a new user is recognized: a federally qualified user. The question whether tribes have jurisdiction over federally qualified users is a non-discrete citizenship identity; tribes have jurisdiction only over tribal members and no jurisdiction over federally qualified users.

The Pilot Station tribal experience in trying to work with the State of Alaska on subsistence is a charade. No one gave us a proper response any time we addressed the governor, commissioner, regional supervisor, or adf&g manager, until we realized the one decision-maker in charge of everything Native was the adf&g manager. The manager has the power to allow tribal members to harvest fish and wildlife, whether tribal food security is in jeopardy or not. After we realized this, we had no reason to ask other state representatives, who only point to someone else about tasks and responsibilities.

During times of empathy, the governor's office will override the manager's duties and allow harvests. In June 2016 Moses Paukan Sr., a respected elder from St. Mary's, wrote a letter to Governor Bill Walker and met with Lieutenant Governor Byron Mallot, the ADF&G commissioner, and St. Mary's tribal members. After this meeting Yukon king salmon harvests were allowed despite the stewardship obligations of ADF&G and treaty obligations with Canada. Unlike this act of empathy, management for resident or federally qualified users puts tribal powers at risk—this separation of powers needs to be addressed. The difference between management and pseudo-management is the power of the final decision-maker.

In the April 2015 letter to ADF&G manager Stephanie Schmidt, Pilot Station emphasized we did not want to extend tribal powers to non-tribal members or federally qualified users. Although the State of Alaska is nonchalant in exercising and extending state powers over tribal members, we are not the same because we do not have the same values; we respect non-tribal members for who they are. We did not want a co-management agreement with the state and especially with the federal government. We were not interested in claiming jurisdiction of federally qualified users; we wanted our tribal powers to serve jurisdiction of our tribal members.

Pilot Station tribe wanted to help the state to manage subsistence, and we recommended USFWS as consultants when subsistence resources become a conservation concern. As it is, USFWS and FSB serve as middlemen between the tribes and State of Alaska. All the federal agencies do is identify, relay, and reaffirm concerns about subsistence and remind the state about duties and who is responsible for what. Their federal presence reminds the State of Alaska of the national interest lands, so regardless if we like it or not, they are here. They have minimum harvest assurances for the tribe and no guarantees for sustained yield harvests for the state. The courtesy of USFWS and FSB to the tribes stems from the U.S. Department of Interior's special fiduciary responsibility; the tribes also have to address their presence.

With realization of ADF&G manager's decision-making power, Pilot

Station tribe made it known that we were done with the governor, the boards of fish and game, the commissioner, and regional supervisor. We wanted to work with the manager with traditional management guidelines to help tribal members. Although ADF&G manager Schmidt emphasized the role of state leaders and regulatory procedures, we emphasized that these were part of *your* state government. Pilot Station explained tribal food security experience with the regulatory process and influence of respectable sportsmen who hold a copy of the state constitution and remind state officials when due process infringes on their convictions. The five ADF&G managers quit because of the burden of their own state regulations.

In our tribal meeting with Schmidt, another state employee reminded everyone that there is no monetary value for subsistence. There is no U.S. dollar amount for traditional Native foods. If an emergency declaration request is submitted, what is the monetary value for subsistence, and how do you identify subsistence users from others? According to ANILCA, subsistence users and federally qualified users are assumed to be the same.

Pilot Station tribe reminded Schmidt that people who need the most help will not ask for it. According to ANILCA, every federal taxpayer qualifies as a federally qualified user. Unlike ANILCA, tribal members are subsistence users. Although Department of Interior will say that tribal membership cannot be used as criteria for subsistence harvests, the actual federal provisions to this guideline are not clear because ANCSA has broad powers that extinguished Alaska Native aboriginal rights. When the needs of the home are not met, elaborate education plans, social service programs, or healthy family initiatives are difficult to achieve. Since the federal and state governments claim dual management, Natives are treated as U.S. citizens, with their daily activities and family livelihoods regulated. Imagine a federal *and* state manager telling the small family farms in the Mat-Su region when to harvest and store their crops, regardless if the crops are in season or ripe. If the harvest should ruin the manager is responsible.

In April 2016 another new manager was hired after Schmidt quit. Before 2010 ADF&G managers lasted more than ten years. The new managers learned the state regulations are cumbersome, difficult, and stressful. It is not pleasant to micromanage the daily lives of Natives. These managers provided testimony promoting state regulation restrictions and quit.

Natives always talk about hunting and fishing. In the letter to Schmidt, Pilot Station tribe concluded that we were willing to work with the state rather than the federal government. Native traditional principles of management compliment the state guidelines of responsibility, even though there are conflicts and legal constraints that keep one from working with the other. The lessons of state subsistence restrictions made us realize these very principles are what the elders tried to explain through language translators as traditional management principles of Native way of life. The Yup'ik laws have never been written. The State of Alaska incorporated these principles into the state constitution as sustained yield. Between tribal and state . . .

1. We agree with sustained yield principles as management guidelines.
2. We agree ANCSA extinguished aboriginal rights to hunting and fishing.
3. We agree Alaska tribes do not own reservations or lands to claim management responsibilities.

We want to work together and use our traditional doctrines. Natives have hunted and fished for as long as many of us can remember. These are not principles of co-management, principles of divide and conquer, or principles of preferential use. This is traditional stewardship of respect. We respect the State of Alaska, but for us to work together, we also need your respect. Unlike use and access, we want management responsibility. We cannot achieve this unless we have jurisdiction. We want to tell our stories.

33 ⪜ One Nation and . . .

"I am from a small village in Alaska. When one is a Democrat or Republican it seems hard to try to work together . . .," I told a roomful of students and moderators. I stuttered. The audience was larger than I had expected.

The high school students were young like me. I heard the microphone echo my words. With no training in public speaking, I tried to rein in my thoughts and convey a reasonable message about the role of government and general consensus of people like me. I looked at the non-Native students and talked about the traditional form of governance that instilled a peaceful life of growing up in a small remote Alaska village. I knew bigwigs from Washington DC were listening. I doubted if anything I said would make a difference; they were adamant about their party affiliations and set in their beliefs of what a government is supposed to be. Do people serve the government or does the government serve the people? I saw friends from Alaska and reassured myself they knew what it was like to grow up Native with our elders' way of life and the notion of how it takes a village to raise a child. We were on a national Close Up high school trip to Washington DC. After five days of visiting congressional offices, a wrap-up session on what we had learned gave many of us an opportunity to voice our opinions.

For me, this was a vacation. I traveled to this session with several students from St. Mary's Mission and Mt. Edgecumbe School. We enjoyed the Smithsonian National Museum of Natural History, the Air and Space Museum, and other significant monuments. The crowds of people all the time, everywhere, were nothing compared to home. The entertaining highlight was the live musical performance of James Belushi in *The Pirates of Penzance*.

In city and tribal council meetings in Pilot Station, it is a Native custom to say a Christian prayer with the notion that there is a deeper faith guiding our worldview and the decision that must be made. The relationship between church and state is precarious. There are many religious denominations, and their comfort and guidance provide solace to those who practice their faith. In a 2017 city council meeting in the Kenai Peninsula, the general custom was to invite any audience member willing to provide an opening prayer. This is a city council thing. Everything was going well until the council realized they were praying to the devil and the person providing the prayer was a demonologist.

When someone has their foot in the door, it is hard to close. This is the irony of the Native identity and the State of Alaska. In Pilot Station the role of the federal government is an invisible one . . . as it should be.

Before 1971, one reason the state and federal government did not want to recognize tribal identities in Alaska was the hassle of dealing with tribal sovereignty. The U.S. government used treaties to recognize certain responsibilities and tasks as a pact between governments, each recognizing the other. As a general procedure, respect is agreed on, civil proceedings are in progress, and above all else each nation is recognized as sovereign. After statehood, the wealth of Alaska resources changed this perspective—besides the fact that the federal government no longer practiced treaty agreements with American Indians. Alaska was rich with resources for Natives to own with the argument that they were here first and should be in charge of their own destiny.

The reservation system in the Lower 48 created enclaves where the land and resources belong to Indian tribes. If Alaska Natives own similar resources within a sovereign tribal pact, agreements will have to be signed recognizing sovereignty. ANCSA settled the land issue, created Native corporations, and discarded all notion of tribal existence. *Tribe* or *sovereignty* were never recognized in ANCSA—these two are not the same as *aboriginal rights*.

When the act was passed and Natives received land and money, the state was pleased with no Indian reservations. Many Natives were pleased the corporations will own the land with the idea of Native control. For many non-Natives, the colonial concept of landownership is the basis of sovereignty, yet most everyone assumed tribal and aboriginal rights were the same. In 1993 President Bill Clinton signed an executive order establishing a list of federally recognized tribes, including 229 tribes in Alaska. After this recognition, the State of Alaska realized the definition of "tribal sovereignty" needed to be addressed. This created a confusing time period between the tribes, corporations, and state, especially with the notion that tribes in Alaska are not sovereign because they do not own land.

As one people, if we ask for economic relief from the any large for-profit corporation, they will quickly kick us out the door and hope we did not start a downward trend on the stocks of the corporation. If corporations owned by foreign countries like Venezuela start providing relief, it is recognition that the world economy is not as complicated as we tend to believe. When natural disasters occur and other countries step in to help, it reiterates a simple reminder: we are human, and when help is needed assistance will be provided. An example is when Hugo Chávez and the Venezuela oil corporation Citgo provided one hundred gallons of heating fuel to many low-income rural Alaska households in 2006. With the high cost of fuel, heating homes during winter is something for which we have all grown dependent.

This relief effort began when Venezuela's president, Hugo Chávez, called President George Bush the devil. Citgo's contribution of home fuel was an effective tool for creating an economic crisis when the economic crisis was already there. Get households depended on the resource, saturate the supply, and as supply dwindles, demand will increase. The Venezuela leader may be a socialist using the idea of spreading the resource to utilize a capitalistic strategy to gain wealth. This idea to spread the wealth is a diversion to remind the average American that the world economy is a little more complicated than we think. As a result, this saturation of supply and increase for demand wreaked havoc on the U.S. economy and ridiculed the economic theory that any corporate intent to make a profit requires exchange of capital.

As a result of this fuel donation, the price of oil skyrocketed from $20 to over $150 per barrel in several short months. Shareholders of oil companies reaped profits never experienced before. Alaskans appreciated the $2,000 PFD dividends as a result.[1]

To be included in mission and vision statements of U.S department agencies is legal representation that implies tribes are in a position to be reckoned with. Many Alaska state departments take for granted that Alaska tribes do not have the same sovereignty as Lower 48 Indian tribes. It is ironic that some federal government departments have a similar view and will not stand up and say tribes in Alaska are sovereign. If Alaska tribes do not have the same privilege as other U.S. Indian tribes, why Alaska Natives continue to be treated as special trusts is a misperception of tribal recognition status.

All Alaska tribes have been given a piecemeal approach by the state and federal government. It is a general acceptance that tribes have some governing responsibilities, social in nature, but they have no sovereignty because they do not own the land. Recent legal changes and disclaimers started to confuse everyone. The land-into-trust program caused tribes to wonder, if the tribes have title to land-into-trust, does that make them sovereign? The land-into-trust program allows Alaska Native corporations to give corporation land to a tribe for special protections. The land is not eligible to be taxed if developed or taken away as an asset. In essence, the land is protected by the tribe as a simple existence of being.

Although there have been many misunderstandings and opinions about tribes, absent of Indian Country the state attorney general admitted in 2017 that Alaska tribes are sovereign. The state constitution does not recognize tribes with the same equality as Alaska residents, but the constitutional forefathers did recognize Alaska Natives as residents. To those forefathers, talking about tribes and tribal members was taboo, and there is no mention of Native rights. That generation of Alaskans had no sentiment for Alaska Native tribes. Alaska Natives are recognized in many U.S. government provisions, but to be included in the state constitution would have given the Native identity special trust with absolute power. This constitution does not apply to tribal members. We need to address this discrepancy.

≋

Places where I have been, things I have seen, situations I have been in, nature does not give a damn who you are. My Yup'ik ancestors did not survive by being sentimental. If Natives were sentimental and sympathetic to the natural world, they would have succumbed to Charles Darwin's theory of survival of the fittest. When non-Native teachers travel to Native Alaska for the first time, it is a culture shock, and many ask: *Why do these people live here?*

When troopers asked Point Hope elders for help to address the one hundred caribou left to waste, the elders experienced the trepidation the state is still trying to impose and instill. When the state implies to Natives to respect animals because that is what Natives are supposed to do, this opens a festering wound of confusion. When non-Natives reiterate a way of life that many in large societies have lost touch with, this creates uncomfortable situations for Natives, who question whether we misinterpreted a lesson from our ancestors. What is the respect the troopers are asking for? Is it the animals we respect?

In an earlier chapter, elder Dan Greene told of respect for the animal as a precautionary safety, implying respect that bear by keeping a safe distance or it could become an ugly confrontation, a lesson of cause and effect with subtle visual cues. The troopers' asking for help contradicts the power of authority that comes with enforcement responsibility. Many believe Natives are supposed to live in harmony with nature. Why troopers try to create a spiritual sense of respect contradicts the state's role of responsibility. Respect for animals is more than a psychedelic freedom of expression.

Many appreciate the wilderness experience of peace and tranquility with aesthetic ingenuity and inspiration. Looking out the window to snow-covered peaks, colorful leaves, cute cuddly baby animals, and flying birds ... serenity. Those who traditionally made the rules and enforce the regulations should realize our Native way of life is not a reality show with entertaining antics to keep everyone's attention.

My Native ancestors passed from one generation to the next the practice and skills of success, not as fun activities, but as skills necessary for survival. To think like a hunter is to be a hunter. Native traditional responsibility is based on successes passed from one hunter to the next. It is, in essence, people management: consensual agreements based on harvest success, internal versus external application tasks to the environment. In Western thought, management of people's activities, what they do and how they do it, is recognized as a necessary tool for resource responsibility. Delegation of authority is not part of the responsibility we all share. From one Native to another, it was never an application of tasks or agreements that you are the only one responsible for everything we do. When we share our catch, we learn that traditional management was a shared responsibility until territorial government and statehood claimed full responsibility and took away Native responsibility.

Natives learned this lesson after they killed the last woolly mammoth. A sensible practice is necessary for survival, and we are responsible for everything we hunt and fish. Targeting animals because they are big and easy should not be our only source of food. Fishing and hunting birds, seals, and other large and small animals created a diverse and rich imagination of appreciating a successful catch as a humble gratuity. A deep understanding that management of resources is not an active task of creating imaginary boundaries and allow one person full responsibility of something we all share. Traditional management was when one hunter, one fisher, told the other that we had more than enough.

Some contemporary non-Natives learned haphazardly amid the cries of many forgotten Native Americans about non-Native hunters who were killing the bison, buffalo, and muskoxen to extinction. It was a close lesson, and it is hard to imagine our wildlife situation if Natives did not voice our concerns. When one Native tells another, "My fish-drying rack is full and I have enough meat," it is a message that we do not need to kill one more caribou, buffalo, muskox, or fish because we could. Because the season is open and we have permission. Perhaps Point Hope Natives killed the caribou because the state gave an emergency order to do so . . . or the Natives killed the caribou to collect antlers to sell.

The State of Alaska continues to claim the state constitution gives them full wildlife management responsibility. What many don't realize is that this language provision was not created in Alaska. It was created in Tennessee, and Alaska used that state constitution as a guideline. This part of the constitution is a Trojan horse for Alaska; the constitution forefathers copied this eloquent language without realizing Alaska Natives' appreciation of Mother Nature is more than respect for animals.

Like a doe instantly struck with a shining spotlight, in the middle of all tribal sovereignty issues is BIA. Since the U.S. government consciously recognized Alaska Natives as part of a special group of Native Americans, they have used BIA as a front for addressing the concerns of Native Alaska. Like a doorstop that unconsciously holds open the door, BIA has been trying to figure out how to address Alaska issues and bowing to every Native dignitary with a kind word. In the Native world, BIA has been interpreting and reinterpreting the meaning of federal policies and reiterating to the tribes that we are here to help you with the best of our abilities, if we can, and if not we will get back to you. The BIA main office is in Washington DC.

Treating Alaska Natives the same as every other Native American was never meant to be complicated. Treat Alaska Native tribes as sovereign but not sovereign. Treat them as tribes but not like tribes.

Traditional Alaska Native cultures never see themselves as tribes but as people. Yup'ik means "real people." Elder Natives learned from early cinema that Natives living on reservations was not a good image. Being restricted in where you can hunt and fish was never acceptable. It is common for elders to say that we are not Indians or tribal members: we are Alaska Natives. A quiet resolution that these Natives did not want to deal with BIA and be stereotyped the same as Natives living on reservations. Many elders have unpleasant stories of having to deal with BIA when there were no other agencies to offer help and assistance. After BIA was dispatched to Alaska to create schools, it has been struggling to identify and clarify its duties. Like every federal agency, BIA goes back and forth to Washington to verify its role and how to deal with tribes.

The traditional role of Alaska Native leadership centers on a consensual agreement between the elders, and the people supported the elders in selecting leaders as wise decision-makers. Anytime there was a disagreement of leadership, elders provided the pivotal duty of either supporting the person or providing recommendations and guidance. This was the traditional role before 1971. Nowadays, it is easy to look to the leaders at the state and federal level and see how non-Native leadership has many challenges. When leaders take advantage of their role as stewards of a people, *government* takes a whole new meaning.

When Alaska leaders take advantage to receive benefits only allowed for a selected few, this creates disdain with the challenges we have in Alaska. During her tenure, Sarah Palin was reluctant to move to Juneau as a full-time governor, which may not mirror any of the merits of her job performance, but we allowed her to live and work from her home in Wasilla and receive per-diem payments while conducting state duties. All state employees should receive similar benefits. For example, as an ADF&G employee, I should be able to work for the Fairbanks office and live in Pilot Station. As a benefit to the state, many rural residents will be employed living in remote communities, promoting economics free from welfare services. The rude awaking of the COVID-19 pandemic made many of us realize that we could work from home no matter who we work for.

Since ANCSA, every Native organization addressing corporations, housing, health, school, and church has followed the same structural framework of leadership. A group of members is selected as a board executive council and a leader is chosen as the chairman. The Native people represented do not select the leaders. In 2016 AVCP changed the leadership of this nonprofit corporation. Instead of appointing a president, the executive council hires a corporate executive officer to run this non-government organization.

The election for the U.S. president is a serious national event. Every three years, we are unfortunate to listen and watch the media frenzy as potential candidates bash their opponents and coax voters with their reasons for representing the people in the highest office. Although every election year follows guidelines of the U.S. Constitution, if a respectable congressional candidate were to legally change his birth name from *Average Joe* to *Electoral College* and encourage people to vote for him as U.S. president, many U.S. citizens are likely to address whether it is true that the person receiving the most popular votes will be selected.

The role of Alaska tribal governments is inevitable. Every time I travel the road system in the Lower 48, it is hard to miss large billboards advertising casinos and Indian gaming, enticing everyone with a chance to win money. Most accept the role of Indian reservations as tribal entities where self-governing activities help generate funds and provide a means to help tribal members—similar to the role of Alaska Native corporations. Unfortunately, Alaska tribes do not have the same mechanism. Alaska tribes have no means to generate funds to help tribal members and instead depend on the generous donation of federal taxpayer funds and state revenue and assistance. The amount of assistance from the federal government is noticeable, but services from the state are not as public because every Alaska resident is eligible to meet the same services. Public assistance is one example; another is tribal child custody cases.

Recent examples of child custody cases and the state Office of Children's Services' working with tribal courts is promising. For tribal courts, the Indian Child Welfare Act provides guidance where the discretion of the case and recommendation of the tribe are valued assets. Actions of OCS used to be similar to actions of ADF&G, where the Native side of the story was often ignored. Unlike OCS, ADF&G works with USFWS as dual managers and the Native has the challenging role to abide with both agencies. Unlike ADF&G, OCS has no federal counterpart yet is willing to work with Natives in the well-being of any child, Native or non-Native, tribal or non-tribal.

NOTES

1. The Alaska Permanent Fund Dividend program is a revenue-sharing program distributed to all Alaskans. The dividend is part of the state revenue created from Alaska's oil and gas industry.

34 Treaty Obligations

"Growing up, we set traps like this and we would catch lots."

I explained this practice of trapping animals to a curious and starry-eyed graduate student at the Center for Northern Studies in Wolcott, Vermont. The concept is simple, yet there is no mention of it in other research papers on trapping this small hand-size critter alive and healthy. The bait and trap methods were not working, and without live samples for scientific observation, Brad could not prove whatever theory he was trying to prove without evidence. Several days later, Brad was all smiles as he caught several mice and voles to start his project. In the grass field behind student quarters, mice and voles followed trails everywhere. As kids, we set traps on trails by digging a hole and setting an empty coffee can as a pitfall. Mice and voles running on trails are creatures of habit.

In Alaska many people assume that since there are not many federal treaties with Alaska Natives, then there are no guilty presumptions and no promises can be broken. An example is the purchase of Alaska and the 1887 U.S. treaty with Russia. Special provisions of this treaty recognize that no intentional harm will come to Alaska Natives. Eventually, the Natives become special trusts and wards of the federal government and have nothing to uphold in the treaty.

Many current treaties with neighboring countries like Canada and Russia include fish and wildlife provisions in which everyone agrees to help manage and conserve. Examples are the Yukon Kuskokwim Goose Management Plan with provisions of the 1917 Migratory Bird Treaty Act, and the Yukon River Salmon Agreement established by the

1985 Pacific Salmon Treaty with Canada. These agreements recognize Native subsistence provisions crucial for food security, and the State of Alaska is recognized with jurisdiction over all Alaska residents. In these agreements, Alaska Natives have no provisional powers to restrict use or deny access to non-locals, non-users, or non-Natives—no power that says, "You are not allowed to hunt or fish here because we say so." No power that says, "Our part of the agreement gives us every right for management responsibility within terms of the agreement." In reality, the Natives have no management power over any user on non-user, and the state does not allow preferential harvests for any user.

The Yukon River agreement with Canada for salmon that spawn in Canadian rivers yet travel through Alaska has no provisions for Alaska Native or tribal responsibility. Pilot Station tribe has offered services to help the state in managing this salmon fishery. There is no record of any state or federal representative who traveled the Lower Yukon to address or negotiate this treaty agreement with the Natives; therefore, it is null and void. When Native fishers fish against state regulations and dare the state to take action, the state will sulk and shy away. There is no penalty when Natives refuse to participate or adhere to Alaska's side of the treaty. Although the state may restrict commercial fish openings and create more economic disparity in the poorest regions in the state, food security will always be a family concern.

The Yukon River Drainage Fisheries Association's summer weekly teleconference meetings recognize tribes. Tribal organizations report real-time updates on fisheries and in-season river conditions to Alaska and Canadian fish managers. In any management scenario, this instant update from communities in the middle of the resource's territory is valuable information. Regardless, the manager is the decision-maker for everything Native.

In 2006 I was a winner of a $100 check from ADF&G as a prodigal resident for the Yukon River calendar contest. The calendar is sent to every Yukon River family to collect seasonal salmon harvest data. Several years later, ADF&G paid me another $100 to use my commercial salmon gillnet at the Pilot Station Sonar Site. ADF&G wanted to test the king salmon catch rates of a commercial gillnet 50 fathoms long compared to a 25-fathom gillnet. I grew up on the river and know how to catch fish with the least amount of effort and sampling error. My CPUE sampling variance is more than proficient. Statistically, CPUE instantly assumes every fisher is the same, whether one is a greenhorn or a commercial captain. My one regret for this sampling test was that I should have allowed the same ADF&G technician to captain both nets as a CPUE statistical procedure. The technician who captained the ADF&G gillnet was a rookie of everything at the sonar site.

When I agreed to use my commercial gillnet, I did not know this data would be instrumental to creating more state regulations. ADF&G agreed to pay me; I insisted I would keep all king salmon for my family and that ADF&G could use my commercial net for this unplanned unscientific salmon comparison. As a commercial fisherman, I use and apply traditional knowledge and skill to my fishing gear to catch salmon efficiently with the least amount of effort. Commercial fishers are happy with lots of fish.

Happy with this opportunity to keep king salmon, I insisted that I would drive and captain the boat with my net. At first, I was going to use my skiff, motor, and sonar gear, but ADF&G insisted that to use different boats was not scientific, with one more statistical variance to account for. So we agreed to use ADF&G's twenty-four-foot Munson aluminum skiff, my commercial gillnet, and ADF&G's gillnet with four of us on board. I was familiar with the Munson. For seven seasons I had worked at the Pilot Station Sonar Site and used this very boat to train new employees. This boat is a custom Cadillac for Yukon fishing; with a partial V-shape hull and power steering, this boat turns on a dime, and stops, slows, and coasts with ease. It is a fisher's boat.

The king salmon comparison addressed the notion that commercial fishnets catch bigger and more female king salmon than non-commercial nets. Both gillnets are eight and a half inches. My commercial net is 50 fathoms long by 45 mesh deep, compared to ADF&G gillnet at 25 fathoms long by 35 mesh deep. For non-seafaring folks, one fathom is equivalent to six feet, and the depth is counted by the number of square mesh as the net hangs in the water. Smaller king salmon size is a statewide concern. With no written methods and procedures, this comparison is ADF&G's attempt to collect evidence that the size of the king salmon is a result of commercial gillnets.

Since 1982 the Pilot Station fish sampling method has been the same. CPUE is a done deal; according to the biometricians, it is a scientific method. To be impartial, the test fishnets are the same depth and length and fished in the same location despite changes in river level, sandbars, and staff. The physical dimensions of a net are measurable attributes of a scientific process and accepted for the sampling procedure. The skill of the captain is another attribute that provides a variance challenge for biometricians and is not considered in the CPUE formula data. I know the skills of every new ADF&G employee who has never fished or driven a boat and motor before. As technicians, these new state employees are on the lowest rung; many are happy to have a job and receive a salary. Any statistical challenge is not a variance, and there is no such thing as ratings guide for ADF&G employees. The physical dimensions of the net and CPUE of the staff are measurable numbers, but there was an unmeasurable attribute special about my commercial gillnet. My net's function is to catch king salmon, but there is something special about my net to catch large Canadian females. It is my business to catch fish where every little skill or application to catch more is considered a trade secret.

At the Pilot Station Sonar Site, ADF&G also monitors river turbidity and water level. The U.S. Geological Survey also monitors the Yukon River with a staging station just below the village. At a 2012 community meeting, U.S. Geological Survey staff provided the average age of the water as sixteen years old in front of Pilot Station. Every normal person sees rain; this rain is newborn water created from hydrogen and oxygen molecules as moisture particles conglomerate within clouds. At the molecular level, the average water age was determined by carbon dating the residual carbon surrounding the hydrogen and oxygen molecules. The river is huge and the volume of water is staggering, but the average water age is sixteen years, and this means that at some area in this huge watershed, the water molecule was formed as snow, rain, or sleet, and the majority of water took sixteen years to reach Pilot Station. Another organization, the Yukon River Inter-Tribal Watershed Council, also collects river samples to monitor pollutants, sediment concentration, and waste. ADF&G is not the only agency monitoring river quality; U.S. Geological Survey monitors geologic aspects, and Yukon River Inter-Tribal Watershed Council monitors environmental conditions.

All Yukon River salmon are anadromous, and by some miracle they all return to the same river stream where they were born. The Yukon River drainage is huge, with countless tributaries and spawning sites for all salmon and other fish species. The sonar site was selected for one reason: There are no other sloughs or river channels salmon can bypass. Every fish on the river have to pass in front of Pilot Station. With the countless tributaries, salmon use their sense of smell to return to the same river tributary where they were born. Many elder fishers scent their nets with a certain Native plant or household liquid detergent to attract salmon. Some younger fishers have taken this practice one step further. I have a collection of river samples from salmon spawning sites I use to soak my commercial gillnets during the off-season, depending on what salmon I am fishing for. I did the same for the king salmon gillnet used for the ADF&G sampling comparison.

Carl Pfisterer has worked on sonar technology since he was a young college graduate and learned the intricacies of everything sonar, including river hydrology, sound acoustics, oscillation of sound traveling in freshwater, use of Didson technology, and the idea of dual beams. For everyone else, sonar is blips, pings, beeps, and movies about submarines. During a tour of the sonar camp for ADF&G and state leaders, Carl was explaining an analog dot matrix paper printout of little wiggle lines as fish. Everything was going well until Carl tried to explain the theory of fish going upriver and fish going downriver. The sonar staff was there to count fish, not the number of fish going upriver or downriver, and the staff ridiculed Carl about the little blips on the paper. Can a fish caught in a fishnet indicate whether it is going upriver or downriver?

Happy with the chance to keep king salmon for my family, I captained the Munson with ease, accounting for the river current and direction of the motor. In less than forty seconds my commercial net was in the water and ready to hit the reverberation band and main route of salmon. There is something about the reverberation band where the river current churns and rolls and creates a challenge for salmon. At Pilot Station, the Yukon River is a single channel, and the force of the current is greatest at this reverberation band where the bend of the river and the sandbar, as a single topographic feature, wreak havoc on physical and statistical characteristics of hydrology. I have never caught one salmon above this reverberation band.

Upriver of the bend is a steep, deep-cut bank, downriver of the bend is a sandbar, and across from the bend is the shale rock cliff where the river has no other choice but to make a churning roll downriver. The shale rock is impenetrable to the current and creates a river force greatest at the nadir. As a result, the river current and force of the reverberation band are greatest just before the sandbar, at the apex of the bend. If the beach side of my net did not hit the sandbar, the river current would pull my net and boat out to the middle of the river. At eight feet of water and over the sandbar, where the river current is not as challenging for salmon, my net was perpendicular to the river and most effective. We drifted for seven minutes and quickly pulled in the net in two minutes. I looked to the beach; there was where Donald and I had run over someone's setnet many years ago. The staff did not know we were also comparing CPUE skills of commercial and greenhorn fishers.

The ADF&G technician captained the test fish gear, and the reverberation band and strong river current quickly pulled the Munson and short ADF&G net out to the deeper channel. The results of the commercial gillnet gear were incomparable. My family was happy with the thirty-eight king salmon. As we pulled in the net, which side of the net the king salmon were caught on is not recorded. ADF&G gillnets do not use scents or attractants, and the test net is only a measurable scientific sampling method that can be repeated by any novice technician where CPUE accounts for deficiency in skills and knowledge. The river water in Pilot Station is a huge mixing zone of molecules from every tributary within the drainage system. The scents salmon follow lead them to their spawning sites. Little bits of cloth are tied along my commercial gillnet. Each cloth was soaked in vials of Canadian river water where Canadian king salmon spawn. I do not use these nets for subsistence fishing. This is my trade secret I never share with anyone. The salmon have more than two thousand river miles to travel.

Summer 2006 was my last season working for Pilot Station Sonar. In 2009 state and tribal relations over king salmon restrictions were not cordial. Several days after my family cut and dried the salmon, Marshall tribal members fished for king salmon against the closure regulations and dared the state to take action. In 1982 BOF passed a regulation reducing the maximum net size to eight and a half inches, and in 2010 the net size was further reduced to seven and a half inches. Following the non-Native logic of why gillnet restrictions are made, we Natives should expect further gear reductions twenty years from now. I don't know what ADF&G or the BOF are trying to achieve.

In the January 2010 BOF Fairbanks meeting, I was one of many Lower Yukon Natives providing testimony opposing any gear restrictions. I had a three-minute time limit. ADF&G staff provided a summary of this net comparison, and the conclusive evidence is compelling that commercial gillnets catch bigger kings. As a Native, it is not my custom to disrespect anyone by talking loudly or raising my voice to try to convince anyone about my ethics. ADF&G gave BOF the reason to reduce the gillnet size. Several months later, in April 2010, FSB passed similar gillnet gear restrictions. After the federal board action, Pilot Station tribe asked the regional federal liaison if FSB can make subsistence regulations without taking public comments, whether they follow ANILCA guidelines or not. With this comment, the liaison asked if Pilot Station could submit an agenda change request to address this. No request was submitted.

In every river in Alaska there is compelling evidence that king salmon size is getting smaller. Although science may eventually claim this as natural, inconclusive evidence of evolution and environmental attributes such as ocean conditions and predatory-prey feeder stock relationship, management by the State of Alaska has been similar for every river system. ADF&G has not responded about the impact of genetic drift and BOF actions. Respectable sportsmen who propose gillnet restrictions blame the gillnet size for the smaller salmon, while many accept global climate change as the cause instead.

The presence of any government official is traditionally shunned by the majority of Alaskans, who prefer less government. This is comforting to the serenity of living on the last frontier. Participating in any board regulatory process where like minds think alike is a challenge. This is never accounted for and difficult for many who have an abstract relationship to the natural world.

A Lower Yukon moose hunting moratorium have provided excellent moose numbers. Natives voluntarily agreed not to harvest moose for five years. Prior to this, moose numbers had been stagnant; recovery growth models and harvesting only males were counterintuitive measures at a time when poaching was a common practice. Moose hunt efforts were time consuming with low success rates. Many had to travel farther upriver, as far as the Innoko River, for a chance to harvest meat. The last year of the moose moratorium was 1998. The moose numbers in this area are now among the highest in Alaska. Wildlife managers allow harvests for three animals with longer hunt seasons, unrestricted gender openings, and hunting of moose calves.

Recently, there is another Native concern wildlife managers are not aware of. There is a growing market of moose antlers sold for cash. The rumor is that the antlers are shipped overseas and sold as an aphrodisiac ingredient. It is not unusual to hear village rumors of Natives in need of cash harvesting antlered moose and leaving the meat to waste. The sale of raw moose or caribou antlers is not regulated; perhaps this is a good time for BOG to consider raw antlers as a regulated product, similar to the ivory market.

The Pilot Station Traditional Council agrees with the State of Alaska on sustained yield principles of management. As Natives, we have no intention of overharvesting or endangering any subsistence fish or wildlife. We agree with the state and are pleased the state constitution recognizes sustained yield as a trust responsibility. This is the first principle we explained to ADF&G manager Stephanie Schmidt.

Management for commercial harvests and cash incentives is another realm.

35 ⋞ Management Options

"You're shaking. Don't laugh, just smile." The autotimer clicked as we watched the shutter of my 35mm camera. "Let's take another shot. Here—trade guns, and you hold the big ones. You caught most of them." We laughed and I told Kevin that this reminded me of Farley Mowat. "Who's Farley Mowat?" I laughed—this thinking like a gussak had some humor after all.

"He wrote this book about studying wolves in the Arctic and running naked with caribou."[1] We laughed, the sun was shining, and the island radiated with peace and quiet, an excellent day for hunting. Kevin VanHatten is an Athabascan originally from Kaltag. We worked for FSL and we were alone in this area of Admiralty Island. Our Native instinct to hunt is part of our culture. With daily deer sightings, most everyone in southeast Alaska knows Admiralty Island is brown bear country; rumors of wolf sightings are rare. There are no wild caribou. Occasionally we hear sightings of moose along the mainland.

The U.S. Forest Service required us to carry high-powered rifles in brown bear country. I carried a Remington 30-06 and Kevin carried a Weatherby 375. Both are lethal to any predator, large or small. The 375 is an elephant gun, and the kick would leave a sore spot on our shoulders. This gun has stopping power to stun and damage any predator who tried to mess with us two Natives. The bullets are soft-point lead with over 280 grains, and any impact would cause the bullet to shatter and cause intentional harm. When we tested the gun on a large rotten spruce, we could not get over the fist-size exit wound.

We had been there for three days, and we wanted picture proof of our catch to show everyone at FSL. We did not expect to kill a raider family smuggling to get at our food. One chewed and ruined our plastic cooler like it was a plastic toy. These mammals will never terrorize anyone else. The FSL staff is familiar with these critters as a nuisance; to everyone else these are just mice. Holding rifles and four or five dangling in one hand with the rest lain side by side on a log, we smiled and pretended to be proud sportsmen.

Mom loved these pictures.

"Not all managers are biologists and not all biologists are managers" was one of the first academic arguments I could relate to. This was once a dilemma posed to early fish and wildlife managers and situations they had to address. Every management regulation decision is scrutinized based on information of perceived wildlife population declines, the basis of what management is all about. These decisions depend on the economics of supply and demand and the rationale whether harvests should be allowed or restricted. I've often wondered how many management choices we learn from mistakes, how many mistakes we learn from making these decisions, and if this is still a learning tool that we can afford to use.

One story I heard while working in the Tongass National Forest was of U.S. Forest Service employees removing logs and wood debris from a fish spawning stream near the edge of a forest clear-cut after the passage of the Clean Water Act. Clean water is clean water, according to presumptions of us humans. I assume Mother Nature's version of clean water is found in molecules smaller than a drop of water. Nature has a dirty mind when she keeps a clean environment. Suppose someone came into your home and cleaned out everything so you could live in a clean bare environment. What the U.S. Forest Service found was that a clean and debris-free stream was not good. All the fish died. There were no logs in the water for little fish to hide from big fish, to hide from birds of prey and bears, to hide from the sun, and to keep the water temperature cool. There were no logs to create mixing zones, eddies, air bubbles, insect coves, and algae growth for little fish to feed.

In November 1992 I was driving alone to Fairbanks from Juneau after my season was over. It was a bright winter wonderland, and the sights of Alaska and the mountainous terrain were mesmerizing. After passing the Alaska-Canada border, the only highway vehicles were truckers and their freight. My vehicle was a small two-door Datsun 210; at thirty-one miles a gallon this little car was an economic upgrade from my gas-guzzling land cruiser. In a straightaway stretch I saw something far ahead. I slowed down because it looked unusual and like something I had never seen except in pictures. I had read of these critters in this part of Alaska but to see it in person and next to the vehicle amazed me. It was walking along the snowplowed road and as big as my vehicle. Before the turn of the century, its cousin the buffalo of the Great Plains was almost hunted to extinction. The woodland bison is bigger and commonly lives in the boreal forests. With snow-covered back, head, and shoulders, huffing and puffing with the cold winter, the size of this animal was formidable. I took out my camera as I drove slowly past. I can only imagine how many wolves could take down this animal.

The stories of the bison, buffalo, and muskoxen all share impacts of non-Native colonization. The buffalo of the Great Plains roamed in great herds; traditional Natives talk of their numbers with reverence of a cultural resource. It has been documented that the muskoxen in Alaska were all decimated before the turn of the century as a result of whalers and explorers. The muskox was reintroduced to Alaska with herds from Greenland and northern Canada. In the boreal forests the bison was hunted to the point of conservation concern, then reintroduced in Alaska with stock animals from Canada. These animals coexisted with prehistoric animals such as the woolly mammoth and provided food security to many Native cultures.

In 2016 ADF&G reintroduced a herd of bison to western Alaska near the village of Shageluk. The bison used to roam and live as wild animals in this area, and this introduced herd is intended to extend the range of the animals. Much of western Alaska, including Pilot Station, maintained reindeer herds before statehood. To help with this reindeer husbandry, Lapland herders were also brought to Alaska to teach this herding method. Reindeer herding is still practiced in the Seward peninsula, near Nome and Nunivak Island. In and near Pilot Station, reindeer herding lasted until 1940, and the last of the reindeer ran off to the wild western Arctic caribou herd. There are no reindeer herds in any Lower Yukon community. The northern Andreafsky hills are assumed to be the extent of the southern range of the western Arctic. Although Natives from Pilot Station, St. Mary's, and Mountain Village have caught caribou near the Andreafsky hills, reindeer herders from communities near Seward peninsula remind Natives not to shoot their reindeer stock as wild caribou.

In a similar situation, the reintroduced muskoxen on Nunivak and Nelson Island roam free and are not herded as domestic stock animals. Nelson Island is closer to mainland Alaska, and muskoxen have walked over the frozen river surrounding the island onto the mainland. In 1990 a Pilot Station Native caught a lone muskox female in a place the locals refer as the volcano mud hills. The hunter returned home and distributed the meat. Although the season was closed, the harvest was illegal. It is not unusual for muskoxen to be spotted near Pilot Station.

Eventually, it is hoped the introduced bison near Shageluk will be eligible for sustainable harvests, similar to muskoxen. Like all wild creatures, the instinct to roam and explore is a natural behavioral creature comfort to learn the surrounding environment. A lone bison female with a radio tracking device roamed beyond the Innoko River drainage, wandered westward toward the Bering Sea, and was shot near the community of Quinhagak. Like the statement that not all biologists are managers, not all Natives are respectable hunters.

How much is too much and how much is not enough? Unlike commercial harvests where the product allows a monetary income, subsistence is a two-sided coin.

Lower Yukon Native families have a good idea of how much salmon to harvest and cache. For large families, fifty king salmon and two hundred chum salmon is more than sufficient, with varying numbers of Yukon pink and coho salmon. This is a lot of fish and Natives will know if they have too much and share salmon with others. The distribution of excess fish is a practice of subsistence. Granted, it is not an effort of conserving the stock but an effort of minimizing wanton waste. When Natives claim they are saturated and the cache is more than sufficient, they ignore all state regulation openings and closures for the remainder of the season.

Season openings and permission for Natives to harvest wildlife at the same time is a non-Native management tool vigorously applied since statehood. The story of my nephew who was charged with wanton waste of moose and my story of throwing away my sister's fish tote of salmon are examples of failure of these management guidelines. When all Natives are given permission to harvest wildlife at the same time, it is easy for the community to get saturated with subsistence harvests. We cannot share any excess because everyone is participating and more wild resources tend to get wasted.

Natives are actively aware of efforts of local organizations in their communities. Like a reservation—that is where Natives live. It is hard to keep secrets, especially with the recent boom of social media. Unlike managers giving Natives permission, if someone is short on subsistence, short on meat or fish, it is not unusual for Natives to provide a communication link to those who have the means to harvest the needs, whether the season is open or not.

One Native management example is to do away with moose hunting seasons, forever.

Although there is a statewide communal hunt program where the Alaska community can participate and provide pseudo-management of annual moose harvests, this sounds like an excellent opportunity for the community to participate in management responsibility. Although this program has been around for many years, communities like Pilot Station and many Native villages will never participate. There are too many overtones of state regulations, and everyone is required to purchase a current hunting license and harvest tag to verify the state's role. Because of the state's claim of responsibility, Natives would rather not participate in something where someone from far away continues to tell everyone what to do and how it should work.

As a Native, the best option is to do away with moose hunt seasons. It is time for communities to vigorously regulate a closed season from March until July as a management option. This will only be effective if local tribes are involved and agree to help monitor hunt efforts and closures during the rest of the year. A time to remind hunters that hunting is closed or not closed and need not to be done in secret. When there is a meat shortage in the community. When someone has the gas and the weather is favorable. This will provide a sense of how much food to cache for the rest of the winter. In addition, tribal participation will discourage wanton waste. More meat can be salvaged, distributed, and preserved in a timely manner, when the family is ready for the surplus relative to other subsistence resources. The state must be willing to extend this obligation for subsistence animals such as caribou, muskox, moose . . . and salmon. Although human population growth is an economic concern regarding our subsistence resources, the unique characteristics of Yup'ik economics is the lack of roads and reliable transportation networks for distribution of store-bought goods for many of our rural villages.

The positive effort of local management is an instant feedback of current wildlife situations and environmental conditions. I know Natives who look to each other and agree that tribes need to get together and agree to this as an option. Although many tribes in Alaska have been trying to get organized and recognized as existing entities, the limited community assets provide everyday challenges.

Every Alaska Native regional corporation has a natural resource department that addresses environmental natural resources—except wildlife and fisheries management. Similarly, whether individual tribes create a natural resource department depends on local available assets. Tribes in Alaska have an option of whether to compact and pool their funds with other tribes toward a regional nonprofit association. AVCP and Tanana Chiefs Conference have a natural resource department that helps with regional wildlife and fishery issues, but they have no management responsibility. They provide recommendations to anyone and everyone.

In the AVCP region, the only tribe that created and maintained a natural resources department was Emmonak Tribal Council. The Emmonak natural resource department addressed fish and wildlife concerns holistically with culture and tradition. One state regulation Emmonak was instrumental in changing was harvests of local beavers. Beaver numbers in the Lower Yukon have always been significant since the nationwide and worldwide protests of the fur market. The supply increased such that the state regulations for beaver hunting, trapping seasons, and bag limits became obsolete. There is no current fur market. Emmonak tribal council submitted a BOG proposal for no open seasons, no closed seasons, and no bag limits. BOG passed this proposal, allowing beaver harvests without imposing conscientious objections. Many residents enjoy beaver as Native food, and regardless of how many are harvested, there are still more and more of them.

Imagine the opportunity this would provide if it was applied to all subsistence resources. The tribal members' assertion to other tribal members is a trust relationship that has always been there, but when obligations are taken away, any conservation effort is the sole responsibility of non-tribal members who do not live in the community. Take, for example, the caribou shot and killed near Point Hope. If the tribes were to recognize the caribou as a true cultural heritage, Point Hope tribal members could help discipline the young tribal members in the best interest of all users. Still, the State of Alaska cannot allow this. The only alternative is to continue to create intertribal fish and resource commissions with the federal government giving tribes pseudo-tribal powers for harvest . . . and require the state to step back and watch.[2]

In the April 2015 letter to ADF&G manager Stephanie Schmidt, Pilot Station tribe admitted that we agree with the state and were pleased that ANCSA extinguished aboriginal rights as the second principle of traditional management. The Bering Land Bridge is accepted as an archaeological gateway for many American Indigenous cultures. ANCSA preempts any claims of aboriginal rights to all Native cultures. Pilot Station tribe admits that we do not represent aboriginal Natives; we represent tribal members, citizens of our tribe. If anything, ANCSA immediately adjudicated Alaska tribes as a misconception of village corporation shareholders. Shareholders are not the same as tribal members.

Pilot Station tribe represents tribal members with a BIA certificate of Indian blood quantum as an enrollment requirement for eligibility. Parents are encouraged to enroll newborns, and an ancestral family tree provides a descendant lineage. Not just anyone is eligible to be a tribal member. This second principle is why tribes need to help manage traditional food security with the state to manage non-tribal members and commercial activities. According to ANCSA, the village and regional corporations receive title to land and tribes have no plenary powers of sovereignty without existing Indian reservations. The third principle of traditional management responsibility will address this.

Alaska tribes need to be involved in fish and wildlife resources and not assume tribal sovereignty for self-preservation of Native identity. Self-determination is an appealing option as a resource management tool—the best interest of tribes is the best condition of the resource. If there is one virtue, it is the fact that tribal members recognize and respect neighboring tribal members nurtured from sharing similar cultural traditions. Not only are cultural aspirations a source for supporting local efforts; all Alaska tribes recognize their community as crucial for tribal identity.

Local efforts such as moose moratoriums and voluntarily minimized king salmon harvests are practiced for the best interest of the resource and are beneficial to Alaska. State and federal regulations have no guidelines for volunteer moratoriums as management tools. When volunteer efforts include tribal elder's absence of consultation or cooperative agreements. We Natives have proven that we do not need federal or state action to take responsibility. We need to utilize this tool as our side of the story. The federal government is most effective as a consultant and must be willing to take action when issues become critical. The State of Alaska must be willing to accept the identity and role of tribes and to concede wildlife responsibility. Perhaps it is time for the State of Alaska to further develop the Division of Subsistence with management authority to work with Alaska tribes.

The State of Alaska bestowed wildlife responsibility to Savoonga and Gamble on St. Lawrence Island. This is a first step to this endeavor. It is only a matter of time before Native Alaska gets our share of the responsibility. We are ready.

NOTES

1. Farley Mowat, *Never Cry Wolf* (McClelland and Stewart, 1963).
2. Due to lack of funds, the Emmonak natural resource department closed in 2001.

36 ⋚ Wisdom of Elders

"Go to school, get an education, learn . . ." This is common advice for young eager minds. Many elders encouraged me with these very words. I thought of this lesson and quietly whispered to Evan, "Someday people are going to be calling you an elder."

What will you say?

⋚

Downtown Pilot Station is located on the Yukon River on a high alluvial land bank. This area is well drained, and the soil is well mixed with sandy loam and silt. At the end of town where the Kwicauq Slough meets the Yukon River is where my grandma Alick, Mom and Dad, and two of my uncles and aunties had their homes. The 1960s was a major period in U.S. and world history, and on local static radios we listened to KNOM Nome or KYUK Bethel. Much of the news focused on statewide and nationwide events. Occasionally the *Tundra Times* newspaper made its way to Pilot Station.

The traditional governing hall or community center was the qasgiq, or the men's house. As the State of Alaska developed its current governing structure, small Alaska Native communities eventually incorporated local governing bodies as an extension of state services. At this time, the state realized that the traditional form of government recognized as village government centered on the elders was not acceptable, especially if state funds are used for municipal services. These responsibilities dawned on state lawmakers as more issues such as health-care services, water and sewer, electricity, transportation, education, welfare, and fish and wildlife were now the state's responsibility over all Natives, despite their traditional ways. The municipal, "city" governing system changed Native ways of leadership.

The state informed rural community leaders that they need to be incorporated into a municipal government to receive state service funds to reassure everyone that no state funds would be misused. The only other alternative was to create a home-rule community, which had strong connotations of non-Native governing responsibility separate from the traditional village system of elders.

A local municipal system must include written ordinances for local projects to address water, sewer, and electricity, and a local tax revenue system as a potential self-supporting income. Regional borough formations were never a realized option for the Yukon Kuskokwim Delta. Although this was discussed to some extent by several regional Native associations, without a reliable resource base as a major economic development incentive, there is no means to support a borough. In other areas of Alaska, oil, mining, and forest products provide economic incentives supporting a borough system of services.

Pilot Station was incorporated as a second-class city in 1969, about the same time as many other rural cities statewide. An incorporated municipal government requires an election system of leadership with written laws. In light of this, Pilot Station elders recognized a new era was about to begin and that their traditional governing system could very well be in jeopardy or replaced. To help document this, Pilot Station completed a traditional qasgiq centered on the elders and Native traditions. At the end of downtown, behind Uncle Leonard's home, a large qasgiq was built. With a large firepit in the middle, the qasgiq was a large steam house and community gathering place where traditional sleds, kayaks, fish traps, and wood-working projects were completed. Dome shaped and iconic as an Eskimo igloo, the qasgiq was host to many songs and stories and a traditional Eskimo potlatch with honored guests from St. Mary's. This qasgiq lasted two seasons, but the traditional stories told there will never be forgotten. Every Eskimo song and dance tells a story.

Stories come in many forms and entertainment. Some have a lesson to be learned, some are entertaining, humorous, scary, thoughtful, and provocative. The most traditional songs provide reverence for many elders. In studying the history of any culture, archaeological finds and artifacts are easily interpreted with current cultural lore and customary use still in practice. In any culture, spooky stories are often used as deterrence for children to avoid mischief and reason to behave and listen to adults.

Introduction to Arctic Archaeology was a college elective class. Before this class, I had no interest in the subject. I was a young student attending the Center for Northern Studies in Wolcott, Vermont. The first sessions focused on major periods of Arctic cultures based on archaeological finds and significance of the make and type of tools. Cherts, obsidians, burin spalls, and Thule cultures were main topics. Besides a faint understanding of obsidians, I had no idea of Arctic archaeology, and this was never discussed in any of my high school history books.

The instructor got to the period of the Arctic small tool tradition and explained the tools and artifacts found. As an example, an artifact was passed among the students: miniature spearheads, blades, and tools were smaller than those of any period. Another artifact was passed, and this got my attention because it was unusual to my Yup'ik mind. The hair on the back of my neck tingled as I straightened in my seat and quietly realized I was holding archaeological evidence of Yu'caauaqs and Ircinraqs.

Before the 2009 king salmon protest in Marshall, there is an Ircinraq story. In many cultures from the Irish to Native Americans, folklore stories about little people and similarities between events may provide doubt to naysayers who find the very existence of these people questionable. Without proof, doubt will always be a challenge. The story in Marshall occurred around Pilcher Mountain during spring geese hunting and involves a little boy found by a hunter several miles from the village. The boy was disoriented and confused and claimed to have been taken by Ircinraq. Although this may be hard to believe, what was interesting was that the boy told a story about a little girl he encountered. When the boy said the little girl's name, it was a name elders had known, a little girl who had been reported missing when they were children.

More than ever, the values between young parents and elders are changing and not practical to today's ethics. Many young Natives accept the mainstream ethics and have grown distant from elders. It is a common response to hear youngsters tell their elders: "You're not the boss." Or, "You're not my boss."

Elders traditionally center family and community values with stories as lessons of respect to support community and family stability. The recognition of elders as community leaders has diminished. The wildlife troopers approaching Point Hope elders to reiterate respect for animals are too late. The damage has already been done. Native respect passed from generation to generation became obsolete when the state government intervened and claimed full responsibility of all Native fish and wildlife. It seems as if we have lost respect for animals, Mother Nature, and elders.

≳

In the April 2015 letter to ADF&G manager Stephanie Schmidt, Pilot Station tribe explained the third principle about why tribes do not own land or reservations to claim management responsibility and why we would rather work with the state than the federal government. Conventional resource management perceptions often create an illusion of external application tasks as the base of management responsibilities.

Take, for example, the Native people of King Cove and the Izembek National Wildlife Refuge. Many Alaska tribes are familiar with the need for a road to the community of Cold Bay, where emergency airline flights are not hampered by inclement weather conditions. The request for a road through the refuge was refused by Secretary of Interior Sally Jewell. If Pilot Station tribe recommended to King Cove tribal members as a do-or-dare, we could continue to be mired with the current situation or be sanctioned for taking action. If King Cove tribal members asked Jewell to step back and watch the Natives build a poorly constructed road, or if the department could consult and help the tribe build a road with environmental guidelines courtesy of a wilderness refuge, what about this third principle that can justify these actions?

Progress toward success is a natural human instinct. The State of Alaska finally realized tribal child custody cases are not issues to be taken lightly and that our children are not aesthetic illusions. They want to work with us on tribal child custody cases. To take care of our children, we must be able to care for our wild resources. If King Cove tribal members told Jewell to go manage the refuge, this was not an ad-lib request. The Department of Interior recognizes many regions in Alaska as federal lands with ecosystem-based management aspirations. Like in Indian Country, this land recognition is the property clause of responsibility—where sovereignty is recognized, the reservations supports this assumption. Another example is ADF&G aspirations to introduce bison in the Shageluk area; if a Native shoots one and gets a citation, another Native will shoot one and dare the state to take action.

In Pilot Station elder gatherings, the concept of hunting and fishing as property management has been confusing since 1960. There is no easy way to describe this for language translators because the Western colonial concept of ownership of fish and wildlife is a challenge for the elders. Native traditional ownership of property or land does not have the same cultural or aesthetic significance as many non-Natives may claim. Over time, as Pilot Station tribe has addressed more child custody cases, we have realized we are responsible for our tribal members, and the elders' idea of traditional fish and wildlife management is *people management*, initiated by the respect and wisdom of elders. Tribes are responsible for tribal members and should be responsible for the actions of tribal members, who we represent not as vested property but as citizens of our traditions. We told ADF&G manager Schmidt we want to manage tribal subsistence hunting and fishing harvests with the state to manage harvests of non-tribal members and commercial fishing. We want tribal members to harvest subsistence foods without fear of an enforcement officer telling them that this is wrong. This is the jurisdiction we are seeking.

We agree that ANCSA extinguished aboriginal rights, and now we have a reason to talk about tribal rights. Tribes in Alaska have no ownership of their land. Although the state will say it manages sustainability and U.S. Department of Interior manages to sustain biodiversity, many times elders have told young fishers they are catching too much fish and we should not exceed our needs. The young fishers look to the elders and comment that ADF&G gave us permission and that they will not allow us to fish next week. When Uppa Kelly was satisfied with our community catch, he would take out his net and be done with fishing and leave Mother Nature to manage the fishery. This is the same lesson elders learned and have tried to teach by example.

These are the Yup'ik laws never written. The Native idea of sustained yield is to harvest what is needed and leave the rest for Mother Nature to manage. There is no proof that Native harvest methods have ever endangered fish or wildlife numbers. Unlike commercial harvests that promote non-Native harvest ethics, the socioeconomics of Native harvest methods helps promote species and genetic diversity . . . and conservation. Absentee management and non-Native harvest regulations, including targeting certain species, encourage overharvesting and decline in wildlife numbers. The impact on salmon numbers for the Kuskokwim and Yukon fisheries is more than sufficient evidence of the effects of non-Native management endeavors since Alaska statehood.

My sister Agnes shrugged with no response when Uppa Kelly asked her, "Why do they want to manage the fish?"

When Pilot Station elders started the qasgiq project, there was another issue that created a rift between Native traditions, and this is what the qasgiq project was hoping to address. In Pilot Station, the municipal government provides the political side of state government. Standing beside the state is the church. Like every congregation, the church also calls for Native attention. Issues of church and state have provided some volatile and interesting history lessons worldwide. The 1969 qasgiq project addressed the attention of both and how Natives used to live before non-Native influence.

In Alaska Native culture, it is a custom for elders to encourage young Natives to hunt and fish and praise and appreciate every successful harvest and show a deep gratuity when a youngster presents a share of the catch. For our youth, it is a reminder that our elders are not forgotten, and this reciprocal nurturing supports each other.

Elders will never discourage young Natives from hunting and fishing. To do so would be counterintuitive to customs and practice of every Native. As young adults, elders did not learn discouragement. Elders will tell young hunters to be cautious, be safe, be careful, travel with a companion, and be observant of the weather and learn from Mother Nature. And if we have more than enough, elders will let hunters and fishers know. We have enough whitefish, but it would be nice to have some beaver. Or next week, we are planning a community potluck and fresh moose and salmon will be nice. It will be a welcome treat for everyone to enjoy.

Uppa Walter Kelly, Wassillie Evan, Noel Polty, Dan Greene, Milo Minock, and several others were Pilot Station elders who led the qasgiq project. As community leaders and Eskimo dance singers, the qasgiq hosted a traditional potlatch with St. Mary's following the same formalities the elders had kept as tradition. As a small child I remember a potlatch for St. Mary's Natives. St. Mary's had planned to host a reciprocal potlatch inviting Pilot Station, but a Catholic priest at the mission told St. Mary's Natives not to hold a potlatch because it was seen as an unchristian thing to do and giving away gifts and food stored for the winter would create community hardships. As a result, this caused tension between the elders, community, and Catholic congregation.

The non-Native priest did not understand the significance of potlatch and assumed these practices were honoring a demigod. The 1969 qasgiq project was a significant event between church and state, elders and tradition, Natives and non-Natives. Traditional potlatch was revived with the qasgiq project, and in 1971 ANCSA changed everything the Natives recognized as traditional ways of community leadership. Native traditions have no written language; many traditional songs provide a parable story difficult to interpret because of cultural differences, language translation challenges, and the storyline. For many a song and dance is entertainment. When the priest saw the Eskimo song and dance revered with graceful praises, this was seen as a religious sect practice violating all holy commandments and ideology of Christian faith. Christian leaders in Alaska did not understand the significance of namesake traditions. Potlatch and dancing were discouraged, and community Eskimo dances was practiced sporadically during the 1950s to 1960s with guarded apprehension. After the 1969 event, potlatch became an annual event between Pilot Station and St. Mary's and helped revive many Eskimo dance traditions.

Most entertaining Eskimo songs are parodies of cultural paradigms. One song created as a lesson of the qasgiq project is a song made by elder Jimmy Paukan of St. Mary's. The first lyrics of the song follows a hymn of reverence with graceful dance moves and a show of respect to Mother Nature and the Native world. It is an Eskimo song and dance like no other. As the tempo picks up with the drumbeat, the dance moves are faster and become alive and entertaining. As the tempo reaches crescendo, the moves look confusing in opposite realms. It is a song about confusing experiences during Jimmy Paukan's lifetime; about heaven and earth, church and state, tradition and culture, present and future, and the people in the midst. The apalluk tells a story about how change is coming and we must be prepared. Jimmy presented this song at a potlatch and just as Jimmy was a special character to people who knew him, the song is a special trademark of his personality, a happy Native person. *Calii* and *pamyua* were repeated many times for elders to hear the song again and appreciate the story of what had almost become forgotten tradition.

Elders know song and dance is a way to express and talk about the traumas of our past to start our healing. Many have found peace and comfort during these events. To be a respected leader is not the same as to be a respected elder. A respected elder is not appointed by the people for leadership skills of serving on any council. A respected elder is recognized for their respect to others, taught by example. It is the same lesson Mother Nature shares when she shows respect and reveals her beauty for everyone to appreciate and tests the skills of those educated with her ways. Compared with the intimidating hunting laws, it becomes difficult to place trust in what Natives should believe and how we should live as a society with our wild resources. Subsistence is a statewide issue.

In 2011 Jesuit priest Ted Kestler provided a newsletter for me to share with our tribal council.[1] Since 1983 Father Ted served many rural Native communities. The newsletter, published in 2002, was a pastoral letter from the Catholic diocese and bishops of Alaska recognizing traditional wild food harvests as important for food security, health, and spiritual well-being. It provides a Catholic perspective on subsistence and implores for an appreciation of different views and recommendations to address this from everyone involved. For difficult topics, traditional Natives prefer long discussions, and this often discourages agency representatives and immediate decisions. Early non-Natives did not have the same patience on fish and wildlife discussions, especially when Natives started telling stories. The BOF and BOG three-minute comment period is a result of this.

At St. Mary's Mission, staff members were volunteers such as Catholic Christians, nuns, and Jesuit priests. The mission has a respected history as an educational institution with a high percentage of successful Native students pursuing higher education and training. As a cultural significant event in 1981, a live performance of a historical play shed light onto what is meant as tradition. Just before Christmas break, the staff performed *Fiddler on the Roof*. Jesuit priest Norman Pepin sang and performed the lead role as patriarch of the play. Although there is some irony in a group of Catholics performing a Jewish play, the message that differences can be set aside for an audience to enjoy a live performance and story about traditions without prejudice is comforting.

Several months later, a Native American visited and told stories about his tribe, customs, and American Indian traditions. As a lone visitor the Indian was proud of his heritage and looked charismatic with long dark hair and a lone feather. Because we were the same height, I was appointed to dress as a warrior with his traditional dress material of leather moccasins, leggings, loincloth, chest plate, and choker necklace. With a painted face the Indian dressed as a chief with full regalia and feather headdress, chest plate, staff, and drum. We were mesmerized as the lone Indian sang and danced. A live performance is entertainment for the soul. As a token of this dress gig the Indian gave me the choker necklace. At the mission, Eskimo dancing and singing were never encouraged; Native traditional dancing and singing were never encouraged in any Christian denomination in Alaska.

NOTES

1. "A Catholic Perspective on Subsistence," *Catholic Anchor Special Supplement*, April 12, 2002, Archdiocese of Anchorage.

37 Story of Tribes in Alaska

"We need your help. Aaron is talking about suicide and we don't know where one of the guns ... One of our guns is missing."

In 2010 Pilot Station tribe presided over a tribal court hearing with the State of Alaska. We lost and recovered the body of a tribal member. The victim was alone, with no witnesses to determine cause of death. Therefore, the state was required to perform an autopsy, but first they had to take custody and send the body to Anchorage. If this happened the body would not return to the community for ten to fourteen days; waiting for the body to return is an eternity for grievance and closure. The family would also have to pay the airline cost to transport the body back to the community. In anguish, the family asked the tribal government to intervene and not send the body out. Several months earlier, another tribal member had been sent to Anchorage for an autopsy and the burden of waiting over two weeks was a difficult time.

Pilot Station tribal judges are elected tribal council leaders. As council secretary I took notes of all tribal court proceedings. If traditional ways of order and justice are to be accepted, a paper trail is necessary to show resilience and authority to address restorative justice. The council had no reason to suspect foul play and sided with the family that the state should not take custody or send the body for an autopsy. This was a somber moment for the two state officials. One quietly conceded and reluctantly accepted the decision and asked everyone if this was what they really want. The other official, on teleconference, commented that without an autopsy the state cannot issue a State of Alaska death certificate. In anguish, family members asked council leaders what our tribe could do to help. A final decision was made in the Pilot Station tribal court proceedings PSTC 07052010, *Family of Bruce M. Beans vs. State of Alaska.*

The next morning a copy of our first tribal death certificate was given to Alaska State Trooper Dan.

Like many American Indians, Alaska Natives did not go unscathed under Western assimilation efforts. The creation of boarding schools and the idea of educating Natives into a civilized culture and way of living created an identity crisis and clash of traditions. Through this era elders kept stories of trauma as hidden secrets. For many, the image of an American Indian tribal member was not appealing to be associated with. It was more appealing to be recognized as an Alaska Native Yup'ik, Athabaskan, Inuit, or one of many other Alaska Native identities. This identity is how tribal existence came to be recognized.

Eventually, somewhere, sometime, the basic virtues and economics of Western civilization came to encompass Alaska Native lives. Unlike treatment of American Indians by the federal government, where the slaughter of the federal Indian Wars and poverty provided the necessary means for treaty agreements and development of reservations to permanently settle Native Americans, Alaska tribes lived and thrived in what was considered a vast, cold, barren land. Americans before the gold rush era considered the U.S. purchase of Alaska from Russia a mistake. Alaska was far away and there was nothing there.

The story of tribes is a story of Native culture and traditions. Natives who once lived a seasonal, seminomadic lifestyle moved to permanent homes within communities and the lives of many were enmeshed. Stories of empowerment from the Alaska Native Brotherhood and Sisterhood from southeast Alaska started a statewide movement and recognition of rural Natives. After Alaska statehood, a new era began when legends of Alaska Native history was made: stories of Howard Rock, the *Tundra Times*, Willie Hensley, State of Alaska land freeze, and Nunam Kitlutsisti. In 1965, aside from the Native statewide effort for civic recognition, the story of tribes was just about to be told from our side of Alaska. As the Alaska Federation of Natives came to existence, rural tribal elders addressed needs for homes, health, education, water and sewer services, and wildlife and fisheries as statewide issues.

In wake of the 1960s Native empowerment movement, President Richard Nixon signed into federal law the 1971 Alaska Native Claims Settlement Act. The final settlement and recognition of Native land-ownership and the creation of Native corporations created frenzy in rural villages. The final hoopla was the cash payment of $962.5 million. Progress was at hand. In 1971, $962.5 million was an unimaginable amount of money, and for non-Native Alaskans this created an envious perception that all Natives were rich. After this settlement, the Trans-Alaska Pipeline created a progressive statewide resource development initiative. Native corporations began selecting traditional lands with resource development potential and divvying up the settlement with glee. The state was pleased to provide corporate oversight with jurisdiction and final management authority for all resource development projects.

In the midst of this frenzy, the voice and concerns of rural elders subsided with the excitement of land selections and talk of money. One issue Alaska Natives continued to address vocally was extinguishment of aboriginal rights. For language translators it was difficult to talk about because the issue was considered settled. Alaska Natives who once helped as language translators became corporate leaders and board members. The talk of the elders in their Native language was trivial compared to tasks of corporate progress.

Like the true virtue of elders and the lessons of living in our small world, the key role of tribes was patience. It is a lesson that the seasons will change and make opportunities to meet food security. Rural tribal leaders attended the largest gathering of Natives at the annual AFN conference, voiced their concerns, and waited with patience as Native corporations grew and settlement payments created excitement among corporation leaders and hordes of lawyers, lobbyists, businesspeople, and resource developers. Tribes waited in patience to see if any provisions of ANCSA would provide services necessary to help tribal members. Some tribes are still waiting.

A leading misconception that Native corporations addressed Native issues was a common sentiment, and many non-Native leaders were pleased no Indian reservations had been created. Although ANCSA also created nonprofit corporations such as Association of Village Council Presidents and Tanana Chiefs Council, elders from rural Alaska continued to address basic services taken for granted and serviced by developed municipal governments. As the municipal governments were being created, many continued to remind the State of Alaska about health care, education, and social services for Native Alaskans. This is when Congress intervened and awoke the tribal identity.

Nonprofit corporations' intent to utilize the tribal identity as a basis for services was never addressed until Congress created the Indian Self-Determination and Education Assistance Act of 1975. Many Native entities agree that this act gives self-determination and self-government powers. Alaska Native entities are familiar with this act as Public Law 93-638. Many Alaska Native corporations use provisions of this act as an entitlement advantage for projects. Unlike corporations, Alaska tribes do not need a disclaimer for recognition. Despite this misunderstanding, some tribes continue to use this provision for tribal projects. Pilot Station tribe has admitted to the State of Alaska that PL 93-638 does not preempt traditional laws of governance. We have never relinquished tribal sovereignty, and we do not need PL 93-638 for tribal recognition. In whose court of law should this claim be settled?

≥

In 1997 Mom was excited and proud to attend my graduation from UAF with a bachelor of science degree in natural resource management. College was exciting for me. In the UAF Rasmuson Library, I worked at the Bibliography of Alaskana, reading articles and entering reference information into the library's computer network. Doing this verbatim, word for word, was one lesson I learned. Western academia takes for granted that what is written and documented is true and applicable to the world as we all see it, and this is the way higher education is achieved. When I was getting paid to read articles, I realized that what is written may also include hidden truths. Like a glass half full of water, what is written can include misinterpreted information, and this made me realize that many traditional unwritten Native stories are true and applicable. I don't know if I succeeded in learning how to think like a gussak.

The elders told their stories, but for people listening without experience, it was difficult to translate or interpret the real message. What we know about Native way of life may have been improperly documented. If the early biblical writers explained in detail the mysteries of the Bible, there would be no more mysteries. Still, this gives a sense of serenity and comfort to those who follow it. I trust my tradition and my culture, but the stories of the elders are filled with trauma and a burden they needed others to know before any path to cultural recovery was possible.

Pilot Station community meetings use a language translator when elders talk. The elders cannot live forever, but every time we lose one elder another stands and talks with a similar message. We have a strong tradition where respect for elders provides more than community stability. This is the heart of a rural tribal government. We know our tribal government was not extinguished with the act of another existing government.

Pilot Station did not wait to address issues. Elders mention that change is coming and we will not be able to hold it back. Change is like the Yukon River; it will create new channels and sand bars, and it will erode lands and take fish racks and homes. We have seen other organizations create many efforts and programs in attempt to address our needs. Many last a season or two and cease to exist; eventually, they are forgotten. Pilot Station elders emphasized that if we want programs to address our needs, we have to do it ourselves. Issues addressed as priorities in neighboring communities are also local concerns; wild food security is a statewide Native priority.

Monetary support from federal and state assistance programs determines the progress and existence of all Alaska tribal programs. As village and regional corporations distanced themselves from tribal members and turned instead toward a demanding shareholder base of profit, stocks, and dividends, many learned that the corporations are required to follow state guidelines of a corporate world. As elders talk about local issues, many realize ANCSA does not apply to tribes.

There is a misconception that the city municipal government is the same as the tribal government. Municipal governments provide services to anyone and everyone willing to pay a fee for any and all city services, such as water and sewer. No fees are collected for tribal services. What created more confusion is the misconception that village corporations were the same as tribes. A corporation represents shareholders with a vested interest in stock portfolio. Tribal membership is a citizenship identity.

With limited federal BIA funds, Pilot Station tribe developed separate from the regional and village corporation. When federal officials remind Pilot Station we must have a tribal constitution to receive tribal funds, we realize our constitution does not apply to non-tribal members. We have no jurisdiction over non-tribal members, and to enforce it would be unethical and disrespectful. Elders talk about how we used to care for each other and share the harvest with our stories. When elders went through hard times, they did not wait to seek answers.

The development and recognition of Alaska tribes have been hap-hazard and fragmented. There are no legal documents that serve as universal guidelines. Each tribe has their own constitution that applies to their own tribal members. Although federal and state laws are meant to represent everyone as one country, one people, the recognition of Alaska tribes without landownership confused trust, obligation, and responsibility. In addition to PL 93-638, other national legal provisions that help tribal recognition include the 1936 Indian Reorganization Act and President Bill Clinton's 1993 tribal recognition proclamation. This led to the 1994 Federally Recognized Indian Tribe List Act, acknowl-edged by the secretary of interior. Before these recognitions, Alaska tribes existed in ambiguity. The 2017 tribal sovereignty opinion of the state attorney general is difficult for anyone to contradict.

Not just anyone can be a tribal member. It is not unusual for tribal members to relinquish membership of one tribe to join another as long as ancestral lineage is documented. Unlike tribal membership, corporation shareholders cannot relinquish corporation shares from one ANCSA corporation to join another. Pilot Station tribe has taken the stance that federal and state laws do not preempt traditional laws. As a tribal court we serve jurisdiction and preside over actions of tribal members in a system of restorative justice. Federal and state laws do not preempt traditional laws when tribal courts are in session; whether tribal laws are written as legal ordinances is beside the point.

July 5, 2010. Two days before the tribal court hearing, my nephew Arlo asked my son Kalen to go and check on his dad at their fish camp. It was 2 p.m., and Bruce had not returned from their family camp in Atchuelinguk River. Just after 4 p.m. Kalen and Arlo returned. With anxious breaths they told their story about finding Bruce's boat floating near the mouth of Blueberry Slough and going into the camp to look for Bruce. Everything in camp was quiet. The smokehouse firepit was cold with burned embers. A fire to smoke the salmon had not been lit for at least a day. The family notified Pilot Station Search and Rescue.

That evening, several boats went out to search. No fresh footprints were found on either side of the river. Many of us who knew Bruce told the rescue team that Bruce always wore his life vest or float jacket. Two boats traveled downriver as far as Hills Island. Just after midnight there was no sign of Bruce.

July 6, 2010. The early morning search-and-rescue meeting addressed body recovery efforts. Volunteers from St. Mary's, Pitkas Point, Marshall, and Mountain Village arrived to help. The Atchuelinguk River is narrow and we had a general area to search, so we did not request to use the ADF&G sonar side-scanner. More than twenty boats dragged the bottom of the river with large grappling hooks. After several hours, my brother Abe told my brother-in-law Terry and I to stay on the beach. It is a Native custom that when there is a search-and-rescue effort, the person we are searching for will not show themselves to immediate family members. In our story, the person we are looking for will not want to be found by family members because of the shame of what has happened. After less than ten minutes, the search crew with my uncle Joe Alick found Bruce. Search-and-rescue boats gathered around Joe's boat and we said a prayer.

When Bruce was recovered, Alaska State Trooper Dan was present taking notes and commented to the search teams about the success of a recovery. In a huge boat armada, Joe Alick leading with Bruce wrapped and bundled, Bruce returned home at 8 p.m.

Before midnight the family of Bruce asked the tribal council to intervene and not send Bruce to Anchorage for an autopsy.

≷

July 7, 12:40 a.m. The tribal court was in session. Beside Bruce's family, also present and providing testimony were two search-and-rescue coordinators, two village police officers, one village public safety officer, and Alaska State Trooper Dan holding the telephone with the Alaska state medical examiner on teleconference. After the tribal court ruling, the medical examiner commented that the state would never issue a death certificate without a body to autopsy.

An airplane pilot for the Alaska state trooper, Earl Samuelson, mentioned a similar situation where the State of Alaska did not issue a death certificate, and the family's estate and assets were never given to the heirs or descendants.

Pilot Station Traditional Village is a tribal government with citizenship duties toward our tribal members. During the court session, a tribal document was given to Trooper Dan with a comment that the Alaska state constitution does not apply to federally recognized tribes or tribal members. It is the same rationale that the Pilot Station tribal constitution does not apply to non-tribal members or Alaska residents. Every Alaska Native descendant is eligible to enroll in any one of the 229 Alaska tribes to receive tribal services and apply for a tribal identification card.

A picture ID card is a recognition of citizenship, providing information on our nationality, like a passport. When we lose tribal members who pass, Native customs have a traditional grieving process and payment of respect to the family, but there is no legal document that shows the loss of tribal members to other governments we share the world with. When we issued our first tribal death certificate, there was one other parliamentary emblem necessary to make it official: a government seal, a tribal government seal. Once certified, the Pilot Station tribal death certificate is recognized by banking institutions, U.S. Bureau of Vital Statistics, and Alaska Native corporations. As a result, the last will and testament of Bruce Beans was recognized and the family estate and assets were settled. In 2014 the family received a State of Alaska death certificate to settle benefits held in trust as Bruce was a former state employee.

Pilot Station ruled the loss of Bruce as accidental drowning. Drowning and loss of life to hypothermia are leading causes of death in Alaska. For elders, loss of life to drowning, natural causes, sickness, or hunting accidents is accepted as part of life. The idea of a person taking one's own life is not. It is unfortunate that the highest national demographic of a suicide victims is Alaska Native males over the age of sixteen. Aaron fit this profile, and when the parent called for help, several tribal leaders responded and visited Aaron. Talk of suicide is difficult for anyone to address. Behavioral health services are nonexistent in rural Alaska. Tribal members need to be willing to admit they need help and someone must be willing to listen to their stories. To start this conversation, we can ask one beneficial but difficult question to our loved ones: "Have you ever thought about suicide?"

We are a tribal government. The Pilot Station Traditional Council tribal death certificate has our own tribal seal and official recognition:

ACKNOWLEDGMENT

In recognition of loss of Bruce Mark Beans, tribal member of the Pilot Station Traditional Council, has respectfully informed the governing bodies of the United States of America, Union of States, and the State of Alaska, that information provided herein as true, and all governing bodies dutifully acknowledge, respect, and honor this certification of the tribal governing body of the Native Village of Pilot Station. We respectfully request all parties honor our loss and the loss of the family to rest in peace eternal and forever.

CERTIFICATION

The Pilot Station Traditional Council, as the federally recognized tribe for the Native Village of Pilot Station, dutifully recognize and certify the beloved loss of one of our own tribal members on this 7 day of July 2010.

Cynthia Fancyboy, President   Elias Kelly, Secretary

38 ⋞ All Things Considered

"I am too young to splash," I told my father-in-law, Albert Beans Sr., and his best friend Anthony Tony. We were taking a steam bath and my father-in-law asked me to splash the boiling water onto the red-hot stones. These two were my elders and I did not want to burn them out of the small hot steam house. I was enjoying their stories. One talked about the Yup'ik who ran out of the steam house naked to see the beluga whales and we laughed.

Many of my Native ancestors would appreciate the entertaining stories of Garrison Keillor and his radio troupe. Storytelling and storytellers are valued in many cultures. Unfortunately, comparing non-Native and Native Alaska is difficult because many situations are not the same. There are no accidents; things happen for a reason.

When I hiked the Chilkoot Trail to learn what the non-Natives were seeking and think about encouragement from elders to go and learn, it took me a long time to realize this sense of Native identity is always with me, no matter where I went or as much as I tried to think like a gussak. Somewhere in this identity is a cultural idea that needs to be accepted so I can effectively communicate to other cultures without adversity. It may seem easy to see similarities in many situations and recognize and applaud innovative challenges to difficult situations, but how can we compare cultural adversity where life is not just being, it just is? When one culture is met with adversity and bossed around by another, it creates resentment. If any Native culture did this, it would be unethical to who we are. Many cultures know the scars of intimidation are difficult to set aside.

The product of every Alaska Native culture is the elders. When elders share stories with Native food, this is the essence of subsistence eloquence passed from one generation to the next. Despite the rural remoteness of Native Alaska, anecdotes of living conditions can be compelling for empathy. In 2009 elder Nicholas Tucker from Emmonak was instrumental in acknowledging the current living conditions in the Lower Yukon.[1] Although Natives in Alaska recognize culture and tradition as a rich and inspirational history of our social customs, the current living conditions in Native Alaska are far below what any respectable civic organization would consider an adequate level. Alaska resources continue to shape federal and state policies. Our wild resources will always be our precious food security source. With this way of thinking, the notion of poverty is not as compelling as many may believe. The times have changed. The current economy in Native Alaska requires payment in cash for groceries and services such as water and sewer, electricity, and fuel to heat homes and run transportation vehicles.

When Moses Paukan Sr., a respected St. Mary's elder, sent a letter to Governor Bill Walker to allow Natives to harvest Yukon kings for food security, the message Moses had hoped to convey was we don't want your help, *we want to help ourselves*. Our elders care for our people.

Sportsmen often look to each other and unconsciously recognize the activities they do as special hobbies of those who can afford the time and expense. To buy rod and reels, hunting equipment, and supplies and the means to go where wild creatures live. A special recognition that these activities are done for a sense of excitement and the ethics of catching that creature is the elixir of life with a vigorous exhilaration of satisfying the needs of life. Subsistence families make a kill to quench hunger. Those who practice catch and release emanate a power of authority. With unsuccessful harvests, sportsmen are not participating to address food security. They can choose not to participate and suffer no great loss. For Natives, choosing not to participate is a luxury of affluence. A Native going to the moon is more of a reality than a Native succumbing to simple riches and catching wild critters for fun and entertainment. Other Native cultures are likely to see the humor.

If the U.S. government approached large successful corporations like Microsoft, General Motors, or ExxonMobil and asked about the well-being and general consensus of American shareholders, they would be ridiculed beyond patriotism that this is not democracy . . . I am an

American. The freedom of Americans was not to cater to or recognize a privileged sector or praise political leaders because of their business savvy. But if the same government approached ANCSA Native corporations and asked about the general consensus and well-being of Native shareholders, there is a lesson somewhere in this dichotomy.

In any human venture, failure is much easier to achieve than success. Many times, I have come home from hunting or fishing without a catch. If there were no special provisions for ANCSA Native corporations, eternal immunity from bankruptcy, large sums of startup funds, support from sister corporations, and tax-exempt status, many would have failed after they were created. The corporation concept forced Natives to become instant corporate leaders with business suits as a necessary image for the business world. The Native traditional idea of a forecast was to look at the weather and decide if today was a good day to hunt, fish, or gather firewood.

It took some time for many to realize that the Native corporations are there to make money and not serve as philanthropists. To be capital driven and self-supporting, whether they are for-profit or nonprofit. Many struggled despite the fact that many Native businesspeople failed to understand that corporations have *no social obligations*. All obligations are to the shareholders. Unlike in free-enterprise corporations, mismanagement is never a concern. In the business world, mismanagement is an accepted practice of those that have folded and cease to exist. Whether they are missed or not is hard to say. There is no reason for ANCSA corporations to fail; the U.S. government created them, and it is often taken for granted that this government is never wrong.

Federal and state democracy does not recognize Native moral obligations or traditional subsistence ethics. When Natives talk about subsistence, the state will pretend to look the other way and the feds will rub their hands and look to the Code of Federal Regulations as guidelines. In the same way, capitalism has no social obligations. Forcing Natives to create and run corporations in exchange for a land claim agreement and loss of wildlife responsibility resulted in controversies about the meaning of subsistence. Federal and state agencies continue to create subsistence regulations. We Natives have grown dependent on someone defining subsistence and when we contradict this definition, we become criminals according to their system.

After ANCSA, the presence of BIA reminded Alaska Natives of another Native identity. BIA is a department providing services to Indians living on reservations. According to Theodore Roosevelt, BIA was created to quell the concerns and quiet the voices of Indians complaining about deplorable living conditions and broken fiduciary promises. In Alaska the same deplorable Native social service programs, health-care conditions, education, and economic situations became the responsibilities of BIA. The statehood act and ANCSA gave every Native a resident identity, but BIA confused everyone when it started talk about Alaska Native tribes being crucial for Native services. For the State of Alaska this existence became a festering identity issue and could not be ignored.

Many Alaska tribes are unique and each continues to develop haphazardly with fragmented services to tribal members. ANCSA allow the state and federal government to legally claim Alaska Native wildlife management responsibility without conscientious objections. Many tribes are in stagnant development phases with uncertain roles in wildlife responsibility and Native food security. In the Lower 48, it is easy to recognize tribes within reservations as existing entities where jurisdiction is an element of sovereignty. In Native Alaska there was a time when nobody knew what tribes were responsible for and it became a stagnant time period. Nonetheless, every little tribal success is one step forward for tribal sovereignty.

For every step forward, comments such as the traditional mindset of prominent state leaders of *one country, one people* were two steps back. This created a confusing sense of belonging. As products of assimilation, Natives have grown to believe that someone will address our needs, voice our concerns, and provide economic stimulus or relief. A belief that someone will support Natives and that all management responsibility belongs to someone in authority. When leaders fly to Native Alaska and ask what we want, there is no assurance or guarantee that they will get on the airplane and return with what we asked for. This charade has given a false sense of hope that the answer to Native problems is the task of someone else, rather than someone living among our own.

Since Governor Steve Cowper admitted the existence of Alaska tribes in 1990, the State of Alaska has taken reluctant steps to try to work with this identity. The state consults with tribes before determining any state services. Alaska tribes cannot be set aside and ignored; we have an identity and this identity can help with who we are.

It is easy for the federal and state government to remind everyone ANCSA extinguished aboriginal rights. Alaska tribal sovereignty cannot be achieved without claiming subsistence as our tribal responsibility. We need our stories as management guidelines to help address community and family values, education and social issues, and wildlife and fisheries management. We need to tell stories about respect as our Yup'ik laws that were never written.

≥

"Eeggigi . . . nutanatam." In the steam house the elders laughed and told a story about why the qasgiq had to be demolished. With an open skylight for light to seep though and woodsmoke to funnel out, the men had to demolish everything because some kid fell through the skylight fifteen feet onto the dance floor. During winter the qasgiq was a little snow-covered dome, excellent for kids to climb and snow slide.

The federal and state governments have been trying to work with Alaska tribes on many tribal issues. Alaska fish and wildlife issues tend to get stagnant and bitter, and we silently accept that we are mired in these current affairs until some issue becomes a news topic and lets us forget what we are trying to achieve. The federal government continues to develop the subsistence program in Alaska, and the state continues to create regulation language for subsistence hunting and fishing within Title V of the Alaska State Statutes.

There are many questions about tribes. The 2017 legal opinion of the state attorney general on tribal sovereignty helped answer many questions. Pilot Station tribe admitted to the state that fish and wildlife management is people management and that we are responsible for our tribal members. We agree with the state on sustained yield principles and that wild resource harvests should not be excessive or wasted.

Alaska tribes need to be trusted with responsibility to our tribal members as our citizens. We learned this lesson when we addressed difficult tribal child custody cases. With lessons learned from the federal Indian Wars, the U.S. government became a middleman between tribes and anyone and everyone else. Creation of intertribal fish wildlife and resource commissions are examples of the federal government helping the tribes to avoid conflicts. Without offending the federal government, many tribes are willing to work with the State of Alaska on tribal services including wildlife, fisheries, and subsistence management. As an intermediary, the federal government should not find it difficult to intervene and provide assistance or recommendations when situations become controversial. As it is now, the only option is to disregard tribal identity and allow federal management for federally qualified users to harvest subsistence resources.

In March 2021, as a solid foundation for partnership, State House Representative Tiffany Zulkosky of Bethel submitted House Bill 123 for the state to acknowledge Alaska's federally recognized tribes. For the safety of tribal members, tribes successfully enforced community travel restrictions during the COVID-19 pandemic as sovereign governments. Without reservations or landownership claims, tribes are responsible for the safety of everyone in their communities. This house bill was approved by the state legislature in May 2022 and signed by Governor Mike Dunleavy on July 28, 2022. We are here to stay.

For wildlife management schemes to work, the State of Alaska must be willing to work with tribes. *Federally recognized tribes* are included in many provisions of the Alaska State Statues except in Title V: Hunting and Fishing. In Title V every Alaskan is recognized as a resident, so a constitutional convention to address any Alaska Native issue is arbitrary—it is only a matter of time before "federally recognized tribes" will be inserted into Title V: Hunting and Fishing.

BIA continues to give federal funds to Alaska tribes. If Congressman Ted Stevens could admit tribes in Alaska are not sovereign because they do not own the land, everyone needs to stand and send BIA back to Washington with one question: *Are the federally recognized tribes in Alaska sovereign?* Tribal services are obsolete if tribes are limited in what they can do.

A simple yes or no answer is more than sufficient, rather than a long-winded response that attempts to confuse fiduciary responsibility. We are not asking for another ANCSA, ANILCA, congressional action, or filibuster, just a simple answer delivered to every Alaska civic gathering by congressional delegates to avoid further disparities and confusion and to set aside notions that the tribes don't know why they are here. Native cultures recognize life as simple to our understanding of Mother Nature. It is our worldview. Autonomous tribal identity is crucial for Native responsibility. Returning with a yes or no is an ultimatum.

I am a Native corporation shareholder. Corporate leaders' promises to protect subsistence because they own the land are empty. Like a fantasy world, the corporation is like the federal and state governments when they say they own the land with imaginary boundaries of responsibility. The corporation has no social obligations. Everyone who believes it does creates the illusion that distribution of wealth and sharing of riches are the definition of subsistence. To cup your hands and your needs will be provided. In a heartbeat I would exchange my Native corporation shares for subsistence.

I am an Alaska Native Yup'ik Eskimo. According to many I cannot hunt and fish whenever I want. When the wildlife trooper looks the other way, the hardships in my community are my responsibility. As a Native, my first instinct, ingrained in the way I grew up, is that I do not trust the state or federal responsibility. When I have seen someone charged with a hunting and fishing crime, I see no wrong, based on what I learned from my elders. I lose trust in what I should believe. Many young Natives are learning to hunt and fish for the first time, young tribal members who learn my lessons taught from my elders: if you are not afraid, I will help you. As more learn this, we learn to help each other. My ancestors know who I am; if you look closely, you will see me in every true Native.

Intimidation by wildlife management is not the answer. In 2018 the formal apology from USFWS and ADF&G for hardships created by strict subsistence regulations was a sign of respect. Many elders had tears when they heard this. It is comforting and a lesson in grieving and healing. The next step is to give back to the Natives that which was taken. As managers we need to tell stories of how we take care of our natural resources to our children and how they can share this story with theirs.

In May 2022, ignoring the existence of the Yukon River Intertribal Fish Commission, FSB approved a management resolution for federally qualified users to harvest Yukon salmon. Claims of non-Natives using the Haul Road Yukon River bridge to gain access to salmon were a leading argument for this decision. This is the same situation of managers' stewarding the resource and expecting the people to do what they decide, nothing more and nothing less. We have another tribal identity challenge to hurdle. We do not want to be recognized as "federally qualified users." Our elders learned that patience is a virtue of respect. It is only a matter of time before our tribal identity will become our management tool.

Our story began many years ago, when our ancestors gathered together and told stories of our way of life and how we help each other; this is subsistence. ANCSA made us forget what our stories were about. When an elder tells a story with a twinkle in their eye, it is reassuring that they care for us and we will never be forgotten. Elders learned that Mother Nature is not the boss. Mother Nature is a storyteller about respect. When elders talk about her, she grows and evolves, she is exciting and promising. Tell this story to your loved ones because we should no longer hold her back and keep quiet. We have come this far, and if we listen quiet, Mother Nature has more stories for each of us to share because we are all a part of her.

In the steam house the elders laughed. One told another story and splashed water onto the red-hot stones, and the steam swirled with pictures . . .

NOTES

1. *Anchorage Daily News*, January 14, 2009.

IN THE AMERICAN INDIAN LIVES SERIES

I Stand in the Center of the Good:
Interviews with Contemporary
Native American Artists
Edited by Lawrence Abbott

Authentic Alaska: Voices
of Its Native Writers
Edited by Susan B. Andrews
and John Creed

Searching for My Destiny
By George Blue Spruce Jr.
As told to Deanne Durrett

Dreaming the Dawn: Conversations
with Native Artists and Activists
By E. K. Caldwell
Introduction by Elizabeth Woody

Chief: The Life History of Eugene
Delorme, Imprisoned Santee Sioux
Edited by Inéz Cardozo-Freeman

Chevato: The Story of the
Apache Warrior Who Captured
Herman Lehmann
By William Chebahtah and
Nancy McGown Minor

Winged Words: American
Indian Writers Speak
Edited by Laura Coltelli

In Defense of Loose Translations: An
Indian Life in an Academic World
By Elizabeth Cook-Lynn

Life, Letters, and Speeches
By George Copway
(Kahgegagahbowh)
Edited by A. LaVonne Brown
Ruoff and Donald B. Smith

Life Lived Like a Story: Life Stories
of Three Yukon Native Elders
By Julie Cruikshank in
collaboration with Angela Sidney,
Kitty Smith, and Annie Ned

Too Strong to Be Broken: The Life
of Edward J. Driving Hawk
By Edward J. Driving Hawk and
Virginia Driving Hawk Sneve

Bitterroot: A Salish Memoir
of Transracial Adoption
By Susan Devan Harness

LaDonna Harris: A Comanche Life
By LaDonna Harris
Edited by H. Henrietta Stockel

Rock, Ghost, Willow, Deer:
A Story of Survival
By Allison Adelle Hedge Coke

*Rights Remembered: A Salish
Grandmother Speaks on American
Indian History and the Future*
By Pauline R. Hillaire
Edited by Gregory P. Fields

*Essie's Story: The Life and
Legacy of a Shoshone Teacher*
By Esther Burnett Horne and
Sally McBeth

*Song of Rita Joe: Autobiography
of a Mi'kmaq Poet*
By Rita Joe

*My Side of the River: An
Alaska Native Story*
By Elias Kelly

*Viet Cong at Wounded Knee: The
Trail of a Blackfeet Activist*
By Woody Kipp

Catch Colt
By Sidner J. Larson

*Alanis Obomsawin: The Vision
of a Native Filmmaker*
By Randolph Lewis

*Alex Posey: Creek Poet,
Journalist, and Humorist*
By Daniel F. Littlefield Jr.

*The Turtle's Beating Heart: One
Family's Story of Lenape Survival*
By Denise Low

First to Fight
By Henry Mihesuah
Edited by Devon Abbott Mihesuah

*Mourning Dove: A Salishan
Autobiography*
Edited by Jay Miller

*I'll Go and Do More: Annie
Dodge Wauneka, Navajo
Leader and Activist*
By Carolyn Niethammer

*Tales of the Old Indian Territory
and Essays on the Indian Condition*
By John Milton Oskison
Edited by Lionel Larré

*Elias Cornelius Boudinot: A
Life on the Cherokee Border*
By James W. Parins

*John Rollin Ridge: His
Life and Works*
By James W. Parins

*Singing an Indian Song: A
Biography of D'Arcy McNickle*
By Dorothy R. Parker

*Crashing Thunder: The
Autobiography of an
American Indian*
Edited by Paul Radin

Turtle Lung Woman's Granddaughter
By Delphine Red Shirt
and Lone Woman

*Telling a Good One: The
Process of a Native American
Collaborative Biography*
By Theodore Rios and
Kathleen Mullen Sands

Printed in the USA
CPSIA information can be obtained
at www.ICGtesting.com
LVHW091040151223
766480LV00001B/80